BURTON BARR

Burton Barr

Political Leadership and the Transformation of Arizona

PHILIP R. VANDERMEER

Foreword by
ALFREDO GUTIERREZ

THE UNIVERSITY OF ARIZONA PRESS
TUCSON

The University of Arizona Press
www.uapress.arizona.edu

First paperback edition 2015

Printed in the United States of America
20 19 18 17 16 15 7 6 5 4 3 2

Cover design by Leigh McDonald
Cover photo courtesy of the Burton Barr Photo Collection

Library of Congress Cataloging-in-Publication Data
VanderMeer, Philip R., 1947–
Burton Barr : political leadership and the transformation of Arizona / Philip R. VanderMeer ; foreword by Alfredo Gutierrez.
pages cm
Includes bibliographical references and index.
ISBN 978-0-8165-3057-1 (hardback)
1. Barr, Burton, 1917–1997. 2. Legislators—Arizona—Biography. 3. Arizona. Legislature. House of Representatives—Majority leaders—Biography. 4. Republican Party (Ariz.)—Biography. 5. Politicalleadership—Arizona—History—20thcentury.6. Arizona—Politics and government—1951– 7. Social change—Arizona—History—20th century. I. Title.
F815.3.B37V36 2014
328.73'092—dc23
[B]
2014007753

♾ This paper meets the requirements of ANSI/NISO Z39.48-1992 (Permanence of Paper)

Contents

List of Illustrations viii

Foreword by Alfredo Gutierrez x

Preface and Acknowledgments xiii

Introduction. Understanding Burton Barr 3
- Burton Barr 6
- History and Biography 7
- Political Leadership 10
- Parties, Principles, and Pragmatism 12
- The Context: The West and Western Politics 14
- The Impact of Western Politics and Politicians 16
- The West, Arizona, and Burton Barr 18

1. Making the Man and Raising the Barr 21
   - Family Background 22
   - New Beginnings: Portland 25
   - Hy Barr and Portland Education 26
   - The Barr Family 29
   - Life in the Military, 1940–1942 32
   - Going to War 35
   - Home, Family, the Army, and the Making of Burton Barr 40

2. Making a Life as a Businessman, Peacetime Soldier, and Family Man 43
   - Working in Civilian Life 44
   - Staying with the Military: Service in the Reserve 49
   - A Political Turn 51
   - A Changing Life 54
   - Family Man 56
   - Moving into a Political Life 60

3. Arizona's Political Structure, Legislative Stalemate, and the Beginning of Reform 62
The Historical Roots of Arizona and Its Politics 63
The Social Basis of Arizona Politics 64
The First Stage of Arizona Government and Politics 66
Political Change and Continuity in Postwar Arizona 68
The Legislative Arena 71
The Historical Role of State Legislatures 72
The Arizona Legislature 73
Political Factions, Power, and Legislative Organization 75
Legislative Inaction, Conflict, and Leadership 79
Reapportionment 85
Barr Enters the Legislature 87

4. Legislative Leadership 90
The Traits of Leadership 92
Burton Barr's Character and Skills 92
The Techniques of Legislative Leadership: Personal and Performance 97
Winning Friends and Influencing People: Techniques for Getting Support 101
Strategy and Leadership 107
Leadership, Values, and Conflict 112
Assessing Leadership and the Legislature 118
The Impact of Situation on Leadership 119
Legislators and the Challenge of Legislative Service 119
The Importance of Legislative Structure 122
Managing Legislative Business 125
Legislative Partners: Conservatives, Democrats, and Senators 129
The Struggle for Leadership: Barr versus Babbitt 135
Burton Barr and Legislative Leadership 139

5. Burton Barr and Policy-Making in Arizona 142
Understanding Barr's Policy Leadership 143
Redesigning Government: The First Steps 146
Reconstructing State Government 149
Fixing Taxes 151
The Rise and Fall of Property Taxes 154
Caring for Health Care 158
From Medicaid to AHCCCS 162

- Water 166
- Air Pollution and Environmental Planning 169
- Education and Mental Health 173
- Laws and Order, Crime and Punishment 175
- Conclusion: Burton Barr as a Policymaker 176

6. Leaving the Legislature and Running for Governor 179
   - Thinking about Running 180
   - Starting to Run 184
   - The Race is On 187
   - A Troubled Campaign 190
   - The Plot Thickens: Evan Mecham Enters the Contest 194
   - The Failed Campaign and the Lost Election 198
   - Power, Campaigns, and History 201

7. An Itch to Serve: Life after the Legislature 204
   - Living with Loss 205
   - Working with the Legislature Still, Very Still 206
   - New Challenges 209
   - Final Days 213
   - Final Words and Larger Meanings 214

Notes 221
Essay on Sources 238
Index 249

Illustrations

Figures

1. Burton Barr's locations with American forces in North Africa, Italy, and southern France 36
2. Major Burton Barr 38
3. Movement of American forces and Barr's units in southern Germany, 1945 40
4. Burton and Charlotte Barr 46
5. Burton Barr and U.S. Army Reserve leaders meeting Governor Ernest McFarland 51
6. The Barr family 58
7. Arizona legislative committee meeting, 1959 77
8. Arizona Senate, 1950s 78
9. Senator Harold Giss and Senate President Clarence Carpenter 81
10. Barr in a rare quiet moment 96
11. Barr and the press 112
12. Legislative action by the Arizona House, 1965–1985 122
13. Barr and district colleagues 131
14. Barr and Reps. Joe Lane, Mark Kilian, Jim Ratliff, and Bob Denny 158
15. The Barr family and President Ronald Reagan 183

Tables

1. Populations of largest Arizona towns and cities, 1890–1920 65
2. Minority influence on Arizona House Speaker elections, 1953–1965 76
3. Political parties and Arizona government, 1965–1985 130
4. Gubernatorial vetoes, 1959–1986 137

Foreword

When Burton Barr was elected to the legislature in 1964, Arizona was a state whose rural population was largely Southern and Democratic but decidedly conservative in its social values. At the time, each of Arizona's 14 counties had two state senators. The House of Representatives was theoretically based on population, but the historical preponderance of rural representatives assured that redistricting would always favor the sparsely populated counties over the two cities, Phoenix and Tucson, that had flourished in the desert. Arizona's governor was largely a titular figure, with real power placed in a plethora of boards and commissions formed by the legislature to guarantee rural dominance of every aspect of government even as the urban population threatened rural hegemony. The so-called one person, one vote decision, *Reynolds v. Sims*, ordering states to draw legislative districts to reflect population was declared by the court in 1964. In Arizona's case the inequalities were extreme: Mojave County had a population of 7,700 and was represented by two state senators; Maricopa County's population was 663,000 and also had two state senators, a ratio of 87 to 1. Predictably, Arizona's rural Democrats refused to implement the order, and in 1966 the court imposed its own redistricting scheme on the state. And then, in the words of the last rural kingpin of state government, Harold Giss, "all hell broke loose."

The urban interest that finally upended Arizona's rural southern dominance was a Republican party based in the most populous county, Maricopa, home to the state's fast-growing capital city, Phoenix. Its first major victory was defeating the majority leader of the United States

Senate, Ernest McFarland, as early as 1952. Their candidate was a young, outspoken, conservative ideologue, Barry Goldwater. In 1966 the greatest concern of the new Republican majority in both houses of the legislature was no longer ideology but governance and infrastructure. The governmental structure that was built to protect rural dominance into the future, in their view, had to be undone and quickly, or they feared their victory might be fleeting. Urban infrastructure largely ignored had to be speedily addressed. There were great challenges to be met, constitutional questions, complex financial issues, competing demands for roads, public schools, colleges and universities in the state's two urban counties, and of course there was the challenge of politics in a majority composed of inexperienced newcomers. Failure seemed likely. But failure hadn't counted on Burton Barr.

The story of how, even as a freshman, Burt stared down Harold Giss and forced the first step in modernizing state government is legend. In a torrent of movement, Burt cajoled, embarrassed, threatened, pleaded, and finally wrangled a simple Office of Budget Director and a requirement for a public state budget for the first time. Once he became majority leader of the House of Representatives, he never stopped. Burt led a constantly evolving coalition of urban Democrats and moderate Republicans in a two-decades-long battle to modernize the state. His legislative accomplishments are perhaps unmatched in any state in the union. It is how he achieved all of it that is his most important legacy. Burt was a hurricane of optimism, a tireless whirlwind who never stopped moving, laughing, joking, cajoling, joyfully urging the hesitant to take steps that they otherwise would not, and somehow always listening carefully to the words of those he led. A friend who served with him as both Speaker and President of the Senate once said of him, "He's the only man I ever met who can talk and listen at the same time." On occasion his humor would have a sharp edge; more often than not his wit, his sarcasm, was the stuff that kept an otherwise angry caucus in uproarious laughter and, before they knew it, agreeing to his constant requests for action. In every complex issue that involved a myriad of interests and a roomful of stubborn characters, Burt could hear every concern and conjure up a legislative scheme that brought a piece of each into it all. Burt didn't believe in running over folks and leaving the dead behind.

Burt was a combat hero of World War II, and it taught him how to persuade the unwilling into extraordinary acts of courage. His battle unit produced three Medal of Honor winners. One of them, Mike Daley, told me at Burt's funeral at Arlington that Burt deserved the Medal of Honor but that he was too busy praising his men to praise himself. Some politicians employ words of hate and derision, words like disgrace, betrayal, destruction, greed, corrupt, hypocrite, and cheat. A generation of politicians have adopted the tactic of derision. It serves to destroy, devour, and overcome an opponent. It is useful for obtaining power, but it is corrosive and self-destructive if one wants to use power to build for the future. And therein lies the contrast with Burt.

I was the Democratic leader of the Senate for twelve years alongside Burt. He was tough, relentless, and hated to lose. He always knew how far to push. At the end of my first session as majority leader of the Senate, we encountered each other as we crossed the mall headed to each other's house; he was bouncing across the mall barking orders at staff who were running to keep up with him, when he saw me. His eyes sparkled, his eyebrows arched, he smiled and shouted out in passing, "They hate you, don't they," referring to my caucus. "Get used to it, kid, they're gonna hate you at the end of every session . . . if you're good." Later that evening the decorated commander at Anzio added, "Once you get your legislative program set, you have to move that baby down the road like a tank, and some people will get run over." He was always cognizant of the folks he ran over; he sought them out and tried to overcome the anger and mend the hurt. He used words too—words of optimism, joy, laughter, and hope—to create a vision of the future that others could believe and share in, and he used those words to re-create and rebuild the state he loved.

Burt's life story can help a generation of new leaders to rekindle hope and embrace the future.

—Alfredo Gutierrez

Preface and Acknowledgments

I knew Burton Barr to be an important figure when I moved to Arizona in 1985, and over the years after his retirement I increasingly believed that someone should write his political biography. In 2003 I recommended this to a graduate student and suggested she talk with Jack Pfister, whom I had heard was researching a history of Arizona politics. She reported Pfister's very generous offer of his research materials on Barr, but soon afterward she left graduate school and the topic. I was finishing a book on Phoenix and thought little more about Barr until the fall of 2009, when I was invited to submit a proposal to write Barr's history. Jack Pfister had recently died, and his family wanted completion for the project on which he had worked, assisted by his colleague Brent Brown. A review committee selected by the Pfister family accepted my proposal, and I gratefully acknowledge receiving research support and the materials that Pfister and Brown collected.

Starting in 1994, the two men conducted interviews with Barr, his family, his employees, and many people in Arizona politics. Over the next 12 years they conducted 36 interviews, collected information on Barr's school activities, his military record, and his father's writings, and compiled newspaper clippings from Phoenix's Burton Barr Library. While working on this and busy with other projects, they wrote half a dozen three-to-six-page drafts on different topics related to the book and created a list of eight chapters, but they did not begin writing the volume they had in mind.

My debt to these men, especially Jack, is considerable. They generated interest in this topic, and most importantly, without their interviews, this book would simply not have been possible. Their research on Barr's youth and military career was thorough and vital for writing chapter 1, and their compilation of newspaper clippings provided a very helpful start for my own newspaper research. But, for all of the value I derived from using these materials, the responsibility for this book is mine, and its failings are mine alone. I decided on, created, and am solely responsible for the entire argument, structure, and text. As indicated in the Essay on Sources, the book rests on the substantial research I did, reading newspapers, locating and conducting additional interviews, examining numerous printed and manuscript records, and consulting the large historical and theoretical literature to put this story into context.

I also wish to thank certain individuals for their direct help on this project. Thanks to Suzanne Pfister for arranging this project, overseeing the funding and transfer of materials, assisting in arranging contacts, and for her continuing support for and interest in this book. I am also grateful to Alfredo Gutierrez, Louise Barr, and David Samuel Barr for generously allowing me to interview them, and I thank Al Kluender for kindly providing his written reminiscences of his experiences with Barr. At an early stage, my colleague Christine Szuter provided valuable advice on publishing options, and Sherrie Schmidt, the Arizona State University librarian, helped clarify my use of and the eventual transfer of the Pfister materials to ASU. Heidi Osselaer was a great help, first in assisting me with crucial research, and later in providing a careful and critical eye in reading the entire manuscript. Peter Iverson read early versions of several chapters, as well as the completed manuscript, and offered his typically insightful and helpful suggestions. Ballard Campbell gave an expert's assessment of chapters 4 and 5. I owe a special debt to Bob Swierenga, for reading the last four chapters, for his great encouragement and enthusiasm for this project, and especially for helping arrange my appointment as a visiting scholar at the A. C. Van Raalte Institute at Hope College. I am very grateful to the institute, its director and staff, and the fellows for providing a wonderful environment and facilities for writing. Finally, I wish to thank Patricia Billings, whose careful, active copyediting was very helpful in improving the manuscript.

Writing can be a lonely business, and I am grateful to friends for listening and asking, "How's Barr?" Most of all I am grateful to Mary. She read and commented on some of this manuscript, and she provided valuable assistance in organizing material from the interviews. But more important, she has been, as always, my patient, thoughtful, insightful sounding board, transforming my experience in this project from solitary to one that was communal and shared.

BURTON BARR

INTRODUCTION

Understanding Burton Barr

Biography, Leadership, and the Transformation of Western Politics

"The history of the world is but the biography of great men."
—THOMAS CARLYLE[1]

"Praise of the political leader as a compromiser *is so rare that, when we find an example of it, it sounds more like satire than sincere praise."*
—GARRY WILLS[2]

"There's nothing forgotten as quickly as someone who retires from office."
—BURTON BARR[3]

In early April 1983, Arizona faced a fiscal crisis, and legislative efforts to find a solution had collapsed. Like the rest of the country, Arizona's economy was in a serious recession, with unemployment at 10.8 percent, but certain features had made the state's economy particularly vulnerable. Employment in Arizona's typically booming construction sector had fallen by a third. Even more striking was the woeful condition of the copper industry, long a key part of the state's economy. Since 1980, copper prices had dropped by nearly half, and these plummeting values drastically reduced corporate revenues, creating an angry, escalating confrontation between miners and mine owners over employment and wages. While this prompted some lawmakers to call for restrictions on strikes, most remained focused on the state's economic condition and its implications for state government.

This situation had been fully evident when the legislature convened in January 1983. In his opening message to the legislature, Governor Bruce Babbitt had declared, "You convene in the midst of a winter of economic hardship and frustration." Noting the slowdown in state revenues and that high inflation had eroded the face value of those revenues, he warned that "economic recovery is still nowhere in sight."[4] Although the governor made specific budget recommendations, the legislature would need to decide on a plan, and with clear majorities in both houses, Republicans bore the primary responsibility for solving the problem. The House Republican caucus opened the session by taking a hard line, voting overwhelmingly against any tax increase, but the Appropriations Committees in each chamber failed to find places in the budget to make sufficient and acceptable spending cuts. Legislators offered various combinations of paring expenses and some revenue increases, but devising a clear and workable solution that could win enough votes proved extremely difficult. As the session wore on, Senate leaders then cobbled together a "sleight of hand" plan to produce a functional but one-time boost in revenue by speeding up the collection of state income tax while delaying the payment of tax refunds. But in early April this effort collapsed under criticism for being unbalanced and too gimmicky.

With the Senate's failure still reverberating through the legislative halls, and with growing fears of legislative stalemate and economic chaos, House Majority Leader Burton Barr moved quickly and adeptly to solve the crisis. He succeeded because he had previously analyzed the problem and prepared a solution, and he was waiting for the right moment to bring it forward. "I always try to anticipate what's going to happen in a session," he later commented. So, although his caucus had voted in January against a tax increase, by February, he had concluded that some form of tax increase would be necessary, and he had been talking steadily with his colleagues about doing just that. He further explained that convincing legislators to raise taxes "takes a tremendous amount of work with them as individuals."[5]

Barr saw the legislative process as both work and art. He talked indefatigably with his colleagues, using his considerable skills to persuade them, but also listening and reacting to their concerns and suggestions. He also knew, "This is a business of timing. You gotta know when to hold them."[6] So while Barr talked about the state's fiscal and spending needs and the danger of inaction, he also waited, letting the Senate pursue a solution. When the Senate plan failed, as he knew it would, he was ready. He presented the caucus with three options, and he was prepared to compromise in order to achieve a settlement.

The stakes were high not only for the state, but also for many Republican legislators. Having spoken out strongly against raising taxes, they found it very difficult to change their position. Here, too, Barr played a crucial role, telling a story from his war experiences to put their decision in perspective.

Representative Joe Lane described Barr's presentation in the meeting of the Republican caucus on this issue:

> Burt stood up in front of the caucus and he said, "You know, a lot of times you've got to do things you really don't want to do." And he said, "I'll give you an example. I was standing on the deck of a troop ship, right off Anzio, and this general came up and put his arm around me and said, 'Son, see that beach over there?' he said, 'Son, you're going to be the first man on that beach.'" Burt said, "Boy, I thought, I don't want to do this." Then he said . . . it worked out all right, but he said, "You've got to stop and think of what you have to do sometimes and what you don't have to." You know that made a great impression on that caucus, on people sitting there. Here they were worried about some little old two-bit tax deal and our political reputation, and here was a guy that was told he was going to get killed on that beach.[7]

Barr's story resonated with his colleagues because they knew it was true. He frequently talked about his war experiences, typically in a self-deprecating way, but legislators knew that he was a decorated hero. They also knew that those experiences had shaped his ideas about teamwork and leadership, and this showed in his consistent emphasis on working cooperatively to get things done. So, despite some misgivings, the Republican caucus and the House voted for a one cent increase in the sales tax.

To win passage of this bill in the Senate, Barr had to use different techniques. When some Republican senators balked at the proposal, he worked with Senate President Stan Turley and Democratic Minority Leader Alfredo Gutierrez to attract Democratic support. That backing had a price, however, for Democratic senators insisted that a Republican proposal to ban strikes by public employees be dropped. When the House had earlier considered the ban proposal, Barr had expressed his reservations but accepted his Republican colleagues' decision to push it forward. Now, with this issue being the only obstacle to repairing the state's finances, Barr supported Turley's decision to drop the strike ban, and the tax increase passed.

The crisis was averted; the public was relieved. *Arizona Republic* political columnist Keven Ann Willey noted the significance of this accomplishment, but, she concluded, Barr's performance in his 19th legislative session "wasn't much different than any other. He displayed his usual wit and wisdom and miraculously managed to rally his troops around even the most politically unpopular proposals. Also, as usual, he got his way on nearly every one of them."[8]

Burton Barr

Burton Barr was a powerful and intriguing Arizona political figure from the 1960s to the 1990s, someone who significantly shaped the state's politics and policies, and whose personal legacy is evident in the enthusiastic reminiscences of his friends and former political colleagues. He attracted many nicknames and labels during his 20-year career as the Republican leader in the Arizona House of Representatives. Not surprisingly, given his complex, larger than life character, his contemporaries struggled to find the right description, the most accurate phrase. Some referred to him with the military title of "the Colonel," reflecting his military experiences, while others characterized him in much gentler, personal terms as "a teddy bear." People described his style with terms like "human dynamo," "tornado," "juggler," a man in "perpetual motion," and the "bionic legislator." According to one knowledgeable observer, he was "the most powerful man in Arizona." Another authority went further, touting him "one of the most effective legislators that's ever been on the scene." Some commentators criticized his approach to leadership, like *Phoenix Gazette* columnist John Kolbe, who, in a striking turn of phrase, termed him "as flexible as overcooked spaghetti." While some opponents complained about his successes, many people lauded his kindness and humor, and Democratic Minority Leader Art Hamilton called him "one of the most decent human beings I have had the privilege of knowing."[9]

Whatever the specific labels observers used, they all recognized his effectiveness as a leader, a skill that grew from several key facets of his life. Born in Oregon in the year when the United States entered World War I, Barr later served as a U.S. Army officer throughout World War II, achieving a distinguished, even heroic, military record and developing a perspective on leadership and pragmatism in the pursuit of larger, shared goals. After the war he remained active for many years in the U.S. Army Reserve, broadening his understanding of the role of civilian authorities. As a successful businessman in Seattle and then in Phoenix, he built friendships and honed his skills in persuasion. When Barr became involved in politics in his late forties, he quickly parlayed those skills and experiences into legislative leadership. First elected to the Arizona House of Representatives in 1964, in the following legislative session he became the Republican majority leader in the House, a position that he held for an astonishing two decades.

Barr became a leader at a key transitional period in Arizona's political history. The state's postwar growth transformed state political loyalties and policy expectations. As the majority leader, Barr played a pivotal role in shaping and passing the legislation that modernized Arizona's government and that instituted vital social and economic policies necessary for the state's progress. Although he served as the Republican floor leader in the House, he constantly worked both sides of the aisle, building friendships with lawmakers in both parties and both houses, and striving to resolve issues rather than to preserve ideological purity. Given his success, Barr was frequently rumored as a prospect for higher office, but he resisted such opportunities until 1985, when President Ronald Reagan asked him to run for governor. Accepting the invitation, Barr left his position of power and moved into a very different political arena. In the Republican primary, he faced withering personal attacks from an archconservative opponent and lost the race. Phoenix Mayor Terry Goddard, a Democrat, quickly recruited Barr to work on projects for the city, and he ended his career working as a consultant with Alfredo Gutierrez, formerly the Democratic majority leader in the Arizona Senate.

At the time of his death in 1997, Barr was still connected to the state's political leaders, and his name was still somewhat familiar to the public. Time has thinned that recognition. Today, Barr's name is known mostly because it graces the downtown branch of the Phoenix Public Library. Many of the important political figures of his legislative years have retired and some have died, new leaders and issues have arisen to dominate the political landscape, and Arizona's demography, economy, and political culture have changed. Yet if the passage of time has dimmed some memories and transformed Arizona's political conditions, this distance has also made it possible to do a historical evaluation of Burton Barr's political career. But what should such an evaluation entail? The transformations in Arizona government, public policy, and political parties during the 1960s to the 1980s have become clearer over time, partly because they are illuminated by developments in their wake, but time may either clarify or obscure the role of individuals. How does one determine Barr's impact in an era of such great change and amid powerful historic forces? What should one expect of a leader in a democratic political system? What constitutes leadership and success, especially within a system of highly structured parties that demand loyalty? To answer such questions for Burton Barr, we must start by considering the nature of history and biography, the character of leadership, and the transformation of politics in the Western region of the United States during the last half of the twentieth century.

History and Biography

People look at the past from different perspectives and see different things. Some historians focus on grand forces and hear the clash of ideologies or movements, allowing them to explain mass changes, like the rise of democracy, industrialization, or the westward movement. Their stories follow larger imperatives, such as the search for economic gain, the power of ideas, the dialectic of class conflict, or the impact of technology. While these approaches are not always deterministic, they generally downplay the role of individual actors in shaping history.

Other historians have emphasized the importance of key individuals. From ancient works like Plutarch's *Lives*, to modern day biographies, writers have recounted stories of "great men" whose actions have shaped the course of history on battlefields, in economic enterprises or cultural endeavors, or in political struggles. American political historians have a rich tradition of touting the impact of major figures. The Founding Fathers are perennial favorites, and libraries are filled with volumes about "great" presidents; even the failed or brief occupants of the office have received generous recognition. Whether because of shrewd choices, good fortune, or simply the power of their position, historians have described presidents and other major figures as the shapers of events that changed history.

But the value of biography is not confined to just the study of "great men" or famous people, or looking for how their lives and decisions affected history. An old tradition used biography overtly to teach moral lessons, like Parson Weems writing about George Washington. Some recent biographers, often subtly, proffer the lives of their subjects as models worth emulating. Other writers recommend biography as the essential way to look at the past. Ralph Waldo Emerson's claim, "There is properly no history; only biography" is an extreme view, but many authors have written history through a biographical lens, seeing the past as the accretion of actions and omissions by individuals, as the result of personal choices and perceptions.[10] This approach demands a broader look at both historical actions and the range of actors. Political developments, for example, can be regarded as the decisions and actions not just of presidents, or even of legislative leaders, but of numerous legislators and an assortment of other political figures. For historical studies of politics, as for studies of the military or of business, this means acknowledging and explaining the agency, or independent actions and choices, of individuals.

So how does thinking about historical causation, societal change, and the role of individuals shape a biography of Burton Barr? From a national perspective, he was not a great or major national figure—not a president nor a senator or congressman. He did not rise higher on the ladder of political office; he lost the only statewide political contest he waged. He was not the acknowledged, sole author of major pieces of legislation, nor did he reach oratorical heights that inspired people to political action. Even within the historical memory of the Arizona public, Barr has a limited stature, dwarfed especially by the iconic image of Barry Goldwater, but also overshadowed by the state's considerable array of nationally known politicians, men like Carl Hayden, Mo Udall, John Rhodes, and John McCain.

Barr's lesser visibility is not surprising, given the large number of state legislators, often with only brief careers, and because developments in Washington, DC, often seem more vital, as well as easier to follow, than the particularistic politics of 50 states. But obvious visibility is not the only reason to examine someone's life. Barr's life story warrants telling because he profoundly affected Arizona's politics, government, and public policy-making, even more than those Arizona politicians with national reputations. And though he did not achieve national recognition, he helped lead a historic, national change in governance. During the 1960s and 1970s, states responded to the emerging needs of modern society and the post-1930s growth of the federal government by modernizing and expanding their governments. Barr's vigorous leadership in this effort provides a case study of this transformation and of the redefinition of American federalism. Barr's political career also clarifies key aspects of legislative culture and procedure, and it shows the changing role of party loyalty and identification in policy-making. Unlike later years, when party preference would be a sure and simple guide to ideological orientation, during the period of Barr's legislative service, parties and party leadership reflected overlapping clusters of views on various political issues. Here, too, Barr's career illustrates those circumstances for Arizona particularly, but also for other states. More importantly, it highlights a style of political leadership focused on outcomes rather than ideology—a pragmatic approach to public policy that is often best appreciated from a distance. "Biography contextualizes a life," wrote political scientist Tracey Arklay, "but can illuminate much more than just that."[11]

A final consideration in assessing Barr's political life is that it unfolded in a state and region that during his years of prominence shifted from being outliers to being pacesetters. Understanding some of the key characteristics of a burgeoning West—such as the nature and distribution of its population, the transformation of its economy, the importance of water, and the role of partisanship—is essential to recognizing Barr's options and choices in policy-making and his leadership style. In turn, appreciating Barr's response to that sociopolitical environment clarifies how and why Arizona and the West developed as they did. These concerns with region, party, ideology, and the legislature reveal why Burton Barr's biography must put his life and work in context. It must be an intertwined story of his political life, the nature of legislative leadership, and the impact of the state and region in which he lived. It is a story in which each part helps explain the other.

Political Leadership

Barr's ceaseless activity, his notable accomplishments, and his personal style evoked numerous descriptions and labels (mostly but not exclusively positive) relating to his leadership abilities. General discussions of leadership often invoke a single set of behaviors, values, and ideals. Historian Garry Wills calls this "the 'superman' school" of leadership, the notion that "a leader can command *all* situations with the same basic gifts."[12] Scholars of leadership, like Wills, reject this concept of universal leadership traits appropriate for all situations in favor of a more complex approach. A leader's effectiveness is certainly personal, depending on his or her individual skills, character, and vision, but it also varies according to external conditions—how well a particular type of leadership works in the context of a particular group, time, and place.

The balance of these traits in effective leadership depends primarily on context—the group or situation in which someone is attempting to lead. For example, leadership abilities needed in a community association differ from those relevant to leading a national group. Heading a volunteer disaster relief organization requires a set of interpersonal and communication skills distinct from those that Dwight Eisenhower needed to fulfill his military responsibilities as Supreme Allied Commander in Europe in World War II. And, of course, people often work in multiple contexts, filling multiple leadership roles. The CEO of a business draws on certain traits in dealing with board members or investors and others when trying to motivate employees. Similarly, effective politicians demonstrate different leadership qualities when working with other officeholders than they do when motivating constituents and winning their votes. Finally, this context for leadership also includes historical era and geographic place.

The second element affecting leadership is the importance of followers. Casual descriptions or simplistic notions of leadership often assume a stark leader-follower dichotomy in which leaders are active deciders and followers are passive—a role that Garry Wills describes as being "dominated or served, mesmerized or flattered."[13] Yet a number of thoughtful studies, including Barbara Kellerman's study *Followership*, explain the active, essential role of followers in decision-making as well as follow-through, and the leader-follower dichotomy is especially flawed in assessing politics. Both Wills and noted political scientist and biographer James MacGregor Burns explain that this simplistic construct ignores democratic philosophy, which posits some give-and-take interaction between leaders and followers, as well as the notion that leaders hold their positions with the continuing assent of their followers. Equally important, the leader-follower dichotomy ignores the reality of democratic politics, for maintaining power requires flexibility.

But how flexible should leaders be? Barr's initial acquiescence in his party's push to ban strikes by public employees prompted no rebukes from his colleagues, but at another point in his service, Barr's willingness to change his views and accept the party position led critics to label him the "Majority Follower."[14] His response to such criticism was a usual one for politicians: that flexibility allowed him to maintain power and fight another day. A less pragmatic and more conceptual defense for accepting the majority's views, even if a leader disagrees in principle with those views, is that acceptance recognizes the majority's authority. Yet too much flexibility, whatever the rationale, can undermine a leader's legitimacy.[15]

People's willingness to follow a leader reflects their sense of shared goals—their needs, interests, and perhaps as well, a larger vision—as Barr demonstrated when he talked about doing good for the state of Arizona. Politics provides a generally different environment for leadership and shared goals than, for example, business or the military, but the great variety of political offices and positions present not one but a diverse set of opportunities for leadership. Elected executives like presidents, governors, or mayors need wide-ranging communication skills, such as persuading voters and negotiating with lawmakers, and the specific context, whether national, state, or local, refines what particular skills are needed. Appointed administrators may or may not require facility in public communication, depending on the nature of their position, but they must be able to manage and stimulate individuals and groups of subordinates.

Effective legislative leadership demands a third mix of skills, the ability to work alone and with others. It involves personal interactions and issue analysis, and it occurs in open legislative chambers as well as behind closed doors. Certain individuals can be more influential working in some areas than in others. U.S. Senator Carl Hayden (1926–1969), for example, boasted of being known as a "work horse" legislator, not a "show horse" orator. But effectiveness and ability to win reelection necessitate other skills as well.

Strong legislative leadership is commonly touted as politically desirable, but the diverse forms and arenas for such leadership can make it difficult for observers to recognize, understand, or appreciate it. The effectiveness of Burton Barr's leadership was quite evident, however, as evidenced by one of his more evocative nicknames: "Mr. Magic." A magician, of course, does surprising things, surmounts seemingly enormous obstacles to achieve the "impossible," and does it with grace and style. The performance involves a ritual and engages the audience, while the method for achieving the solution remains a mystery, or "miraculous," as Keven Ann Willey wrote in her column about Barr's ability to rally lawmakers and avert crisis in 1983.[16] As a label for political leadership, then, the description "Mr. Magic" is positive and congratulatory. It reflects success in achieving outcomes, public approval, ritualized forms and interactions, and acceptance of some uncertainty about how the result was achieved. This fits well with a politics that emphasizes outcomes and stylized interactions. By one standard or by one cultural approach to political leadership, then, this is a laudable style.

This political magician approach to leadership conflicts with other notions, however, since it does not necessarily and clearly include factors like the role of followers, articulated priorities, public discussions, and transparent negotiations. The terms "magic" and "magician" may suggest sleight of hand, diversion, trickery, or even fraud. This style can seem like hocus-pocus, a show, a sham without substance. Beyond objecting to flashy methods, people often criticize a politics of magic as obfuscating political differences and encouraging arrangements or deals that paper over differences, rather than promoting open, public debates over principles. Barr's severest critics, those who held this view, called him a "philosophical prostitute" for changing his positions and making deals.[17]

Parties, Principles, and Pragmatism

The history of American politics overflows with vivid examples of different leadership and political styles. Perhaps the most familiar are leaders known for their ardent advocacy for certain principles (sometimes ideologues), and whose legislative actions connected especially well to external audiences. For example, Senator Barry Goldwater achieved a national reputation as a champion of conservative politics, while Senator Ted Kennedy mobilized liberals across the country with his Senate speeches. Other noted legislators were adept conciliators (some of the "magicians"), working primarily within their institutions. Henry Clay, for example, was in Congress for much of the first half of the nineteenth century and earned the sobriquet of the "Great Compromiser" for his role in resolving major political controversies. More recently, Tip O'Neil, a successful Speaker of the U.S. House (1977–1987), explained in typically understated fashion that Congress included "countless brilliant lawmakers," but, "My own skills had more to do with powers of persuasion and with getting things done."[18]

Complicating the division between compromise and the pursuit of principle has been a historically conflicted engagement with the political party, the primary organizing framework of American politics. Some critics have perceived parties as a threat to the individual's conscience and an obstruction to achieving policy ends, while other commentators have viewed party affiliation pragmatically, for example, as the best means for securing particular policies, and party defenders have equated party loyalty with adherence to principle. Americans' views of parties have changed over time and varied by place. During the early days of the republic, the term "party" had a negative connotation and was attached to groups whose actions seemed to threaten the operation of republican government and the public good. Beginning in the 1830s, economic development, social differentiation, and a growing appreciation of democratic possibilities led Americans to employ parties to organize the popular will. They quickly created very elaborate party structures and participated at impressively high levels in party activities and various forms of political life. These new democrats (both Democrats and Whigs) championed parties as a necessary means to organize and implement public preferences, and they expected elected representatives to heed the public's voice.

Views of party and leadership blended in interesting ways during this era. The forceful actions of President Andrew Jackson prompted his supporters to organize the Democratic Party and his critics to dub him "King Andrew." His successor, Martin Van Buren, was not a successful or important president, but he was notable both for defending parties and for being an early "career politician." These attributes won him the nickname "Little Magician," but it was mainly his political opponents who used this, and they viewed his skills, ideas, and actions as chicanery, not leadership. Still, Van Buren's pro-party perspective dominated American political culture in the years after he left office. In the early 1900s, the intensity of party loyalty began to decline, and anti-party sentiment began rising among voters. By the mid-twentieth century, political scientists criticized declining levels of party voting on issues in Congress and began calling for a "responsible party system" in which parties would stand firmly for specific policies. The patterns in some state legislatures, such as Arizona, were even more complex than those in Congress. Party voting in those state arenas was sometimes higher, but they also saw notable changes in partisanship and party strength, as well as occasional factional splits in which a minority party controlled a legislative chamber. By the 1980s, however, the levels and intensity of partisanship began to increase generally, and notably within Congress and state legislatures.[19]

Ideas about the legitimacy of parties have shaped expectations about who should hold office and how policies should be made. In turn, these ideas have influenced popular notions of leadership. But different times and places have prompted different questions and reactions. Harry Truman's bluntness dragged him to abysmally low public approval ratings in the early 1950s and limited success with Congress, but 25 years later Presidents Gerald Ford, Jimmy Carter, and Ronald Reagan all invoked him as a leader to emulate. The practice of politics and political leadership has also been affected by the strength of party loyalty, the capacity of party organizations, and the relative strength of the two major parties.

The style and success of Burton Barr's leadership not only illuminate his personality and ideas, they also help explain the larger political context, showing ideas of leadership within and outside of the legislature, the structure of Arizona government and its challenges, and views of partisanship and policy. Barr's career is additionally instructive because his considerable success, the criticism it engendered, and his ultimate defeat span an era of significant change. His gifts perfectly matched his time and place: a postwar era that saw shifts in party loyalty, a region that experienced enormous growth and fundamental cultural change, and a state that needed to improve its government and address serious policy questions.

The Context: The West and Western Politics

The West has fascinated the American imagination, fueled by cultural expression in dime novels, television, movies, and even video games. Although this region is a patchwork of various climates, topographies, demographic patterns, cultures, and histories, and although, as David Wrobel notes, Westerners disagree about who "fits" as a Westerner, there are important reasons to talk about "the West" as a region and to use it as a context for evaluating politics.[20] First, nearly all of this large area is arid, and so water is a prime and vital consideration in the West. For the region's leaders, the complex issues of water location, storage, and management have been at the forefront of discussions about economic, social, and political development. The West's aridity, combined with its vast land area, means that most of the region shares a similar physical-spatial characteristic: population concentrated in cities, and significant distances between residents of lightly populated rural areas. In addition, west of the Great Plains, most rural areas that are arid but not desert have been used for ranching. The region's shared topography also created common economies and experiences of forestry and mining in the mountain areas. Still, water is the resource that most defines the region, and Arizona shared fully in this Western pattern of water's political, social, and economic impact.

Western states are also linked by historical development. They experienced stages of development at similar times: settlement and statehood occurred in clustered years from the mid-nineteenth century to the early twentieth century, and World War II injected every state with population and economic development. Finally, Western topography and settlement opportunities fostered the growth of diverse cultures and lifestyles. Western residents shared a sense of distinctiveness and difference, a common individualism. Their mindset was framed by the traditional sense of opportunities available to settlers and newcomers, and by the struggle, joy, and success of building new communities. Ambivalence tempered these positive attitudes, as new residents felt disconnected from areas they had left, distant from the rest of the country, and in a subordinate relationship to it. With an economy that relied on exploiting resources to be sent and processed elsewhere, and that depended on economic decisions, especially financial ones, made in the East, many Westerners, including Arizonans, considered themselves victims of a domestic colonialism.

This promoted a politics of protest, but these "voices were drowned out by those of neighbors and other westerners eager for federal 'interference.'"[21] Building on a nineteenth-century tradition of federal involvement through the military, control of Indian reservations, and management of federal lands, Westerners demanded the establishment of federal facilities and aid for internal improvements, especially projects for water control and storage and for hydroelectric power. Encouraged by the Newlands Reclamation Act (1902) and supported by subsequent funding, the federal government built numerous dams, including major ones like the Roosevelt Dam on the Salt River and the Hoover (formerly Boulder) Dam on the Colorado River. These early twentieth-century projects played a decisive role in remaking the West, touching Arizona in direct and profound ways.

Federal assistance grew even more important during the 1930s, when Western states benefitted from federal spending far out of proportion to their populations or tax revenues. The pattern continued after 1939 through spending on military facilities and defense manufacturing plants, a decision influenced by security, climate, and political considerations. This transformation intensified as Cold War defense spending and the policy of decentralization boosted the development in Western states, notably Arizona, of the aerospace, electronics, and defense industries, along with military facilities.

The postwar construction of airports and highways, combined with major innovations in communications, boosted the economy and shrank the region's vast distances, bringing its people closer together and nearer the rest of the country. Arizona benefited from closer connections with California, while aviation dramatically accelerated the growth of the Tucson and Phoenix metropolitan areas. Western communities, like those elsewhere in the nation, sought and benefited from federal policies on home mortgages and construction, suburban growth and urban redevelopment, and health care. And, as in other regions, this growth in the West produced gains and losses, more jobs and income but growing sprawl and pollution. By the late twentieth century, the West had transitioned from a peripheral to a core region.

But while the region benefitted significantly from federal support, Western attitudes toward the federal government were never uniform or simple. Nineteenth-century frustration with subordinate territorial status and delays in winning statehood linked to the continuing federal role in owning and managing huge amounts of Western land were evidenced in the Sagebrush Rebellion of the 1970s. The expanding regulatory role of the federal government, especially in areas such as the environment, generated additional opposition. Beyond a general complaint about insensitive and intrusive federal authorities, Western politics tend, as Jeff Roche observed, "toward the individualistic, and westerners are often leery, if not distrustful, of centralized authority."[22] Concerns about federalism reflected not simply an antigovernment attitude, but sometimes a preference for using state rather than federal or local authority. A major postwar development involved the expansion of state governments, and Arizona offers us an excellent example of how Western states shared in this experience.

The Impact of Western Politics and Politicians

The political importance of the West resulted from its population, leadership, and political culture. In the postwar era, the region's population grew three times faster than that of the rest of the nation. This included nearly every state in the region, but especially California and Texas. Those states were primarily responsible for the region's prominence on national political tickets, and they also supplied numerous congressional leaders, but many leaders came from other Western states, including Utah, Nevada, and Arizona. Western politicians achieved prominence partly because of strategies like portraying regional balance among the party's leaders. Those politicians also had more leadership opportunities because they served longer in Congress, which reflected their interest and ability to win reelection. But while necessary, longevity was not a sufficient basis for gaining leadership positions. Particular skills and values were also crucial.

The popular, media-induced perception of Westerners as heroic, sometimes stoic, but often bluntly frank was personified by men like Barry Goldwater. The more characteristic trait of Western political leaders, however, was and remains their ability and willingness to balance different factions and interests. Their relatively greater electoral security facilitated this. In addition, because many Western states had smaller populations, their leaders were more likely to know each other, encouraging a more personal basis for political interaction. This condition was important, for example, in Arizona. Western political culture also encouraged an ability to see various sides of policy disputes, a give-and-take attitude toward negotiating them, and a willingness to make deals. Samuel Lubell described the vital leadership role during the 1930s and 1940s of "border-state" politicians who practiced a "balance of compromise . . . between the Democratic extremes."[23] Their negotiating skills and their ability to position themselves in the political center passed on to Western politicians in the postwar era—not simply or automatically, and not to everyone, but it was a predisposition and skill set encouraged by the Western political climate.

This climate was partly affected by the region's considerable change in partisan preference. Most states were Republican before 1930, but the Depression and New Deal brought Democratic victories. This trend was reversed in the first two postwar decades, with most states becoming more competitive. As national politics shifted to the right in the late 1960s, Western states led this trend toward the Republican Party. According to Michael Malone and Richard Etulain, this confluence with national trends also represented a Western experience of "shedding of postfrontier, confrontational politics and their gravitation toward a conservatism based on suburban and middle-class values."[24] Yet beneath this visible pattern lay a more complex political reality.

Starting in 1968, Republican presidential candidates captured nearly every Western state in every election, even while Democrats were winning numerous gubernatorial, senatorial, and congressional races. In part, this evidenced greater voter willingness to change: by the late 1970s, roughly a fourth of Western voters switched their support from one party in the presidential election to another in the following off-year election. Even more voters—over half—split their tickets between candidates at different levels of government.

While split-ticket voting and shifting party strength between elections occurred in many states, those patterns had begun earlier and developed more strongly in the West. In those states party ties had always been comparatively weaker, and while many individuals identified strongly with one of the major parties, third parties drew more support than in other regions. Moreover, many progressives actively criticized parties, and various states passed laws that weakened their control of the electoral process.[25]

Having weaker party institutions and loyalties encouraged a politics that focused on personalities and individuals. Candidates increasingly created their own organizations and campaigned separately. Barry Goldwater initiated this effort in Arizona, using his plane to fly 1950 gubernatorial candidate Howard Pyle across the state, and two years later himself in his own campaign for the U.S. Senate. Over time, as historian Paul Kleppner noted, "Personality-focused campaigns became the norm, rather than party efforts or issue-driven movements," which gave a significant advantage to incumbents.[26] Developing reputations and records somewhat independent of their parties, these officeholders were more able to win than were non-incumbents of their parties, sometimes handily. In Arizona after 1956, all but one of the 26 incumbent governors and senators running for reelection were successful.

Weaker party ties also affected governance. Without the linkage of party loyalty or a fear of consequences from seeking personal rather than collective purposes, officeholders acted more independently, and different branches of state government were more likely to clash. Legislators in most Western states tended to have less time in office than lawmakers elsewhere, but their legislative experience differed even more because they had fewer institutional support services for their legislative work. The difficulties of governing were accentuated by the region's heritage of direct democracy. In the late nineteenth and early twentieth centuries, most Western states enthusiastically endorsed multiple methods for enhancing the power of citizens over officeholders. They supported direct primaries to nominate officials and recall procedures to remove bad officials. More striking was their adoption of referenda and initiatives as alternate methods of enacting laws. As intended, these direct legislation methods did provide alternative paths for pursuing public policy, but they also significantly complicated the activities and strategies of state legislatures.

The West, Arizona, and Burton Barr

Arizona's character and culture are a unique blend of traits, but they also echo the basic patterns of Western history and politics. The last of the 48 contiguous states admitted to the union, Arizona developed its own balance of protest against its perceived colonial status and ardent pursuit of aid from the federal government. Despite its small population, Arizona's political leaders soon achieved national importance, as U.S. Senator Carl Hayden rose in seniority and influence after 1926, while his colleague, Senator Ernest McFarland (1941–1953), served as the chamber's majority leader. Arizona's postwar growth resembled the surge experienced by the largest Western states of California and Texas and the boom in several smaller states like Colorado and Washington. As much as that of any Western state, Arizona's history demonstrates a general shift from postfrontier, colonial, confrontational politics to suburban conservatism and the pursuit of growth. But the state's political path cannot be so easily pigeonholed. Its partisan shift during the 1950s and 1960s from the Democratic party to the Republican was also accompanied by limited party loyalties and frequent split-ticket voting. The transformation of state government and the development of major policies involved complex interactions and decisions. Arizona politics during these decades remained contested and complex.

Burton Barr was a crucial figure during this political era. He faced major and fundamental changes like shifting party affiliations of voters and officeholders, and a dramatic rise in the importance of legislative districts. The House, his legislative chamber, remained reliably Republican, but party factions and personalities always play a role in state politics, and they figured prominently in Barr's experience. A further complication was the Democrats' relative strength in the state Senate, plus their control of the governorship for 14 of Barr's 22 years in the legislature. Arizona's tremendous growth in its urban populations, its desire for economic expansion and diversification, its pursuit of federal money (particularly for water projects), and its objections to federal regulation confronted Arizona lawmakers with major policy choices, and Barr shaped those decisions. Senator Jon Kyl claimed that Barr "stood astride the most dynamic period of growth in the state's history," and John Kolbe, the conservative Phoenix journalist, voiced the opinion of most people when he noted that Barr "wrote the legislative history of this state for 20 years."[27]

Arizona's circumstances and pursuits were not typically American or even Western, but the questions of governance and policy facing the state were at the heart of national and regional debates. For example, the need to deal with rising urban and suburban problems was complicated by the limited capacity of state government and the legislature.[28] Examining how Burton Barr dealt with these challenges, how he forged a leadership style and defined legislative priorities, how he helped build the capacity of state government, and how he worked with people from a wide range of political perspectives in Arizona, speaks also to the experiences of other states and of the nation during this period of transition, and to what we can hope for from political leaders. Studying Barr's role in Arizona politics also moves us beyond the traditional "Goldwater prism," seeing everything in a predictable, dichotomous liberal-conservative split, which was similar across the country, and beyond envisioning everything in Arizona as a consequence of that interesting man's life and actions. The reality of Arizona and Western politics was far more complex and fluid than this framework would suggest. As Jeff Roche rightly argues, "Westerners crafted unique definitions of liberal and conservative, forged their own connections between culture and politics, and redefined the relationships between economic and political power."[29]

Barr's life story illuminates the transformation of postwar Arizona and the nature of political change. He was an exemplar of the politics of conciliation and a model of effective legislative leadership. That style and those values were not something he picked up as convenience; they reflected his core being. For him, as much as for anyone, leadership was personal. His leadership skills developed out of his family background, his experiences during the Depression and World War II, and his work. It was this personal history that brought him to Arizona and to eventual political success.

CHAPTER ONE

Making the Man and Raising the Barr

"Biography is a system in which the contradictions of a human life are unified."

—JOSE ORTEGA Y GASSET[1]

"He loved to tell war stories. This was not an area of his life that was secret by any means. It was, I think, truly the defining part of his life. And I think it made him the person he was."

—STEPHANIE BARR STRASSER[2]

Burton Barr's political life is part of a larger story about political leadership and transformation, but understanding that story requires knowing where he came from, the familial, social, and political landscape of his past. Biographies vary in focus and intent, but they all recount stories of their subject's early life, their family, home, and education, because these experiences are always formative in some way, helping to shape character, values, and relationships. In this respect, Burton Barr's later life and political career are no different.

Yet, as an adult, Barr refused to talk either publicly or privately about that part of his life. His daughter Stephanie questioned him about his family history, but in stark contrast to his frank and lengthy conversations about many other subjects, his childhood and family were topics "he just didn't really feel like discussing."[3] His parents and brother were a mystery to his wife and children—literally. He seemed to have had virtually no contact with them for the last 30 years of their lives, and his parents never met their grandchildren. He did not attend his parents' funerals, or his brother's. This startling behavior, particularly when contrasted with his devotion to his own wife and children, raises questions about his parents and upbringing, but there is no direct evidence to explain it. The pattern of his early life offers no clear signs of a particularly tense or conflicted relationship; he did not rebel in any obvious way. Perhaps there was some Rubicon moment in the 1940s when he moved away from them, or perhaps the patterns of their lives simply sent them in different directions. Since Barr provided very little oral record and no written documents relating to his family, we must rely on fragmentary references he made and the limited material available in public records. But while the causes and nature of the division are uncertain, the important influences upon him and the basic course of his life up to adulthood are clear.

We can also understand aspects of his life by looking at when he lived, by considering the era in which he was born and raised, and, most importantly, the time in which he entered adulthood. The impact of historical events on people varies by their stage of life. This was particularly true for Barr, who was part of what Tom Brokaw famously called the "Greatest Generation." There are caveats to this notion, of course. History is filled with conflicts, and every generation faces some serious challenges. What distinguished this generation is that it came of age during crises and conflicts, the Depression and World Wars, that were grave and proximate. Living through these extraordinary events as they were entering adulthood gave the people of this generation a unique set of experiences and a particular perspective. For Barr, growing up in the Depression separated him from his family and encouraged him to see the world a different light. But his military and war experiences had far greater importance, shaping Barr's sense of himself, his desire to act, his sense of purpose, and his notions about leadership.

Family Background

Burton Barr was born on October 14, 1917, in Portland, Oregon, but his family roots were much further east—in eastern Europe. The only information on those origins comes from some basic demographic records, which provide an outline of the story. His mother's father, Isaac Hurwitz, had been born in the Pale of Settlement, a region of the Russian Empire stretching from Lithuania to the Ukraine on the Black Sea where Jews were legally permitted permanent residence, and by the mid- to late nineteenth century that population exceeded five million people. The creation of the Pale in 1791 had been intended to segregate Jews, and perhaps to reduce conflict with non-Jews, yet anti-Semitism remained prevalent there, as in other parts of the Russian Empire. The assassination of Tsar Alexander II in 1881 sparked the tinder of that prejudice into violent attacks on Jews, or pogroms, and restrictive legislation. In response to these assaults and restrictions, more than 150,000 Jews left Russia in that decade, by 1914 the total had reached 2 million, and nearly all immigrated to the United States.

Isaac Hurwitz was one of those Jewish immigrants. Born in the Pale in 1868 to parents also born there, he was 18 years old in 1886 and had just married. His wife, Bessie Meyerson, had been born in Latvia, and her parents came originally from Latvia and Germany, but at some point not too long after her birth they had moved to Poland. Whatever the precise circumstances that encouraged the family to move and initially brought the young couple together, the pogroms and restrictions pushed them to move further. In 1886 the parents, Isaac, Bessie, and Isaac's brother, Jacob, left their violent and threatening homeland to seek a new life in the United States.

The families probably travelled overland to Hamburg, Germany, and then to New York City on one of Hamburg America's steamships. Their destination was truly a different world. The nation's wealthiest city and its financial center, New York also boasted a burgeoning manufacturing sector, with its clothing trade being easily the city's largest industry. New York was the world's busiest port and served as the primary entry point for the millions of immigrants attracted to America, especially after the opening of the immigration screening station at Ellis Island in 1892. In each decade from 1880 to 1910 the city's population increased by a third, reaching 4.8 million in 1910. Immigrants composed a major part of that increase, streaming in from all over Europe and beyond, so that foreign-born residents constituted about 40 percent of the New York population, and their children made up roughly 25 percent.

Many immigrants who landed in New York quickly moved on to other places across the nation. By contrast, New York was the end destination for most Jewish immigrants, especially those from Russia, so their numbers and share of the population grew considerably. In 1880 some 80,000 Jews lived in New York; by 1910 they numbered about 1.1 million. Their experience also differed somewhat from that of other immigrants because they arrived as families and intended to stay in America, whereas other groups included a high proportion of young men and a substantial number who returned to their homelands.

Seeking to re-create their familiar worlds and customs, Jewish immigrants clustered on the Lower East Side of Manhattan, especially in the Tenth Ward, which became known as the "Jewish Tenth Ward." Increasingly crowded conditions there encouraged outmigration to other places in the larger New York area, particularly across the East River to Brooklyn. Jewish immigrants shared more than neighborhoods. Because Russian laws had prevented Jews from owning land, they had been urban dwellers, not farmers, and other occupational restrictions encouraged them to work in skilled crafts. As a result, Thomas Kessner notes, Jews in New York were most involved in clothing trades, which provided the occupation of "one of every three arriving Jewish workers."[4]

The Hurwitz family likely fit this pattern, although the evidence of their individual behavior is very slim. The clearest tie is occupation, for Isaac was connected with the garment industry, working for a suit and cloak factory, while his brother Jacob worked as a jobber in clothing. Within several years of Isaac and Bessie's arrival, a daughter, Ella, was born, and over the next 20 years the couple had six more children, all of whom lived to adulthood. By 1910 the family's circumstances had improved to roughly middle class status. They were living in Brooklyn, in a house owned by Bessie's mother, along with Bessie's brother Samuel and his family, as well as Isaac's brother Jacob. Isaac had become the proprietor of a grocery store, while Jacob worked as a real estate agent. As further indication of the family's economic success and mobility, Ella studied piano with Paula Gallico, a pianist of some reputation, and worked as a music teacher.

Hymen Max Barr's background was similar. His parents were also Jewish and emigrated from Kiev, Russia, to the United States. They were living in Brooklyn when Hy was born in 1888, followed by two siblings, Sam and Ida. The family assimilated to American culture fairly quickly. The name Lubarsky was Anglicized to Barr at or soon after arrival in the United States, and the family was only nominally observant in religion.[5] Hy attended Cornell University, followed some years later by his brother Sam. This was an unusual university: as a land-grant school, it provided education in practical fields, such as agriculture, veterinary science, and education, yet as one of the elite Ivy League schools, it also offered a liberal arts education. It was socially progressive, admitting women in 1870 and offering scholarships to worthy students across the state. Hy's ability to win admission to Cornell, excel in his studies, and graduate with a degree in English reflects both personal and cultural values, ambition and distinction. In 1908 he won the university's Barnes Shakespeare prize, and in 1910 he won another prize for his paper entitled "The World and the College," which hints at Hy's breadth of vision.

After graduation, Hy and Ella Hurwitz married, and not long after that, they left New York. Like their families' experience a quarter-century before, this venture involved a major change in circumstances, a hope for the future, and a long migration to a new place. They crossed not an ocean but a continent, moving to Portland, Oregon, where Hy would begin a new job as a schoolteacher. And unlike their parents, whose migration and community were defined by their Jewish identity, Hy and Ella moved to a very different kind of community and increasingly adopted an American identity.

New Beginnings: Portland

The vibrant city to which the young couple came had a distinctive character and culture that would shape the family's opportunities and values. Established in the mid-nineteenth century, Portland grew steadily and then boomed from 1890 to 1910, when it was the third-fastest-growing city in the nation. Although surpassed by Seattle as the leading city in the Pacific Northwest by 1910, Portland continued to grow at a healthy pace, reaching a population of around 250,000 by 1920. It boasted a high level of home ownership, congenial neighborhoods, and culture: a 1920s survey put it 22nd of 150 cities, based partly on the high rankings of its schools and library services, which were also reflected by census information on the city's high literacy rate. The leading city in Oregon, Portland shaped the state's political culture and fostered its expanding use after 1902 of direct democracy measures like the initiative.

Portland is a river city built at the confluence of the Columbia River, a broad water route accessing much of the Pacific Northwest, and the Willamette River, which runs the length of Oregon's fertile Willamette Valley. Portland railroads strengthened the city's connection with this hinterland and facilitated the export of agricultural, timber, and lumber products. Thus, Portland served as both a commercial and a financial center for the region, but its few manufacturing businesses were small-scale enterprises. As a result, the labor movement in Portland was comprised primarily of dock workers, not factory laborers. In general, Portland was prosperous, and historian Robert Johnston notes that "some authorities even listed Portland as the third wealthiest intermediate-sized city in the country."[6]

The city's population was relatively homogenous, especially compared with New York and other large cities. A large majority of its residents were immigrants or children of immigrants from northern Europe; relatively few came from southern or eastern Europe, and even fewer were Asian or African American. Church membership, which was slightly less common than in Eastern cities, included a sizable majority of Protestants, but the city also contained a significant Catholic population and a small but influential

Jewish community. "In Portland, as in other Pacific Coast cities, German Jews were among the generation of merchants that founded the town; in the nineteenth century they helped create a civic order in which office holding and private voluntarism fortified social stability."[7]

In the 1890s Jewish immigrants from eastern Europe began settling in South Portland, an area on the western side of the Willamette River and south of the original city settlement. Largely craftsmen, peddlers, and small businessmen, they created their own organizations and joined community associations like the Elks and Masons. As their community's population grew, they joined the city's expanding population movement to the east side of the river, where nearly all of the post-1900 growth occurred. This largely middle-class area boasted numerous parks and schools; nonresidential activities were located on the periphery, and the proportion of its single-family homes that were owner-occupied was nearly double the rate for other midsized American cities. It was to this rapidly growing area that Hy and Ella Barr moved in 1910.

Hy Barr and Portland Education

What drew them to this section of Portland was Hy's new position as a teacher at the Fulton Park School in the somewhat older, northern section of east Portland. After two years he moved on to become principal of Fernwood School (1913–1914), then of Buckman School (1915–1916), and finally of Irvington School, a position he held for the next 26 years. This migration represented upward mobility in the school hierarchy, especially the last move, for Irvington was then the prime neighborhood on the city's east side. Its solid, relatively large school buildings demonstrated a serious investment in education and served as a community center and a source of public pride. The initial building, constructed in 1905, was a two-story structure of 21 rooms and five furnaces. In 1932–1933 a substantial brick structure replaced the original building.

Hy's career grew steadily. In the 1920s he became very active as an author, publishing a short text on Oregon geography (1929), coauthoring an operetta, *Cinderella and the Cat* (1928), and coauthoring a third volume, *Redskin and Pioneer: Brave Tales of the Great Northwest* (1932), which was part of Rand McNally's American Life Series. More useful for his career advancement was his administrative work. In 1927–1928 he served as one of Portland's assistant superintendents of schools, an additional, part-time position. Starting in 1925 he also served as the part-time director of research, which involved writing speeches for district officials and school board members. In 1943, when the board decided to make this a full-time post, Hy left his principal's position and worked solely as the director, which he continued to do until 1956 when he retired. He maintained his connection with education but shifted his focus, earning a degree from Reed College in 1945, and later lecturing at Reed, the University of Portland, and Multnomah College.[8]

As an educator, Hy Barr left a valuable mark on the community, creating programs and articulating an educational philosophy that emphasized both the value of education and the importance of responding to the needs of individual children. His views followed the teachings of progressive educators like John Dewey and fit the Portland school system very well. A 1926 study by the Federal Bureau of Education concluded that Portland had "developed one of the finest and most progressive school systems in the county," and noted specifically the importance of "progressive people" in creating a supportive "school 'atmosphere.'"[9] Throughout his career, Hy Barr preached the philosophy that "teachers should teach students and not subjects." "Great teachers," he argued, were not put off "by the difficulties of learning and behavior that certain children present. They consider these a challenge and tailor methods to reach these children." Believing that both schools and homes "are educational institutions and must work together," he visited the home of every student, and he helped organize the city's Parent-Teacher Association.[10]

Barr's belief that education should be egalitarian and shaped to individual students led him to support special training for what he estimated to be "about 2 percent who are mentally below par" or "slow-minded."[11] For the next higher level, students who were more able but still had limited abilities, Barr recommended solid training in vocational schools. Recognizing that physical problems could also hamper children's success, he favored schools designed to meet their needs and even supported conducting school "at the bedside" of seriously ill children.[12] He recognized the impact of bad dental health on student progress, leading to the establishment of a school dental clinic.

Despite hard economic times in the 1930s, Barr defended the cost of education, and even argued that the nation spent too little on it. In advocating school funding, he argued, "Every pupil, whether he be the poorest child on the poorest farm or the richest child in any city block, should have an equal chance to have a good education." Having well-trained and "adequately-paid teachers," a "modern curriculum," and good buildings were essential for ensuring "a nationwide citizenship which will measure up to the needs of our time."[13] Schools were crucial, he argued, for "spreading understanding and tolerance between races and nations." Linking overt forms of ethnic and religious prejudice to thinking in simple stereotypes, Barr identified the solution as "merely 'stopping to think.' "[14]

In his writings, Barr linked education to pressing social and political problems. Just as he promoted education as a method for eliminating ethnic and religious prejudice, so too did he connect education with building citizenship and patriotism. He wrote passionately about international relations and the possibility of creating "a world without war." He noted the terrible cost of World War I in lives and money—money that could have been used productively in many areas, including education—and he endorsed a view widely held in the 1930s that armament manufacturers had played a key role in fomenting war. Looking at growing international tensions in the 1930s, he cringed at the prospect of another major war, and he described protests against American involvement in any future conflict. His analysis was reluctantly realistic, and he sadly predicted American participation, but he admonished his readers "never to give up the struggle to abolish [war]."[15]

Public schools were themselves the subject of two major political struggles in the 15 years after 1910, and Hy's position in the Portland school administration made him a participant.[16] The first controversy ran from 1911 to 1920 and involved the mandatory vaccination of schoolchildren for smallpox. Public opposition to this policy exploded in 1914. After several cases of smallpox were reported in the southeast part of the city, and eastside schools followed the city health officer's recommendation to exclude unvaccinated children from school for two weeks, parental protests shut down the schools. A 1916 initiative to prevent a vaccination requirement for schoolchildren failed in the state but passed in Portland, with strong eastside support. Finally, in 1920 the school board plan to exclude unvaccinated children for 21 days prompted another initiative campaign, but this protest effort lost decisively, ending the controversy.

A second struggle over public schools had to do with the broader purpose of public education. After a slate drawn from the city's professional and business elite lost a school board election in 1921, an initiative was proposed in 1922 requiring that all children be educated in public schools. The familiar telling of this story attributes the initiative to anti-Catholic sentiment and opposition to parochial education, with the state's very large Ku Klux Klan membership as the driving force behind the measure. But Robert Johnston's careful study of the controversy concluded that democratic populist elements initiated this measure and that Masons were the most influential group of supporters, and it argued that proponents considered this an attempt to advance democratic equality by breaking down both ethnic and class barriers.

Voters passed the compulsory public education initiative in 1922, but both the Oregon Supreme Court and the U.S. Supreme Court struck it down. The proposal, like the Klan, disappeared, but it highlighted the importance of public education in the state. Hy Barr was not a visible participant in this campaign, but the debate raised questions of equality and tolerance, which he later wrote about at length. And, like the battle over vaccination, it made clear the strongly politicized nature of education during Hy Barr's early years in Portland and, thus, Burton Barr's home environment.

The Barr Family

The Barrs were initially quite mobile in Portland, moving to new rental homes as Hy changed schools every several years, but after he became the principal of the Irvington School in 1917, they stayed in the same home for the next 20-some years. Surprisingly, the family rented—apparently at least into the 1940s—rather than buying a house. This was a bit unusual, since Hy's salary was sufficient for such a purchase and because home ownership was the overwhelming pattern in their neighborhood. Whatever the reason for this decision, it did not reflect a tenuous connection to Portland. Besides the bond from Hy's work, their ties to the city expanded a year after they arrived, when Ella's family moved to Portland. Isaac, Bessie, and their five children, plus Isaac's brother Jacob, rented a nearby house. Isaac first worked for several years as a clerk, then as a hat maker, and finally as a tailor. Jacob was employed as a clerk and then salesman for clothing firms, and the children held various jobs in sales or as clerks, stenographers, or bookkeepers. The connection to the Barr family in New York was more tenuous, but Hy's brother, Sam, maintained contact with him, and later made regular visits to Portland to see Hy and his family.

Isaac, Bessie, and Jacob did not become U.S. citizens, and thus could not vote. While many immigrants did not immediately take steps to become naturalized citizens, it is slightly unexpected for this family, given how long they had lived in the country and that they had never intended to return to Russia. This does suggest some limits to their assimilation into American society, although they did modify their name to Hurwitt. Both Hy and Ella were citizens, of course, since they were native-born, but there is no voter registration record for either of them, which is highly surprising, given

Hy's focus on citizenship. The question of assimilation also relates to religious identification and practices. Although there is no information suggesting their regular religious observance, when Isaac died in 1933 and Bessie in 1963, both were buried in a Jewish cemetery. Neither Hy nor Ella belonged to a Jewish congregation or association, nor were they buried in a Jewish cemetery. More strikingly, Hy was cremated, a practice that violated Jewish law and practice. While not definitive, when added to the thrust of Hy's public writings, these factors strongly suggest that the Barr family had only minimal connection to Jewish identity or religion.

Besides serving in the role of a principal's wife, Ella taught piano lessons to local children. In 1914 she gave birth to her first son, Wallace, and in 1917, Burton was born. With two children, Hy established as principal of Irvington School, and the Hurwitts living within walking distance, the family was relatively settled in Portland. Both Wallace and Burt attended Irvington School, of course, under the watchful eye of their father. Given Hy's role as a principal, his emphasis on the home-school connection, and the high expectations of people that he often expressed, little of his children's performance and behavior would have escaped him. One of the few childhood memories that Burt later recounted to his children was having to stay at his desk until all his homework was done, and he described his father as being very strict. When school was out of session in the summer, the family would sometimes go to the ocean, where they would pick berries, and later Burt would make jam with his mother. Not surprisingly, she also taught him to play piano.

After graduating from Irvington School, both boys attended Benson Polytechnic High School, first Wallace (1927–1931) and then Burt (1930–1934). While this choice might seem surprising for children of a classically educated and academically oriented father, it makes sense in view of the school's high reputation. Begun in 1908 as the Portland School of Trades, it combined college preparatory education and vocational training in a way that mirrored Hy's progressive educational views, and it provided insurance against hard economic times. The school expanded its programs, adding a printing department in 1920 and radio training in 1923, and by 1940 it was the largest school in Portland.

Both boys were active in extracurricular activities at Benson, but Wallace, who was shorter than his classmates and wore glasses, was less athletic. Wallace was in the Drama Club and the band, as well as in the International Relations Club and the Public Speaking Club, and the *Benson Yearbook* praised him as "one of Benson's best orators." Burt played on the golf team and was considered a good tennis player, particularly in doubles, on a team with a chance to win the league championship. His success in these sports was helped by his summer jobs caddying at a local golf course and working at a tennis club. (He also held a more arduous job one summer, working 14 hours a day to sell and deliver meat.) Besides being a member of these two athletic teams, Burt wrote for the pep staff and was a member of the Ben Scribes Club (a writing club); he also joined the Public Speaking Club and was a member of the Minutemen group, which was probably another forensic activity. His vocational track at school was learning how to operate a printing press and linotype machine. He later joked about this training as "a good thing to fall back on when the brain stopped growing," but in a more serious vein he characterized Benson as a place that "taught Shakespeare with overalls."[17] His senior yearbook listed his ambition as a "writer," his qualifications as "unknown," and his likely future as a "meter reader."

Graduating from Benson High in 1934, in the depths of the Depression, Burt was admitted to the University of Washington and began his studies as a business major. His decision to attend a university in another state is slightly surprising. The Seattle school was academically superior, but out-of-state tuition was higher at a difficult time. Whether Burt went for academic reasons or to distance himself somewhat from his family, his Washington experience was relatively brief. He dropped out for financial reasons, which suggests that family financial support was unavailable, although Burt might have been less than fully dedicated to his studies. Instead of returning home, for the next two years he worked in various places, most memorably as a bellhop in Palm Springs, California, where he found employment and entertainment in carrying the bags of movie stars. By 1937 he had sufficient savings to return to school, this time at the University of Oregon.

Burt lived at the Sigma Alpha Mu house, which was a Jewish fraternity. More than 40 years later, when the *Arizona Republic* researched and published a lengthy sketch of his life, the journalists reported that Barr had joined the fraternity. Barr denied that he had been a member and said he only lived there on the recommendation of a friend from Palm Springs. He escalated the dispute by demanding that the newspaper's publisher fire one of the reporters. Barr's reaction was uncharacteristically impolitic. Perhaps his identity had caused him tension during those years. Oregon fraternities generally did not accept Jews, and if he had been identified as Jewish, this might have restricted his alternatives to staying at Sigma Alpha Mu. He might have resented that, but it does not explain his strong reaction so many years later. As a student he evidenced no religious identity, and perhaps he imbibed his father's belief in assimilating into

American culture. Near the end of his life, Barr mentioned something obliquely to a friend, suggesting he had explicitly rejected his mother's religious views. As an adult he defined Jewish identity as being religious, not ethnic, and he became a baptized member of the Episcopal Church, like his wife and children. In this sense, then, he was not Jewish.

If anti-Semitism played any role in determining Barr's residence or the policies of fraternities at Oregon, it did not prevent Sigma Alpha Mu residents from becoming some of the top student leaders. This included Barr, who was selected as chairman of the Homecoming Weekend for 1939. He filled this role very successfully and won public praise from university officials for ending a tradition of student vandalism following the game. Barr again studied business, focusing on accounting. He graduated in 1940, but his grades worsened in his last semesters. He later joked that he was allowed to graduate on the condition that he never practice accounting. While obviously an exaggerated, self-deprecating assessment of his record, it also obscured why his performance declined: because his attention was being drawn to larger problems facing the world.

Life in the Military, 1940–1942

Barr's college experience was shaped not only by classes and organizing campus events, but also by his experience in the Reserve Officer Training Corp (ROTC). Although he later claimed to have joined for the money—it paid $1.25 a week—it is highly unlikely that his decision was simply financial, for armed conflict was already raging on several continents, darker war clouds loomed on the horizon, and the American military was being readied for some kind of action. In 1937, when Barr returned to college, the Spanish Civil War had begun, drawing American volunteers, and Japan invaded China; in 1938 Germany took over Austria and Czechoslovakia; and in 1939 war broke out in Europe. Barr was more than just aware of these developments, he focused on them and their causes. Instead of studying accounting, he was reading accounts of what the American, French, and German governments had done after the previous European war.

Although the American public was generally leery of involvement in foreign wars, national defense had substantial support, and Barr's involvement in ROTC was not unusual for the time. The modern, campus-based ROTC program had begun in 1916 and expanded through the 1920s and 1930s to more than 300 schools, producing some 6,000 reserve officers per year, an essential core of officers that the army would soon need. The army's strength grew slowly during the 1930s, reaching around 180,000 men by 1939, when European hostilities inspired a funded expansion to 227,000 (and 235,000 in the National Guard). Congressional enactment of the nation's first peacetime draft in September 1940 authorized an army of 1.4 million soldiers. Reserve officers played a key part in training these increased numbers of soldiers. The University of Oregon ROTC program only offered infantry training, and Barr did well in this program, rising to cadet lieutenant colonel. After graduating from college, Barr reported in June 1940 for active duty at Fort Lewis, a major army facility south of Tacoma, Washington.

Barr's college experience as a campus leader and then a successful ROTC cadet gave him a preliminary sense of how to combine organization, command, and amiability into leadership, but the next five years would transform that understanding and define his character. His later autobiographical reminiscences would touch lightly on his college years, but their detail and tone of his accounts regarding his military experiences show how fundamental these were to his life. His daughter Stephanie noted the striking contrast between his unwillingness to reveal anything about his earlier life with his eagerness to talk about his army service.

Barr's military experiences and his notions of leadership were also shaped by a fortuitous circumstance. When he first reported to the officer of the day for duty as a new second lieutenant, he encountered the commander of the day, Lieutenant Colonel Dwight D. Eisenhower. A nervous Barr saluted Eisenhower, who asked Barr where he wished to be placed, meaning what he wanted to do. Anything the officer wanted, stammered Barr, and Eisenhower assigned him to be platoon commander of A Company, in the first battalion of the 15th Infantry Regiment, which Eisenhower commanded. The placement was highly consequential for Barr. It gave him a modest personal connection with a soon-to-be powerful and famous man, but it was far more meaningful because Ike provided a model for leadership. At a time when many Americans, including military men, felt that America could and perhaps should avoid the war, Eisenhower was forcefully clear. As Ike drilled his men for the war he was certain was coming, Barr remembered him saying, "If any of you think we are not going to war, I don't want you in my battalion. We're going to war. This country is going to war, and I want people who are prepared to fight that war."[18]

Eisenhower's no-nonsense approach, his understanding of a leader's responsibilities, and his notion of how to get things done offered Barr a fundamental lesson. While Barr's company was on the shooting range one day, Eisenhower came to inspect them and found a soldier who had not filled in his score book. "Who," Barr later asked, "is to blame? The kid? Oh no. His platoon leader is to blame, and I heard Eisenhower's voice say, 'Barr, come here!'" Standing out of earshot of the men, Eisenhower chewed out Barr so thoroughly that 40 years later Barr claimed to "remember every word of it." Since Eisenhower was scheduled to eat lunch with A company that day, Barr decided to avoid being Eisenhower's second lunch course, but as he headed over to sit with B Company, he heard Eisenhower call his name:

> I went up to him a second time, and he said, "I'm going to tell you something, Lieutenant, and you'd better listen carefully. This morning you did something wrong, and I bawled you out for it. That was the end. We don't carry grudges around here, not for an hour, not for half an hour, not at all. Now, you eat lunch with your own company." Suffice it to say, I did, and I never forgot that. I've practiced it, too. Whatever people think of me politically, I don't think you'll find anybody who'll say that I carry grudges. So I learned something fundamental from Eisenhower.[19]

Barr learned other lessons as he interacted with the future president, as he discovered how to relate to a superior. In a confused military exercise on a very hot summer day, Eisenhower delightedly viewed the surrender of many opposition soldiers as victory, but Barr recognized the GIs' primary motive. Gathering his courage, Barr told Eisenhower the unpleasant truth: "Colonel, all these guys want is to get on a truck. If you've got enough trucks to haul all of them, you'll get all of them to surrender." Eisenhower paused, laughed, and agreed.

But the colonel was not really a jovial man, and military rank mattered. In October Barr was with a group of second lieutenants at the officers' club, all singing rather lustily as they celebrated his birthday. Suddenly, an apparently annoyed Eisenhower appeared from a private room at the back of the club, and as the singing instantly stopped, Eisenhower asked Barr why his group was making so much noise. After he explained that they were celebrating his birthday, Eisenhower said, "Fine, you come with me," and started back toward the rear of the club. A nervous Barr followed him and found Mamie Eisenhower, along with the other ranking officers and their wives. Eisenhower then turned to Barr and said, "Now, Lieutenant, we are going to celebrate our birthdays together." He bought Barr a drink and led him in singing several choruses of "Happy Birthday" and "Roll Out the Barrel," his favorite song. Barr joined in, cautiously. Characteristically, he later followed up the experience by memorizing all of the verses to the second song.[20]

Going to War

Eisenhower left Fort Lewis the following month, beginning his rapid rise through the military command hierarchy. Barr stayed in Washington, continuing to train soldiers, winning promotions, and waiting for combat. After two years, now a captain, Barr participated in Operation Torch, the army's first operation in the European theater. This American-British invasion of French North Africa began on November 8, 1942, with three forces landing at Morocco and two at Algerian ports (see figure 1). Despite some initial hesitation and internal divisions, French forces controlled by the Vichy government eventually offered resistance, resulting in some heaving fighting and nearly 500 Allied deaths. The major battle involved French forces in Casablanca, where Barr had been part of a team setting up a forward command post. Firing ceased late on November 10, and on the following day five American officers drove to the city to accept the French surrender. One of the officers was Captain Barr, who carried an American flag into the city as cheering crowds lined the streets.

With the Allies now in control of Morocco and Algeria, the Germans moved from Libya to invade Tunisia, and American and British forces moved east to contest them. Barr served as a staff officer during this period and assisted in setting up forward command posts. American forces gained considerable experience during this initial campaign. When the Axis forces in Africa finally surrendered on May 13, 1943, the Americans and Barr were ready for the next step in the war—the invasion of Italy through Sicily with Eisenhower as the Supreme Commander of the project.

Preparation for the invasion occurred at locations across North Africa, and on one occasion Eisenhower met with General George Patton and General Mark Clark in Port-aux-poules, a small Algerian town. Finding Barr's name on a list of nearby personnel, Eisenhower had him summoned to the cottage where the generals were meeting. "Petrified" to see his former commander, now a four-star general, Barr walked up the steps, and "Ike comes down and he puts out his hand." As Barr saluted and then shook hands with the general, Eisenhower grinned and asked the new major, "Barr, how did you get promoted so fast?"[21] Although struck by the irony of the question coming from a man whose rapid promotions had launched him over the heads of many senior officers, Barr restrained himself from making the obvious retort until his later retelling of the story.

During this period Barr learned useful lessons about the difficulties of planning and the qualities of leadership. One of his tasks involved waterproofing trucks so that when they were offloaded from landing craft, they

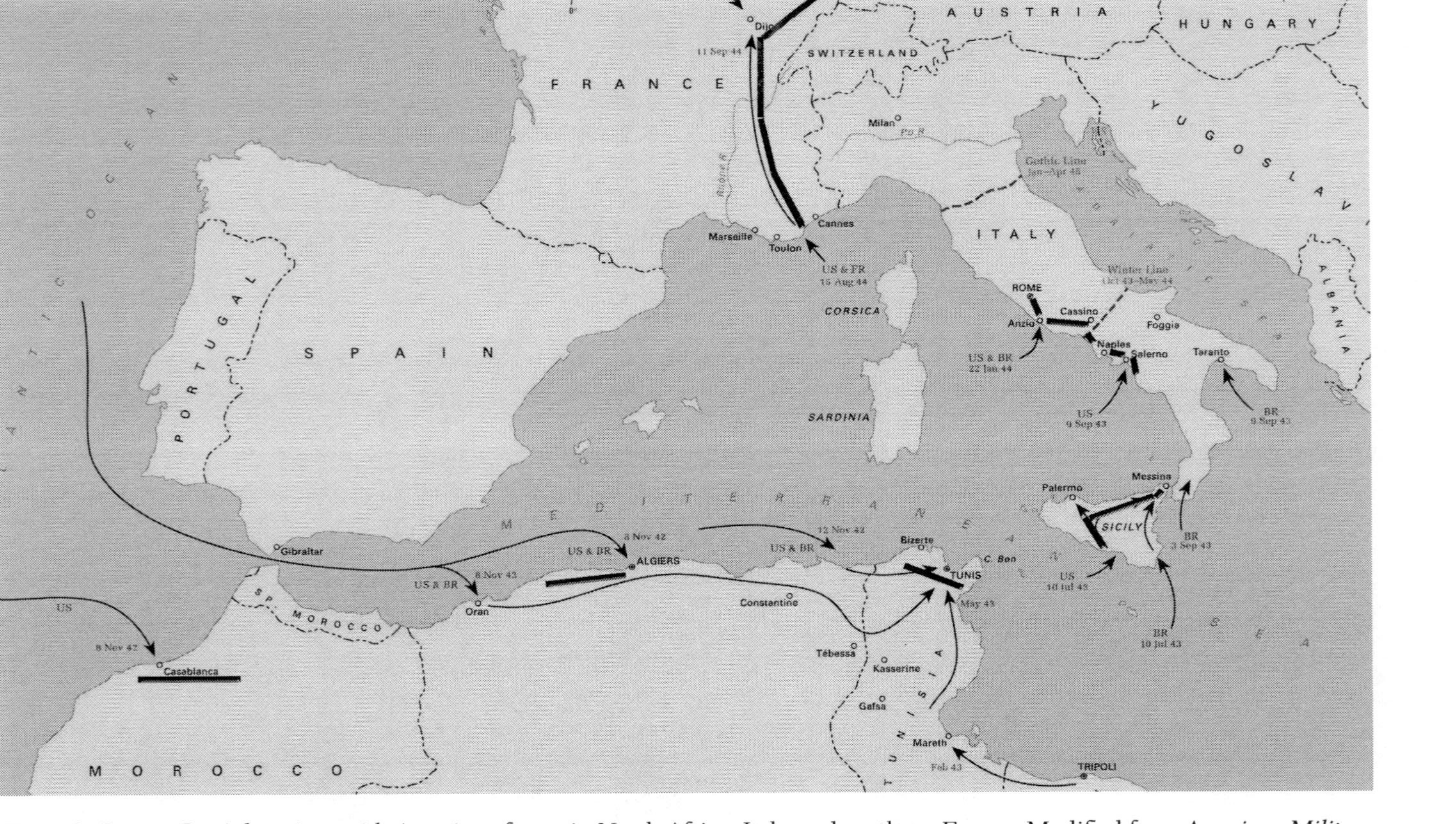

Figure 1. Burton Barr's locations with American forces in North Africa, Italy, and southern France. Modified from *American Military History*, vol. 2, *United States Army in a Global Era, 1917–2003*, Richard W. Stewart, ed. (Washington, DC: Center of Military History United States Army, 2005), 134–35.

would be able to roll through the surf onto the beach. His team developed the method, tested it, and then arranged to demonstrate it for General Omar Bradley. On the day of the demonstration Bradley arrived with Lieutenant General Theodore Roosevelt Jr., and sat on the beach waiting to see how this technique would assist the Allied invasion of Italy. The landing craft appeared, dropped its landing bridge, and a five-ton truck pulling a 155 mm howitzer moved forward—and suddenly disappeared under the water. Moments later the driver popped up and swam to shore. It turned out that the section of shore chosen for the demonstration had not been sounded, and instead of a shallow bottom, it had a 20-foot drop-off. Barr, his commander, and the entire staff were dumbfounded. General Bradley stood up, and with a deadpan expression, he turned to Barr and said, "Thank you, Major Barr, that was most interesting."[22]

Barr and his group overcame problems like this, and as executive officer of the 15th Infantry, Barr participated in the invasion of Sicily, which began on July 9, 1943. By August 17 the Allies had won control of the island, and in early September they made several landings in southern parts of the Italian peninsula. Barr served in the 34th Division as a plans and training officer in the major aim of that campaign—to capture Naples. The relatively quick success of the Sicily and southern Italian campaigns led to Italy's surrender and raised Allied hopes, but conditions changed for the worse. Germans deposed the Italian government and replaced Italian forces, and then, as the fighting moved into the mountainous terrain of central Italy, the Allies faced a more costly and difficult struggle.

In January 1944 Barr was part of an Allied force that attempted to go around this deadlock by landing further north on the west coast of Italy at Anzio. Here and in the nearby battle at Monte Cassino, Americans saw some of the most desperate fighting of the war. Heavy German artillery and mortar fire caused severe casualties, and for his service in this arduous fight from the initial planning on November 30, 1943, until February 16, 1944, Barr received the first of his two Bronze Star medals, "for meritorious service in combat."[23] Besides praising his tactical judgment, courage, and energy, the commendation also lauded his "personality and efficiency" in coordinating very successfully with varied allied forces. Barr emerged from this campaign uninjured, but he was close enough to the fighting that German shelling destroyed a barracks with all of his clothes. After the Allies finally broke through German defenses in these areas in May, he participated in the drive to Rome and then north to the Arno River. Years later, after reading a newly published history of the war in Italy, Barr told one of his Arizona House staff members that he had been part of a reconnaissance mission that strayed, and they became the first three Americans to enter Rome.

Planning for the invasion of southern France had begun in 1943, but the Italian campaign and the invasion of northern France took priority. In the summer of 1944, however, with progress in Italy going more slowly than Allied leaders had hoped and with the D-Day invasion forces bogged down in Normandy hedgerows, the Allied command decided to push ahead with the third invasion of Axis territory, this one in southeastern France. Barr rejoined his 15th Infantry Regiment in the 3rd Infantry Division, which was part of the force that invaded southern France in mid-August. Within a month, this force had driven past Lyon and far enough north to connect with General Patton's Third Army, which was heading east to Germany.

Figure 2. Major Burton Barr. Burton S. Barr Collection.

As the army reorganized its forces and reestablished its supply lines for the push into Germany, Barr received new orders. In mid-October 1944, he was sent back to the United States, to Fort Leavenworth, Kansas, to receive additional training at the Army Command and General Staff College. Barr also used the occasion for a nonmilitary purpose. On November 1, the day he arrived at Fort Leavenworth, Barr got married. His wife, Charlotte Bennett, had been born in Montana in 1915, one of six children of a postman in the interestingly named small town of Plentywood, in the northeast corner of Montana. Charlotte had moved to Washington, probably attracted by the employment opportunities as war production boomed there in the late 1930s, and had met Burt while he was serving at Fort Lewis. Clearly, the couple had been corresponding while he was overseas, but we know nothing of what they communicated, except for their obvious intention of getting married.

Barr's stateside training ended in early February 1945, and he rejoined his unit, which was still in France but readying for a drive into southern Germany (see figure 3). He returned as commander of the 1st Battalion, and he led his soldiers through very heavy fighting during the next three months. Barr participated directly in combat, risking his safety to oversee operations and also to save wounded comrades; his commander described him as "almost fearless." In April he was involved in almost constant fighting. In Neustadt he reorganized a rifle company that he led in a charge on a German stronghold, shooting several enemy soldiers and personally capturing three others. In the grueling battle for Nuremberg on April 19, he ignored heavy sniper fire, running 1,000 yards to lead a platoon in preparation for an attack. He then charged and silenced a gun emplacement and directed his platoon across the area without any casualties. For his bravery, "gallantry in action," and quick thinking during these episodes, he won another Bronze Star and two Silver Stars.

The war in Europe ended in May, and in August Barr was among the first soldiers returned to the States, partly due to injuries he had suffered. He spent part of his 30-day recuperation leave with his parents, but his transition to civilian status was halted by additional health problems, and he was hospitalized with jaundice from bad yellow fever shots, and with pneumonia. After recovering, he went to Quebec in October on a final tour for the army when he suffered a gall bladder attack, an episode that ultimately required surgery. At the end of November, he was transferred to a hospital in Utica, New York, still ill but scheduled for discharge. When his father learned of this, he wrote to Eisenhower, who intervened on Barr's behalf, and Barr was transferred to a hospital in Van Nuys, California,

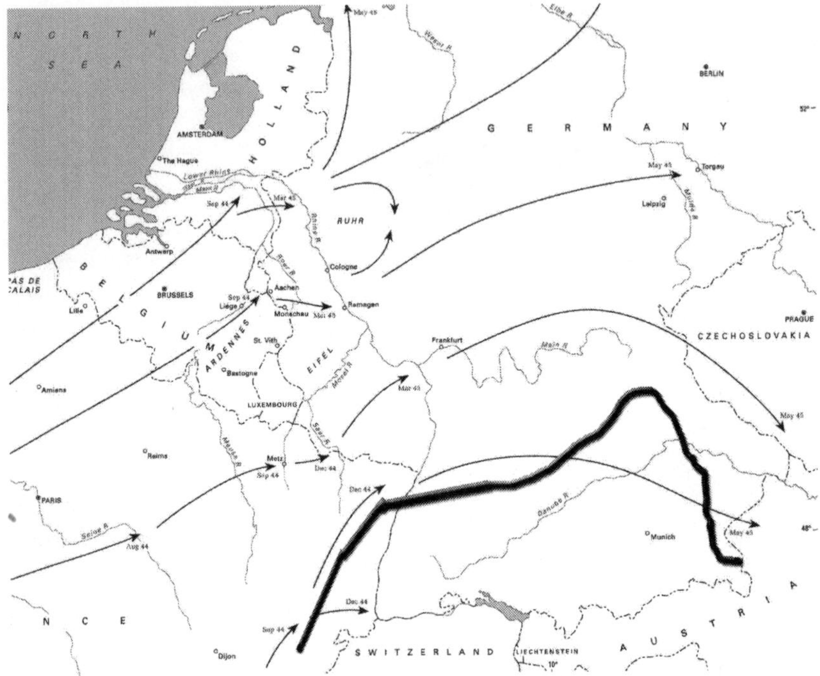

Figure 3. Movement of American forces and Barr's units in southern Germany, 1945. Modified from *American Military History,* vol. 2, *United States Army in a Global Era, 1917–2003,* Richard W. Stewart, ed. (Washington, DC: Center of Military History United States Army, 2005), 147.

where he received treatment for circulation problems in his right leg. He remained in the army for another eight months, until he was finally healthy again, and he was released from active army service in August 1946.

Home, Family, the Army, and the Making of Burton Barr

In 1946 Burton Barr was 29 years old, and his personality, perspective, and values were well established. In later years he remained virtually mute about his family and upbringing, both with his family and with the public, making it hard to draw conclusions about that stage of his life. Nothing in the available evidence suggests any childhood trauma, but he clearly separated from his parents and even from his brother Wallace, who served as a captain in the Marine Air Service and evidently maintained contact with his parents. This distancing began when he left for college, seems to have continued—perhaps understandably—during the war, and then became explicit and absolute after the war. Was it caused by cultural or religious differences, or by personal conflicts? Burt once mentioned that his father was a disciplinarian, and a friend concluded there was no love between the two men. His father's attitudes about peace and war may also have caused division; a friend said that Barr went to war "because of" his father. If so, Burt's postwar involvement with the army reserve could have been further cause for this division. Whatever the reason that Barr later cut himself off from his family, the person he became as an adult showed the deep influence of his family and his upbringing.

We can discern some influences on him even without detailed evidence and personal testimonies. His family was eastern European Jewish and had moved to New York City, living within an interrelated ethnic, religious, and economic community. But his parents' educational successes set them on a divergent path, and their move to Portland removed them from that close community and distanced them from their ethnic and religious roots. This separation seems clearly to have been an intentional decision, although their desire for ethnic independence and for assimilation into broader American society likely grew over time. His father spoke and wrote about the importance of diversity and tolerance, and neither he nor his family demonstrated a Jewish religious identity. His parents also sought education, mobility, and opportunity for their children, and instilled in them a sense of individual responsibility.

Burt seems to have lived these values growing up. He did well in school, was athletic and popular, and absorbed his parents' beliefs in education and assimilation. Although his father kept his job during the 1930s, Burt was aware of the problems of the Depression through his own work and by observing society around him. But what shaped him more than anything else was his experience in the military. His second wife Louise said that "he talked about it constantly"; his son Mike reported likewise that "he talked about it all the time."[24] Mike noted the importance to him of "fighting for a bigger cause," and Louise observed:

> The camaraderie in the military was such a good atmosphere for him, and working with those men and leading those men, I mean he just seemed to shine doing that. The standards at the battle fields have stayed with him. As far as I know it was always reflected in almost everything he did.[25]

Barr's experience in the military was transformative, then, as it was for many who served in World War II. Fighting for a great cause, sharing life and death experiences with a group of men, dealing with fear, showing courage, and periodically seeing the absurdity and humor in situations created memories and friendships that lasted a lifetime.

But for Barr it involved more. The military offered him opportunities for leadership, and he found these essential. Louise reported, "He was so proud of the fact that he had learned his leadership, you know, under distress, and under battle." One of his company commanders, Mike Daley, described several key skills that Barr had learned. First, he discovered how to plan successful operations that reached their objective and had the fewest casualties. Second, he "instinctively knew what people could do, and he would give you assignments that he thought you could handle." Don Isaacson, a legislative staffer for Barr in the 1970s, stressed that Barr's military experience led him to respect "the contribution of people who maybe otherwise wouldn't be respected, [which] led him to appreciate nearly everyone." Barr used humor, as Daley noted, "at his own expense, of course, not anybody else's."[26] As he used humor, he also deflected praise. Telling stories about Daley and Audie Murphy, both Congressional Medal of Honor winners under his command, Barr said, "They're brave, I'm not. I'm just a guy."[27] Yet it was Barr who recommended them for the medal, and Daley and others claimed that he should have won that same award. Finally, Barr showed kindness in numerous small ways, and he demonstrated what others commonly called "decency."

Of course, wartime and peacetime are different. The dangers of gunfire are not the same as wounds from verbal criticism or being stymied by opposition, and people are markedly more willing to make sacrifices when they know their survival is at stake. Effectiveness in working with others does not necessarily constitute leadership, and military leadership differs from political leadership. Yet the primary skills that Burton Barr learned in North Africa, Italy, France, and Germany were the same ones he would attempt to employ in a peacetime context and eventually in political office.

CHAPTER TWO

Making a Life as a Businessman, Peacetime Soldier, and Family Man

"He was a great salesman."

—EDDIE BASHA[1]

"I think he took some of his interest in politics from some of those associations he developed through his army reserve services."

—LLOYD CLARK[2]

"The most important thing to him in this world was his family and his kids, and that was the A Number One priority."

—PETER BURNS[3]

When Burton Barr was finally released from the army in August 1946, he returned to a status he had not held for over six years. At that point, he had served roughly half of his adult life in the military, matured into an able leader, risen considerably in rank, and fought in a conflict that changed the direction of world history. Given these successes and the strong emotions generated by these experiences, it would not have been surprising if Barr had chosen to remain in the military. Instead, he opted for civilian life, working as a salesman and then manager for a national refrigeration company. After moving to Arizona, he helped develop a successful business in the 1950s and 1960s, and in the process established strong and important friendships. He also built contacts through his service in the army reserve. Barr developed a wide network of people who knew and respected him, and in 1964 business colleagues and neighborhood friends persuaded him to run for a seat in the Arizona House of Representatives. His election and then quick success in the political world created a new focus and coincided with changes in his personal and business life in 1969 that would dramatically alter his future. Over the next 25 years, Barr balanced his activities, focusing on politics when the legislature was in session, and business when it was not, and always being attentive to his family. While his business and military activities had initially fostered contacts and leadership skills, his family became the center of his life, giving it a new balance, perspective, and joy.

Working in Civilian Life

By October 1946 the war had been over for a year, and during that time Burton Barr had suffered through a nightmare of health problems. He had been incapacitated, hospitalized, and treated for hepatitis, jaundice, pneumonia, gall bladder failure, and poor circulation in his legs. He never discussed this experience, the exact problems, or the treatment, but years later, friends remembered that, on several occasions when Barr had to remove his shirt for some reason, his abdomen showed numerous scars. He later joked about this, saying that he had decided not to stay in the military because he had a habit of getting shot, but this was mainly his way to deflect concern for him or praise for his medals. On some other occasions he suggested that the military was too "rigid," yet his subsequent service in the reserve seems to cast some doubt on that explanation. In serious moments he must have considered a military career, given his considerable success, rapid mobility, and penchant for command, but the postwar policy of drastically reducing the size of the military might have dissuaded him.

Barr probably had some sense of this limitation when he first came home, for the career possibility he mentioned was working in the State Department.[4] After a year of medical problems and inaction, however, he was ready for something other than government service. And so, out of the hospital and freshly discharged from the army, he went to seek work in Seattle, where his wife had been living since the time before they were married. The city had boomed in the 1940s, first because of wartime manufacturing and then because of Boeing's postwar shift into the burgeoning market for passenger aircraft. The company's growth fueled economic expansion throughout the area, fostering new businesses and pulling in new residents.

Barr was one of many people attracted by the area's prospects. His college training and degree were in accounting, and he did have skill with numbers, but his wartime experiences had shown him that his greatest interests and skills were in dealing with people, not in keeping the books. So, instead of an office job looking at numbers, he found a sales position with a restaurant supply firm, where he learned about food equipment, as well as about customers and selling. Years later he would tell people the key lesson he learned from the supply firm's owner: as one of the company's salesmen described his conversations and potential sales opportunities with prospective clients, the owner interrupted and said forcefully, "I don't want weather reports. What did you sell?"[5] Barr absorbed this message, which reinforced the pragmatic, objective-focused training he received in the war, and relying on his personality, intelligence, and wit, he did well in his position.

After several successful years, he began looking for other opportunities, and he found one in San Francisco with the Hobart Company, which manufactured machines for food production, such as grinding, cutting, and mixing, as well as many items like dishwashers and refrigeration units. Learning about these products expanded Barr's knowledge of the business, but he was restless and ambitious. A year later he took a new position as the regional sales manager for McCray Refrigeration, which sold cold storage and refrigeration equipment.

In 1951 Barr was selling refrigerated cases to grocery stores throughout the West. One of those places was Phoenix, in the Salt River Valley of central Arizona, and for Barr, an ambitious man of 34, the city held many attractions. Like Seattle, the area was booming, but Phoenix was not simply experiencing growth, it was aggressively pursuing it. Starting in 1948, the Phoenix Chamber of Commerce's Industrial Development Committee began recruiting businesses from elsewhere in the country to move to Phoenix. What helped make this possible was a skilled workforce drawn partly by the lower cost of living and, for some, by the health benefits from the dry air and warm climate. Lower taxes on manufacturing and storage of manufactured goods, plus passage of a right-to-work law, added to the attractiveness for some firms, and the presence of increasing numbers of vacationers and visitors boosted other economic opportunities.

One of Barr's Phoenix clients, Paul Parmenter, managed a food equipment sales company started by his late father. Now owned by Paul, his sister, and his mother, the company sold grocery store and restaurant equipment, as well as institutional kitchen supplies. With possibilities for growth but without his father's assistance, Paul was struggling. For example, he had been unable to resell a load of refrigerated cases for grocery stores that he had purchased from Barr. Barr recognized a mutual opportunity. He persuaded Parmenter to hire him as sales manager and vice president, within a few months he had sold all of the cases, and he became a key part of Parmenter's expanding business.

Figure 4. Burton and Charlotte Barr. Burton S. Barr Collection.

The dramatic expansion of Phoenix and its suburbs during the 1950s fueled an increase in shopping locations that catered to automobile traffic. Shopping centers built at major intersections provided general parking for all of their businesses and were anchored by grocery stores. As a result, the number of grocery stores grew even more rapidly than the Phoenix population, and the Frank Parmenter Company was kept busy servicing this expanding market. Barr focused on selling them Tyler refrigerated cases and Hobart meat slicers, saws, and scales. The business continued to boom, and in 1955 Barr hired an additional salesman, Larry Shelp, fitting out a Volkswagen van with small items such as butcher knives for meat cutters, and aluminum platters and pans to use in meat cases. Barr also expanded the business by selling cases and other items to liquor stores, bars, and the rising number of convenience stores—Circle K, U-tote-M, and Put & Take stores.

After 1960 the grocery business changed dramatically and in ways that benefited Barr. In 1960 about 90 percent of the Phoenix area's nearly 400 grocery stores were single stores, with only three chains of regular grocery stores: Bayless had 26 stores, Safeway had 14, and El Rancho had 9. In the succeeding years chain stores expanded rapidly, particularly three locally based chains: Fry's, Smitty's, and Bashas'. Barr benefited from that centralization and expansion, particularly because he was closely involved with all three owners. Don Fry, the owner of several grocery stores in Oakland and south of San Francisco, had come to the Phoenix area in the 1950s because of his son's health. In 1960, bored with semi-retirement, he bought a local grocery store that had gone bankrupt. A banker at Valley National Bank connected Fry with Barr, who sold him equipment for the entire store. Within the next few years Fry bought an additional four stores, and then more, and in all of them he installed equipment bought from Barr and the Frank Parmenter Company.

The role of friendship in Burton Barr's business successes was even more apparent in his work with a second Phoenix chain, Smitty's Markets, started by Clyde Smith. Barr and Smith became good friends, and Larry Shelp, Barr's partner in later years, remembered that "they spent many happy hours arguing about what Clyde should put in his next new store." Burt would propose a new idea, and Clyde would object, "but, I tell you, Burt was a salesman. He would convince him. And most of the things . . . Clyde Smith tried in his stores did work." Another example of Barr's friendship building and persistence involved Ted Babbitt, a member of the big, prominent family that had started the Babbitt Brothers Trading Company in 1889 and grown it into a multifaceted enterprise with ranching, real estate, shipping, and merchandising operations in northern Arizona. Ted ran the company's grocery store businesses and expanded these stores in the postwar period. Barr was told that it was difficult to arrange meetings with Babbitt, a warning that he took as a challenge. As one of Barr's employees recalled, "Burt met him, liked him instantly," and after several more trips "we began selling them Tyler refrigerated cases." The two men became friends, they and their wives socialized together, and after Burt's son was born, Ted became his godfather.[6]

Barr's bond with Eddie Basha also went far beyond a business friendship. The initial connection was with Eddie Basha Sr., who with his brother Ike had begun a grocery business with a single store in Chandler in 1932. Barr's friendship quickly extended to Eddie Basha Jr., once Eddie Jr. returned to the Valley in 1959 and began working in the family business after graduating from Stanford University. And with the death of his father in 1968, Eddie Jr. controlled the company. As he later described the relationship, "The friendship of Burton Barr and our family was so rock solid, so formidable, that any time my dad opened a store—and after my dad's death, any time that I and our people opened a store here—it was always Burt Barr who did all the fixture work." They bought Tyler fixtures from Barr, and Barr's employees did the piping work. "We never asked for anybody else to submit a proposal to us. It was automatic and axiomatic that Burt Barr would do the Basha jobs." Basha considered Barr a great salesman because he "made a point of calling on customers and selling the product that he had." He attributed Barr's success to his "infinite storehouse of energy" and to being a "hands-on type of guy."[7]

Richard Kaplan, who worked for Barr after 1971, noted other characteristics that contributed to Barr's success. The most important was integrity: "He was a very honest man. Very, very honest." Barr was also loyal and committed to his customers. Beyond accepting the categorical imperative that "the customer is always right" lay a more personal element. Kaplan marveled at "His people skills; his ability to befriend people; his ability to make [anyone], whether it be an employee or prospective customer, feel that they are probably the most important person at that particular time." Time and again, Barr stressed to his employees that everyone should be treated with respect. He modeled this in how he treated them, including in subtle ways, like remembering the details of their personal lives. Finally, Barr demonstrated a terrific memory. "Burt never wrote a thing down. He never carried a pen. But he had this amazing capability of remembering everything that was thrown at him."[8]

The skills and values that Barr developed and displayed in his business affairs would be equally crucial in his later political success. Honesty, salesmanship, attention to personal details of individuals, and an excellent memory were also vital skills for a would-be politician. His eagerness to meet people brought him contacts and friends throughout the Salt River Valley and the state, and traveling helped him learn more about where he lived. One of the main forums for building business contacts in Phoenix was the Chamber of Commerce. After the war, this group had spearheaded the drive for economic development and government efficiency, and its membership of over two thousand men and women included the area's most influential citizens. Barr belonged to the chamber, although he did not pursue a leadership role in it. He did not become a member of many other groups that businessmen and women commonly joined, such as fraternal organizations like the Masons or business service groups like the Rotary Club, and the only social club he belonged to was the Coconino Country

Club in Flagstaff. But he was connected to another group that provided social occasions, required a time commitment, and reflected his continuing interest in the military: the Reserve Officers Association.

Staying with the Military: Service in the Reserve

At the end of the war, Barr had decided not to pursue active military service as a career, but he did not wish to sever his ties with the army—nor did the army wish to lose him. In September 1946, a month before he was discharged, he was temporarily promoted to lieutenant colonel in the infantry, and five months later, that appointment was made permanent for five years. Barr's new military role involved serving in the expanded army reserve program, a postwar compromise between maintaining a sizable Cold War military while reducing the cost. But, despite the efforts to increase training and provide more financial inducements to participants, the size and nature of the reserve remained the subject of an ongoing organizational and political struggle.

Soon after relocating to Washington in 1946, Barr threw himself into promoting the reserve. He spoke frequently to clubs and organizations in the Seattle area, explaining the reserve and supporting recruiting drives. He also organized the 104th Infantry Reserve Division. His success in Seattle was matched in Spokane, in eastern Washington. In a letter of appreciation, Barr's supervisor praised his high standards and example, writing that "what measure of success the Organized Reserve Corps School in Spokane is now enjoying can be attributed to your ability to impart enthusiasm and confidence in your co-workers."[9] Shortly after leaving Washington for Arizona, Barr's five-year appointment as a lieutenant colonel expired; he accepted an indefinite appointment to that rank in January 1953, and in August he reported for duty in Arizona. Promoted to the rank of colonel the next year, in April 1955 he was named commander of the 59th Reserve Infantry Regiment, the largest army reserve unit in the state.

Within months of taking his command, Barr faced the prospect of losing it, for his unit was threatened with deactivation. The problem was not specific to his unit but a condition that had for some time plagued the entire reserve system: enlistments were too low to maintain units at full strength. The army's proposed response—to disband and combine units—was one logical option, but Barr vigorously opposed applying this remedy to his unit. He claimed that his division was being unfairly singled out, and that this was additionally unreasonable because he had recently made approved expenditures on recruitment and training for his unit. Ultimately his arguments convinced the army, and the 59th persisted. Barr then turned to solving the problem of lagging enlistments. He organized the Javelina Association, a civilian organization to support Arizona reserve units, and he very actively supported a statewide program promoting reserve enlistments. In his unit's newspaper, Barr warned against "the public apathy toward military service that naturally follows periods of international conflict," he explained the importance of service, and he touted the new opportunities for service as causing "so little inconvenience to their civilian lives."[10]

Though he advised potential recruits that reserve military service would be only minimally disruptive, Barr's reserve service consumed much of his attention and energy. His secretary at the Parmenter company, Barbara McMillen, quipped that if she had answered his phone saying "Headquarters, 59th Infantry," she would have been correct half of the time. But beyond his enjoyment in building up the reserve, Barr also found in this group the camaraderie that he had valued so much while on active service. His wit and easy manner added to his effectiveness as a commander. At the end of a day spent on duty, he opened his quarters to officers interested in conversation over beer; he offered Olympia, a tribute to his time spent in Washington state. Barr regaled his guests with war stories, often told with himself as the butt of the tale.

His time with the Javelina company also brought new experiences, including interactions with various public officials, such as Governor Ernest McFarland (see figure 5). In 1957 McFarland was coming to review the troops, and Barr, knowing that it would be hot and that the governor liked orange juice, arranged to have a container of fresh juice placed in the refrigerator of his guest quarters, which were guarded. But after the governor came to his quarters and Barr went to retrieve the juice, he discovered that the guard, who had been standing outside all day in the heat, had drunk all of the juice. Barr first spoke angrily to the officer in charge, but he later saw humor in the incident and remembered when commanders had dealt generously with his own mistakes.

Service in the reserve brought Barr into contact with both politicians and politics. His sensitivity to the ties between the military and politics was certainly heightened when his former commander, Dwight Eisenhower, was elected president in 1952. In addition, the Cold War and the conflict in Korea made foreign policy and military strategy top political issues. The conclusion of the Korean War reduced tensions, but the political debates over reserve service persisted, as even Eisenhower pushed for reductions in size. Occasionally, a personal connection with Congress developed, as when

Figure 5. Burton Barr and U.S. Army Reserve leaders meeting Governor Ernest McFarland. Burton S. Barr Collection.

Senator Richard Russell, chairman of the Senate Armed Services Committee, came to Arizona and spoke to the Javelina company. But most political connections for Barr and the reserve were local and state, particularly with governors. Lloyd Clark, who served with Barr in the reserve, concluded, "He took some of his interest in politics from some of those associations he developed through his army reserve services."[11] With units in most cities and towns across Arizona, and with Barr commanding them in summer training camp each year, he got to know a great many people.

A Political Turn

By 1964 Barr was 47 years old, and he had been a member of the military for 24 years, including 18 in the reserve, from which he would retire in

1965. He had also held the same job with the Parmenter Company for over a decade. It might be tempting, though too simple, to say that his life lacked excitement, but it would be fair to conclude that he was ready for new challenges. The first of these arrived when several members of the Republican precinct committee from his neighborhood asked him to run for a seat in the Arizona House of Representatives. Their request was not entirely out of the blue, since Burt's wife Charlotte was very active in district politics, serving on the precinct committee. (One neighborhood leader later remembered that Burt was initially known for being Charlotte Barr's husband.) But Burt was initially cautious.

In considering this possibility, he weighed the demands of the office and his chances of success. His friend Clyde Smith advised him against running, arguing that the duties would interfere with his business activities. When Barr raised this concern with the committee members, they told him the legislature met for only 63 days and that the work was relatively undemanding. And while it would require Barr to spend some time away from his business, they emphasized the value of having a business leader serve in the legislature. Winning the election was Barr's second concern, and the committee also reassured him about his prospects. They noted that this was an open seat because the incumbent had just vacated it to run for the state corporation commission. Furthermore, the recruiters explained, Barr would face no opposition in the primary, and in the general election the district always elected Republicans. So with those assurances, Barr agreed to run.

But the party workers were wrong. No sooner had Barr announced his candidacy than Dr. Charles Kalil, a member of the extremely conservative John Birch Society, declared his intention to seek the Republican nomination. While the party workers and Barr might not have predicted Kalil's candidacy, they probably should have expected opposition from someone in the Society, for in recent years its members had been very active in politics. In 1961 key Society members and their allies had organized a Stay America Committee that ran a slate of candidates for Phoenix mayor and city council. In 1962 a Glendale car dealer named Evan Mecham rode the enthusiastic support of the Birch Society to win the Republican primary nomination for the U.S. Senate and then lost the race to the incumbent senator, Carl Hayden. And in 1964 Mecham was running hard to win the Republican primary for governor (ultimately, unsuccessfully), charging that the administration of Republican governor Paul Fannin was guilty of waste and unethical behavior, and publishing a newspaper claim that his opponents were the Republican "bosses." And more generally, in Arizona, as in many other states, Barry Goldwater's campaign for the presidency had inspired conservatives of various stripes to seek control of the Republican Party.

Barr's opponent had some initial advantages. A doctor who had served briefly on the Maricopa County Commission and then for four years on the state Oil and Gas Commission, Kalil had greater name recognition as a candidate and a group of society members to work for him. Barr's strengths were his ideas, personality, and commitment. Though a fairly mainstream Republican, Barr could also campaign as an outsider and a businessman. In announcing his candidacy he identified business and economic growth as his top issues: "I am genuinely interested in the effort to bring more industry into the state. In order to spur the economic growth Arizona must have a state tax base and responsible, orderly government at all levels."[12]

Barr then took this message to the voters of his district, going door to door. From June, when he declared himself a candidate, to the primary election in September, and then again to the general election in November, he walked his district every day, asking voters for their support. While his primary opponent may have been better known initially, Barr's energy brought him into contact with voters, and his personal skills won them over. His skill in peddling refrigeration equipment to grocers involved selling both the equipment and himself; as a candidate, he was selling himself and his ideas. It was a labor intensive process, but he had the time and, it turned out, the interest and determination. So, while the recruitment committee had been wrong about the lack of primary opposition, they were right in selecting an energetic candidate, and they were right about the district. Barr beat Kalil in the primary by a 3 to 1 margin, and he handily won the general election, garnering 4,305 votes (66.7 percent) to 2,147 for his Democratic opponent, James I. Dugan.

As Barr entered the legislative chambers in January 1965, he found himself in an unfamiliar environment. Worlds apart from his recent experience mass marketing himself in the election campaign, it also contrasted with his work experiences, where he would move from talking to one business to meeting with another across town. The legislature was a place of rules and rituals; it was a hierarchical system, with veterans holding power and newcomers expected to stay quiet; and it was a place where knowledge was power. While resembling the military in some respects, the absence of a formal command system meant that relationships between participants were vastly different. Barr soon connected with a group of Republican freshmen legislators. Their shared reaction to their legislative experience and a desire to effect change gave Barr a sense of common purpose and the camaraderie he relished.

Barr enjoyed his first term, and in 1966 he ran for reelection. His effort was complicated by a substantial redrawing of his central Phoenix district, which almost doubled in size. Barr again took to the streets, meeting some voters already familiar with him, but dealing with many others for the first time. Like his previous campaign, this one was hard fought, and it resulted in a clear victory for Barr. The election also brought Republican control of both legislative chambers. After the final caucus decisions were made, Barr emerged as House majority leader, inaugurating a new role for Republicans in Arizona and a new phase of his life.

A Changing Life

By 1968, when Barr ran for a third legislative term, he was on the verge of facing changes that would fundamentally alter his life. The first of these concerned his marriage. On the surface, Barr's wartime marriage to Charlotte seemed happy and successful. They lived in a stylish and comfortable home close to Piestewa (then Squaw) Peak. Designed and built for them in 1955 by architect Al Beadle, it was roughly 2,000 square feet, relatively large by standards of the time, and they enlarged it in the early 1960s. Shaded by long eaves but with floor-to-ceiling windows that kept the rooms well lit, it had an open floor plan, a fireplace, and a wet bar that made it ideal for entertaining guests. Charlotte was an effective host in social and business occasions, yet Larry Shelp felt that she was always somewhat distant, "not someone you could get close to or intimate with very easily."[13] Eddie Basha was closer to the couple and realized that the marriage was troubled. The cause of this unhappiness is unclear, since this was another personal matter that Burt kept very private, but friends concluded that it concerned children. Whatever the specifics, Burt's desire for children seems to have been an important reason why the marriage fell apart and a key part of Burt's subsequent life. The couple separated informally in late 1968 and formally in April 1969, and seven months later Charlotte filed for divorce. The final decree divided the couple's assets roughly in half, with Barr providing $1,000 per month alimony, and Charlotte moved back to Washington.

During the same period, Barr made a second major life change: he left the Parmenter firm to start his own business. He did this because of several growing concerns, rather than a specific crisis, and it also reflected a greater effort to be assertive in his life. The Parmenter company was booming during the 1960s, as the Valley's population expanded and the economy grew. Barr was an excellent salesman and manager of others. He believed that visiting clients was essential, but as Eddie Basha noted, "Paul Parmenter was virtually a recluse and you hardly ever saw him." Barr found this increasingly problematic, and he would complain to Basha "how frustrating it was that he couldn't get Paul off his duff to go out and call on the trade."[14] Larry Shelp agreed, adding that Parmenter "had a lot of old friends and customers around the Valley, but he was not doing that much, and Burt was running the entire company."[15] The company's pay structure was a second, worsening irritation. While the company's profits were rising, the bonuses to salesmen were not. Their complaints put Barr in the middle, struggling to get Parmenter to pay more generous bonuses. Barr proposed a profit-sharing plan as a solution to this recurring argument, but Parmenter and his family refused, leaving Barr unhappy but powerless to change things.

Dissatisfied, Shelp and another salesman, P. J. Benning, decided to investigate starting their own company. After locating a possible building to rent, and fearing that Barr and Parmenter would discover this, they told Barr of their intentions. He understood and tried again, unsuccessfully, to get Parmenter to offer better pay. A month later Barr told Shelp that he wanted to join their enterprise. The separation benefited all parties, since Parmenter was being pressured by Hobart to sell their products exclusively, while the new split-off company, Maverick Store Fixture Company, handled the products of other manufacturers. Although Barr's divorce settlement reduced his assets, he was able to come up with his majority share of the startup money. Under his direction, the new company was immediately profitable, and it grew rapidly thereafter.

Focusing on the burgeoning supermarket business, the company expanded from refrigeration to providing these stores with equipment for their bakeries, delis, and produce departments. Maverick's full service approach was unique in the area. As Richard Kaplan noted, "We provided the equipment, the installation; we provided the drawings; we provided a lot of the layouts that they did not necessarily have the capability of doing themselves in those early years. We worked with some engineering companies, and we did a lot of our own drawings and our own engineering drawings."[16] As president, Barr was responsible for customer relations and supervising expenses. He was not involved in detailed planning or layouts for the stores; he left that to his partners. It was a division of labor that worked well.

The company's growth coincided with Barr's greater role in the legislature. Larry Shelp felt that Barr became "totally involved in the legislature," but Richard Kaplan disagreed. He reported Barr's active involvement in the business and ascribed it to Barr's ability to compartmentalize his life, "taking his political life and just setting it aside for a moment, and then actually getting down to business and taking care of business at hand." This separation was not always possible to achieve, particularly in the mid-1970s, when the company's growth exceeded its structure and personnel. Kaplan remembers going to see Barr several times a month while the legislature was in session, carrying a large stack of checks and payables to sign. "He'd be on the floor; he'd vote; and then he'd run off the floor; he'd run back into his office and he'd yell, 'Kaplan, are you ready?' And he'd sit there and—you've got to envision a stack of payables a foot high for tens of thousands of dollars—and he'd scribble his name on these checks."[17] Then Barr would have to race back to the legislature, and during the next pause, he would return to his office to finish signing checks.

Although this exercise greatly amused Barr's legislative secretary, it was obviously not good business practice. So, despite his desire to maintain control over all expenditures, Barr soon created an alternate system for authorizing payments while the legislature was in session. As his company prospered in the late 1970s and the 1980s, with his good partners and a larger, capable staff, Barr was able to scale back his business work and focus more on politics. More and more, when he came to the office after being at the legislature, he would talk politics, about what bills had been passed, or complain about "that so and so down there, I wish I could ship him back up to Pinetop or where he's from."[18] In 1980 the Retail Grocers Association of Arizona created an award for the Supplier of the Year, and Barr was its first recipient. This award primarily recognized his work in the industry and his active membership in the association, but also because he had encouraged people in the food industry to be politically active. Finally, in 1986, when Barr was 69, he and co-owner Larry Shelp arranged to sell the Maverick Company to Richard Kaplan for payments over the next ten years. And for the first time in 40 years, Burton Barr was no longer in charge of selling.

Family Man

The third aspect of Barr's life that changed was his personal life: he remarried and had a family. Even before his divorce from Charlotte was final,

Burt began seeing Louise Trammel, with whom he shared many interests but whose life experiences differed greatly from his. The daughter of teenage itinerant farmworkers, Louise had attended Phoenix schools and then gone with her mother to Germany, where she worked for U.S. Army Intelligence from 1958 to 1962. Returning to Arizona, she completed a degree in accounting at Arizona State University in 1965 and began working for an accounting firm. After four or five years she passed the exam to become a certified public accountant, one of very few women CPAs in the state. During the same period Louise became involved in Republican Party politics, especially in the Young Republicans, serving as the national committeewoman. It was at these meetings that she met Burt, who was a very popular speaker for the group. The two were married in January 1970 in a civil ceremony in Las Vegas. According to Louise, having children was a condition of the marriage. And according to Larry Shelp, she also insisted that Burt play a major role in raising the children, and that she be able to continue her accounting work. Burt happily agreed. The couple had three children in rapid order—Stephanie, Michael, and Suzanne—and she did continue her career. After initially working at home, she opened her own firm, and in the 1980s the *Phoenix Gazette* named her one of the top twelve women in accounting in Phoenix.

Burt was an active father and took that responsibility very seriously; indeed, he seemed to consider it his primary role. Everyone who knew him saw his devotion to his children and believed his claim that "they all come first," which is what his children also remembered. He tended to them from when they were born, burping the babies and changing their diapers. As they grew older, he was the transportation director, taking them to the Sotel Jewish Preschool. The family joined a nearby Episcopal church, Christ Church of the Ascension, where Burt was baptized and where he served as an usher, and as the children grew, they participated in choir and other parts of the service. Burt continued to start his day by giving them breakfast and getting them off to school, and he remained part of their days; his daughter Stephanie remembered occasions when he picked her up from school at noon and took her out for lunch. To his son Michael, he was "omnipresent," and he was "here to play or there to take care of us or do whatever it was that we needed to do."[19] He strongly encouraged each of the children to participate in many extracurricular activities, and, mirroring his own childhood experiences, they were involved in a myriad of sports. Louise recalled, "It was Burt's motto that they were going to be well-rounded individuals."[20] He did more than encourage this; he participated, always as an audience, sometimes as a driver, and occasionally, even as a coach.

Figure 6. The Barr family. Burton S. Barr Collection.

His primary expectation for his children concerned their education. He required them to finish their homework before doing other things, accompanying the admonition with a rare recollection of his father's similar instructions to him. They were expected to do well in school and go to a good college, but the choice of school and career was theirs. Michael concluded, "He was proud that we were all doing well."[21] Burt's approach to parenting contrasted with that of his father, whom Burt once described as quite strict. The children reported that Louise was the disciplinarian, because Burt never wanted confrontation. But while Burt was more inclined to be lenient, Stephanie noted that he "could give you a look" that would be painful, because "you just didn't want to disappoint him." Even "worse than any punishment" he might mete out, however, was "having to *explain* yourself to him." Burt was also a "worrier," concerned about their friends, and waiting up at night for Stephanie to make "sure that whoever was dropping me off didn't linger."[22]

Just as he was active in their lives, Burt also made his children part of his life. He regularly brought them to the Maverick office to eat lunch or even spend the day. They knew the workers well, especially his partners, Larry Shelp and Richard Kaplan, whom they considered "like family." Even more significantly, he involved them in his legislative life. He not only brought them to his office, where his desk was replete with framed pictures of them; he had them sit in the House gallery. Munching hamburgers, they would watch the floor proceedings. His son Michael reported that his father would "always open those sessions with special introductions of us, and it seemed like everybody around there knew us really well."[23] He took Michael's Cub Scout den on a tour of the capitol and brought them to meet the governor and secretary of state. He talked about his family constantly to his staff and friends. His legislative aide, Nikki Corral, remembered, "He would take any of his kids' calls and Louise's calls any time. We'd call him off the floor—we had standing orders—'If my family calls, you get me.' He was always available to them."[24]

People recognized Burt's devotion, marveling that he would leave or even adjourn a meeting to attend a child's event. For Barr, the priorities were simple: he explained that if his "legislative life ever got in the way of my family, I'd quit in a minute." Conscious of his late start in having children, he joked, "I've got to be the only person getting ready for retirement, Cub Scouts, and Brownies in the same year." As the children grew older, Barr's energy did not falter. In his sixties, he and Stephanie won a father-daughter dancing contest.[25] But maintaining this close connection meant making choices. An article in the *Arizona Republic* in 1982 explained that "Barr is not one to participate in evening speeches or political social events, because they would take time away from his family."[26] Instead, people came to the house; Michael called it "politics central" for Arizona. "It seemed like every night that somebody would come by, some politician or another lobbyist, and they would all talk."[27]

During the summers Burt had more time for the family. Louise and the children would spend a month or two at Coronado Island in California, with Burt staying for a while and then flying back and forth from Phoenix. And Burt found other opportunities to be with the family. Besides taking occasional trips, he bought a boat with Larry Shelp, which he used to take the kids water skiing; and in the winter, they used the family cabin near Flagstaff.

Moving into a Political Life

Burton Barr's postwar career initially had two tracks, business and the army reserve, and through these he developed skills and ideas that shaped his personal life and, very notably, his later political career. When he left the army in 1946, he went into sales. Although he changed employers several times over the next six years, he remained in largely the same business: supplying food processing equipment, primarily to grocery stores. Barr learned his products and the grocery business, he was a good salesman, and he established close relationships with individual owners. His success rested firstly on his exceptionally engaging personality, and secondly on the principles he followed. He believed deeply in satisfying his clients, he insisted on treating everyone with respect, and he was scrupulously honest.

His participation in the reserve provided something different: an emotional link with his wartime experiences, which remained a central part of his identity throughout his life. And it offered a camaraderie somewhat like what he had found during the war and that he deeply loved. Working with a group of men in a command situation was a joyful experience for him, and getting to know this group expanded his social life too. His reserve service also involved a public role. He wrote and gave public addresses on policy matters, while his role as commander brought him into contact with people in politics and started him thinking more about political topics and a political life.

Barr's almost inadvertent move into political office changed his life. He first found himself in voter-based politics, going door to door to win voter approval. That had some familiar elements of salesmanship to it, but the number of voters he needed to contact limited the quality of the personal interaction; it was sales, but in a high volume environment, which differed from his business experience. Yet he discovered that he loved this interaction too. Serving in the legislature was an experience quite unlike that of campaigning. It was, in some ways, the perfect environment for Barr. It provided camaraderie (predominantly male), it had a limited group of participants to learn about and interact with, and it offered the chance to do something, to solve problems to advance the public good. But if the legislature would eventually prove ideal for Barr, that would not have been the case earlier, and it was not fully apparent in 1965, given the structure of Arizona government and its political culture. Both of these would change, and Barr would play a crucial role in bringing about the changes.

CHAPTER THREE

Arizona's Political Structure, Legislative Stalemate, and the Beginning of Reform

"The rural counties, they were in charge, they were in charge."

—BURTON BARR[1]

"In effect, the governor's office was a ceremonial position."

—ALFREDO GUTIERREZ[2]

Democratic leaders, Senators Harold Giss and Clarence Carpenter would not accept "any change that would take from them the absolute power to determine the health or fate of any State agency or institution."

—J. MORRIS RICHARDS[3]

"Republicans spent their life writing speeches on losing in Arizona. And so, all of a sudden, the Republicans win."

—BURTON BARR[4]

The structure and ethos of the Arizona government that Burton Barr encountered in 1965 were rooted in the state's initial character. The three factors of population, economy, and political ideology had shaped the state's early government and political loyalties, determined the distribution of power, and framed limited expectations about public policy. Little changed over the next three decades. The enormous growth in the state's population and economy during the postwar era did produce a notable shift in party preferences, as Arizona voters chose Republican candidates for president, congress, and governor, but politics within the state were more complicated.

Although it was increasingly obvious to many Arizonans that the state government was woefully inefficient and unable to handle contemporary problems, and despite the many examples of innovation in other states, repeated calls for reform went unanswered. Years passed with little improvement, as the state's traditional powerbrokers used their control of the legislature to block change. The legislative structure, rules, and procedures facilitated this by enabling key individuals to stymie the policy-making process, but the fundamental reason this condition persisted was because of the severe malapportionment of the legislature, primarily of the Senate. Representation in the House did reflect some of the changes in Arizona, and as Republican membership and dissatisfaction with the legislative stalemate grew, the House became an arena for coalition politics, changing rules, and policy innovations.

By 1963 forces within and outside the legislature finally forced action on a few measures, but efforts to reform state government withered. Political conditions in the state changed fundamentally after 1964, when the U.S. Supreme Court required all states to apportion their legislatures using a one-person, one-vote standard. This, along with the expansion of voter rights and the enfranchisement of Arizona's minority populations, reallocated power, changed the nature of political representation, and created the possibility for innovative policy-making and governmental reform.

So, when Burton Barr entered politics and the legislature in 1965, it was at a time when the demand for reform was rising, and when achieving it was suddenly possible—but not inevitable. Well suited for legislative life, he transitioned smoothly into leadership on a major aspect of government reform in 1966. That success established his reputation, winning him a leadership position in the next legislature and beginning his impressive record of reforming government and enacting major public policies. To understand the political challenges that Barr faced in the 1960s and the significance of his achievements, one must examine the deeply rooted conditions that had shaped Arizona and its politics, and then consider the structure and character of the Arizona legislature.

The Historical Roots of Arizona and Its Politics

Arizona's political world grew from its geography and history. Its unique pattern of settlement, the distribution of its population, and the early decades of economic development dominated by agriculture and mining shaped the initial expectations, opportunities, and behaviors of its people. Their Populist-Progressive values shaped the state's constitution, its decentralized governmental structure, and the use of direct democratic methods.

The Democratic Party was the dominant force during Arizona's first three decades of statehood, attracting the affiliation of most voters and winning most public offices, and nothing during these years much altered the patterns of party affiliation, political values, or differences over issues. Massive urban population growth and economic developments in the postwar period stimulated major political consequences.

The shifting balance of power between the two parties constituted one dimension of this political change. Starting in the early 1950s, Republican presidential, congressional, and gubernatorial victories broke the Democratic monopoly on the state, but power and politics in state government were far more complicated. GOP successes grew with the rising number of urban residents, who supported certain reforms. Urban Democrats generally supported a reform agenda, but rural Democrats were often conservative and fought a rearguard action against change. These ideological and factional party divisions, combined with the rigidity of the state's political structure, meant that Arizona politics were ripe for change.

The Social Basis of Arizona Politics

Arizona's political geography reflects the overlay of historical and spatial factors: the initial location of its indigenous population; the Spanish and Mexican settlement in southern Arizona; the discovery of minerals, largely copper, in central and southern areas of the state; the availability of water in the central region; and the influx of migrants from other parts of the United States, Mexico, and Europe seeking opportunities and wealth. Arizona's settlement was unlike that of many states to the east, with their well-watered lands that yielded a wide and thick distribution of farms, hamlets, villages, towns, and cities; and it also differed from states where access to a lake or major river fed the growth of a major commercial port city. Instead, the extent of Arizona's mountainous and desert terrains, its general aridity, and the location of its resources produced a pattern of disparate population clusters. In 1910 half of the territory's population lived in four counties, while the other half was relatively evenly distributed between the other ten counties. Tucson and Phoenix grew primarily because of agriculture and to a lesser extent, commerce; the other cities were the byproducts of mining, while smaller towns served more dispersed ranching and farming areas.

In Arizona, as in many Western states, mining drove much of the growth, starting in the mid-nineteenth century. It not only shaped the population distribution but also drew in flows of immigrants from as near as Mexico and as far as Cornwall, Britain. Individual miners initiated the exploration for minerals, but mining quickly became the province of big businesses, most often major corporations. These corporations brought substantial financial investment and a demand for workers with engineering skills, and they employed a sizable industrial labor force. Conflicts between companies and workers prompted strikes and the organization of unions, forging a crucial part of Arizona's culture and mettle. As vast economic enterprises and as *the* employer in many mining towns or cities—indeed, they were often the reason for a town's existence—mining companies like Phelps Dodge and Kennecott directly affected Arizona politics starting in the territorial period, and remained the foundation for political divisions in the subsequent years. Mining targeted various metals, but by far the most important of these was copper. High levels of copper production in four locations in the state supplied the population base for different cities and counties (see table 1).

Farming drew other groups of settlers to Arizona Territory, particularly to the Salt River Valley in central Arizona, and further south, to Tucson, where the Spanish had first settled in the eighteenth century. Despite limited rainfall in the desert valleys, their rivers provided enough water for irrigated agriculture, supplemented by groundwater. The substantial flow of the Salt River, an extensive system of canals, and completion of the federally funded Roosevelt Dam on the Salt River in 1911 supported the growth of Phoenix and an array of towns scattered across the Valley. Tucson, the older city with better rail links, was initially larger and more important, but by 1920 Phoenix had become the dominant city and the commercial center, complementing its political role as the state capital. Two smaller towns, Yuma and Flagstaff, served similar but lesser commercial roles in the southwest

Table 1. Population in the largest Arizona towns and cities, 1890–1920

Towns and Cities	*1890*	*1910*	*1920*
Bisbee-Douglas	1,535	15,456	19,121
Globe, Miami, Superior	803	8,473	16,197
Clifton-Morenci	1,358	9,874	9,163
Prescott, Jerome	2,009	8,185	9,040
Tucson	5,150	13,193	20,292
Phoenix	3,152	11,134	29,053
All Salt River Valley towns	4,537	15,859	40,207

Source: "Decennial Censuses: Arizona, Counties, Cities, Places, 1860—1990," Bureau of the Census, 2001; Clifton-Morenci estimates from Charles Sargent, ed., *Metro Arizona* (Scottsdale: Biffington Books, 1988), 44, 50–51; Salt River population from these and other local sources.

corner and northern area of Arizona, respectively. Finally, the northern and eastern parts of the state were primarily engaged in cattle ranching and sheep raising, along with some farming.

The Arizona population was layered by chronology and geography. The initial Indian population was spread across the state but was most numerous in the central and eastern areas, and by 1910 it represented roughly one in seven Arizona residents. When the territory was first acquired from Mexico in the mid-nineteenth century, Mexicans had lived mostly in southern Arizona, especially in the Gadsden Purchase area, but over the next six decades the development of mining and agriculture drew them across the territory. By 1910 Mexican-born residents constituted a seventh of the Arizona population, and perhaps an equal number were Mexicans of U.S. birth. African Americans and Asian Americans were far less numerous, each constituting less than one percent of the territory's inhabitants.

The remaining two-thirds of the Arizona population in 1910 were Anglo Americans, but that group included an array of cultures and backgrounds. Mining especially attracted streams of European immigrants either to work the mines or to "mine the miners" as merchants or suppliers. Scandinavians and native-born Americans from the Midwest came to the towns of Superior and Miami; Jewish merchants who had traveled from San Francisco joined Cornish and Irish miners in Tombstone and Prescott, Southerners from Texas to Tennessee came to farm or ranch, while Mormon settlers migrated south from Utah into eastern Arizona and into the Salt River Valley. On the eve of statehood, Arizona ranked only forty-fifth in population (compared with being fifth in area), but its 204,000 people represented a range of cultures and livelihoods.

The First Stage of Arizona Government and Politics

Arizona achieved statehood in 1912, during the heyday of anti-colonialist feelings, denunciations of Eastern corporate interests, and concerns over misuse of power. These sentiments were fully apparent in the state's main economic and political struggle, as miners and miners' unions confronted the powerful mining corporations. This conflict played out in the state constitutional convention, where members wrote a number of protections for labor into the constitution. Concerned about the potential for misuse of government, especially by mining and railroad interests, the convention members fashioned a decentralized governmental system. They created a relatively weak office of governor, with limited opportunities for appointment or removal of officials; established many elective offices, even including a state mine inspector; and dispersed authority to multiple independent boards and commissions.

The constitution writers also believed that more democracy would solve governance problems, so they empowered citizens by providing the new measures of direct democracy such as initiative, referendum, recall, and the direct primary. On various occasions during Arizona's next century, these popular powers proved critical, but never more so than in the earliest days of statehood, when voters reinserted judicial recall into the state's constitution after President Taft had removed it, enfranchised women, and prohibited liquor.

In the first two decades of statehood, Democrats were the stronger political force. Led by George W. P. Hunt, an indomitable, mustachioed politico of considerable girth and progressive views who was elected governor seven times, they controlled all three branches of government for most of this era, drawing broad support from miners, ranchers, Mormons, and immigrants from the South and from Ireland. Republicans, who won the backing of mine owners and managers, and garnered greater support from urban residents, especially transplants from the Midwest and East, had limited success overall, except in 1920, when they swept the state offices and won control of the state Senate. In other years, the GOP found little to cheer about in election results, winning only 10 to 15 percent of the legislative seats and none of the other state elective offices. But elections for governor were quite different. Republicans concentrated their efforts with some success on the contests for the state's top office: they not only won three of the ten races, they were also competitive in each contest, averaging 48 percent of the vote.

Reaction to the Depression and an influx of new residents in the 1930s turned Arizona into an overwhelmingly Democratic state. Voter registration, which had averaged two-thirds Democratic, now jumped to 87 percent for the party of Franklin Roosevelt. Democrats mobilized voters from various groups, including new young voters and in-migrants to the state, but they also gained from the conversion of Republicans. Some of those gains reflected popular endorsement of New Deal policies and the appreciation of federal dollars, but other converts simply followed a pragmatic aim of trying to influence the party with all the power. The gains in registration carried over into elections, as Democrats swept every state office and virtually shut Republicans out of the legislature. But, while cooperating with federal programs, accepting federal assistance, and modifying the tax system, Arizona Democrats did not use their near-total control of state government to address emerging problems. Nor did they follow the example of other states by expanding or restructuring state government.

The state's most vital issue, which simmered and periodically boiled over, was water; specifically, securing more water for the state. Both parties shared this goal, and in the 1920s Arizona began a decades-long struggle with six other states, but mainly California, over rights to Colorado River water. Arizona rejected the 1922 Colorado River Compact's water allocation plan, but Congress adopted it and funded construction of the Hoover Dam. In 1944 state leaders bowed to political reality and ratified the compact, but the allocation of water remained unsettled until a U.S. Supreme Court decision in 1963. The state's congressional delegation then united to achieve legislation in 1968 authorizing the Central Arizona Project, a system of canals, pipelines, and dams to distribute Colorado River water to the state, but acquiring funding would be another battle. During those same decades, Arizonans also dealt with water supply within the state. Five dams were constructed on the Salt and Verde Rivers between 1925 and 1946, significantly boosting the water storage capacity for agriculture and for new urban residents. The construction of dams and the pursuit of water from the Colorado became more urgent because Arizonans were overusing their groundwater. Starting in 1945 the governor urged the state legislature to grapple with this worsening problem, and in 1948 the legislature finally took the first meager steps to address it. But effective solutions to the interrelated problems of groundwater and surface water would require more foresighted and courageous policymakers in the future.

Political Change and Continuity in Postwar Arizona

Arizona also resembled many Western states because World War II helped initiate a new economic era. Federal spending on military facilities and defense manufacturing plants, and the example of planning by California cities, awakened Arizona to fresh opportunities. Cities first and then the state worked vigorously to revise the economy by recruiting aviation and electronic businesses. Phoenix initiated the strategy in the 1940s, Tucson followed shortly thereafter, and in the late 1950s Governor Paul Fannin began a statewide effort. Arizona's traditional economy—agriculture, ranching, mining, and forestry—related to rural Arizona and its natural resources, but the new, booming economy was urban. It brought a massive influx of people, who filled and created jobs, and bought and built homes. And it meant that by the 1960s, the state's policy priorities, like those of other urbanized Western states, were shifting to economic development, urban infrastructure, and the problems of suburban growth, sprawl, and pollution.

The demographic and economic transformation of Arizona also changed its formerly predictable political world. Republican voter registration jumped to 25 percent in 1952, 34 percent in 1962, and 42 percent by 1970. Reversing the trend seen in the 1930s, Republicans now regained the affiliation of some who had pragmatically identified as Democrats, as well as benefitting from in-migration, especially by Midwestern Republicans. But party loyalty was comparatively weak among Arizonans, as voters split their tickets at a higher rate than other states, and some regularly voted for the other party's ticket. Bolstering the historic pattern of limited loyalty was a new municipal form: in Phoenix, the Charter Government Committee, a nonpartisan group, ran the city government from 1949 to 1975.

So, while registration during these decades denoted a general shift in party preference, the more meaningful changes in behavior came earlier. The electoral shift began when Republican nominee Howard Pyle won the governor's race in 1950 and again in 1952, and the Republican victory circle widened to include Barry Goldwater for the U.S. Senate, John Rhodes for a U.S. House seat, and Dwight Eisenhower for president. This initiated a run of GOP victories in presidential and congressional races. Republicans improved their showing in legislative races during the 1950s, winning a third of the House seats and 10 percent of the Senate. GOP candidates for state offices also ran better, and in 1966 they won a majority of their races.

Notwithstanding the importance of changes in party registration and electoral success, a much more complex political reality lay beneath partisan labels, as the composition and values of both parties altered during the immediate postwar years. Some shifts were tied to arguments over new policies, as Arizonans responded to national debates about unions, civil rights, and social entitlement programs. But urban Arizonans also demonstrated interest in efficient and responsive government that could consistently provide necessary services. Immigration and different types of jobs brought new people with different political experiences and expectations to the state. The electorate also expanded through the political mobilization of African Americans, Mexican Americans, and Native Americans starting in the 1960s and 1970s.

This latter expansion would bring additional liberal voices to those of Democrats who had supported New Deal policies, but into the 1970s the party retained some loyalty from many "Jeffersonian Democrats," a label traditionally used in Arizona and elsewhere in the nation by those favoring a restricted federal government as well as certain limits at the state and local level. Arizona Democrats attentive to national politics tended to be more liberal, while conservatives and moderates generally dominated among Democrats active in state politics, especially in the legislature. Caught between changing national and state trends, by the 1950s these mostly rural legislators were commonly called "Pinto" Democrats, after the horse of two colors, since they retained the Democratic title but often voted Republican in national or state races and generally opposed change.

Arizona Republicans commonly pushed for economic development, favored lower taxes, and criticized labor unions, but they too were a diverse group, made more so by the addition of recent immigrants living in Phoenix and Tucson. Some held classical free market views and harbored suspicions of government—much like the common, simplistic depiction of Barry Goldwater's views—but others saw the need for state government action, like providing state assistance to attract businesses and support economic development and advancing equal protection support for minority groups. Most importantly, many Republicans favored a more modern and efficient state government, rather than one that was traditional and minimalist. These divisions created tensions within each party but also interesting opportunities for cooperation.

Arizona's political culture, the basic set of ideas about governance and who should govern, reflected the initial migration streams into the territory, its relatively slow growth from the 1850s to the 1950s, and the impact of conditions in a frontier and desert area. Drawing on a model created by Daniel J. Elazar, political scientist David Berman explains Arizona as a blend of "traditionalistic" culture, evident in its reliance on a paternalistic hierarchy and endorsement of limited government, and "moralistic" culture, which emphasizes "the common good and the implementation of shared principles."[5] Elazar also argues that "social and family ties are paramount in a traditionalistic political culture," and the patterns of Arizona's political leadership show these as having influence but not being determinative.[6]

Arizona's relatively small population in the nineteenth century, along with the arduous conditions of early settlement, meant that pioneer families often developed close personal connections and appreciated their shared experience and status. By the early twentieth century, those families, as in other states, began savoring old stories, promoting history, and constructing a shared identity. Members of these families accepted the responsibilities of public leadership roles for themselves, their kin, and members of other pioneer families. Moreover, their economic success gave them the stature to win wider public endorsement.

Thus, into the 1950s men (for the most part) from these families dominated Arizona politics. Carl Hayden, who spent 42 years in the U.S. Senate after serving 12 years in the U.S. House and holding local offices, carried on the legacy of his father, Charles Hayden, who had founded Tempe in 1871, played a major role in its early development, and also held local offices. Senator Barry Goldwater's family had arrived in the territory in the 1860s: his uncle Morris was elected mayor of Prescott and then to the legislature, while Barry's father Baron became a public figure in Phoenix. The Udalls were a prominent Mormon family in several places throughout Arizona. David Udall represented St. Johns in the Territorial Legislature, his sons Levi and Jesse were judges on the state Supreme Court, and U.S. Representative Stewart Udall (1955–1961) from Tucson was the first of many third-generation Udalls to hold public office.

Family and tradition were important in arranging leadership, but Arizona also welcomed and groomed new political leaders. In part, this reflected settlement-era mentality, when sharing and cooperation were required for progress and even survival. It also spoke to the desire for growth and the recognition that this aim was best served by encouraging rather than obstructing the advancement of newcomers. Burton Barr exemplifies this kind of leadership. Arizona's acceptance of new political leaders also shows in its relative openness to the involvement of women. As historian Heidi Osselaer shows, by the 1950s women had become "legitimate politicians," and within the state legislature they were "drawing powerful committee assignments [and] introducing important legislation."[7] So, while family and friendship ties helped some Arizonans obtain political success, newcomers could also apply.

The Legislative Arena

While Barr's political activities were broadly shaped by Arizona's political system and culture, in many respects the legislature was a political world of its own. The role and power of legislatures in most state governments had waned in the twentieth century, but conditions in Arizona lay somewhat outside of national trends. Within a relatively weak state government, and facing a weak executive branch, the legislature held primary authority, yet the method of apportionment, notably for senators, led to domination by rural counties and economic interests that resisted change. Bipartisan coalitions governed the House, where chairs and senior members exercised suzerainty over their committees, ignoring the desires of committee members or the interested public. Legislative activity was stymied by various obstacles. The conditions of legislative services, particularly the limited facilities and support staff, made lawmaking difficult in both houses, but legislative progress was frequently smothered by the Senate, which was completely controlled by Democratic Senate Majority Leader Harold Giss. But court-mandated reapportionment eventually transformed the legislature, most notably the Senate, spurring momentum for change.

The Historical Role of State Legislatures

State legislatures occupy a singular place in governance and politics. While legislators are elected individually from districts, they serve as part of a group that represents an entire state. This collective responsibility distinguishes their political functions from those of individuals elected to statewide offices, and it means that the skills they need also differ from those required of state-elected officials. The legislature's role has also altered greatly over time. In their classic study of American legislatures in 1966, Malcolm Jewel and Samuel Patterson observed, "We are living in an executive-centered [political] world," for "in the twentieth century the broad outlines of public policy tend to be formulated by executives," but they also noted that this was not always the case.[8] Indeed not. In the nascent American nation, state legislatures were the overwhelmingly dominant branch of government. During the nineteenth century, legislatures were regarded as the "peoples' houses," the embodiment of popular will. Even as government expanded and became more complex, the public still considered legislatures to have the primary responsibility in making public policy.

Ideas about the proper structure and duties of government began to change dramatically during the late nineteenth century, however, and Progressive Era exposés of legislative misdeeds fueled public concerns about governance. As the public increasingly perceived legislators as representing only parochial interests or as the tools of special interests, it came to view executives more favorably. Governors now appeared as the best representatives of the people as a whole. Their role resembled the new example of the dynamic business leader, they had the endorsement of a statewide electorate, and advances in communication and transportation enabled them to connect directly with voters. Historian Jon Teaford notes, "Governors were emerging as the policy leaders and chief legislators of their states."[9] In their drive to improve government efficiency, they sought the advice of social scientists and other experts, and into the 1920s they advanced the reorganization of state governments. The key to their enhanced power was their authority in budgeting and directing states finances.

In the first two postwar decades, many states expanded the power of the executive, lengthening the governor's term of office to four years, and, in some cases, consolidating state agencies. Legislatures also began to professionalize, shifting to annual sessions, reducing the number of committees, raising legislators' salaries, and providing staffs, most notably in the form of legislative councils. These trends accelerated from the early 1960s to the mid-1970s.

The Arizona Legislature

Arizona's history differed in some important ways from this national pattern. The state's Progressive Era constitution had created a weak gubernatorial post, with a myriad of offices, boards, and commissions not under the governor's control, and this system remained in effect into the 1970s. The governor's suite in the capitol building neatly symbolized the office's limited importance. The secretary to Governor Ernest McFarland described it as being "really primitive" and inadequate in size and features, noting that reporters standing in the hallway could hear conversations being held in the office. A decade later, Governor Samuel Goddard (1965–1967) found the rooms scantily furnished, but because his budget did not include funds for furniture, he had to borrow tables and chairs from the offices of the Highway Patrol.[10]

Confronting a weak executive branch, and especially a weak governor, the legislature could do mostly as it wished, but generally it wished to do very little. That attitude reflected the preferences of conservative political interests, which retained considerable strength in that branch of government. Constitutional provisions, as well as the legislature's internal organization, rules, and procedures, also hindered any inclination to meet demands for change. Finally, demographically influenced political shifts produced tangled factional divisions that further complicated legislative efforts.

The legislature's inertia was encouraged by its system of apportioning representation, and this reflected Arizona's initially small and persistently clustered population. Representation in the lower house included a democratic dimension, for although seats were apportioned by county, each county received one additional representative for every numerical block of votes (starting at 2,500 in 1932) cast for governor in the previous election. This scheme underrepresented areas with lower turnout (partly because some citizens were disfranchised), but representation roughly reflected population differences and growth. The weakness of this method was a perpetual increase in the size of the House, which rose from 52 seats in the 1930s, to 58 in the 1940s, and then to 82 in 1953.

Even compared to the House's imperfect system, representation in the Senate was egregiously inequitable. Arizona resembled various states in adopting a "little federalism" model for its legislature, apportioning Senate seats to areas, usually counties, rather than by population. In states with many counties and a distributed population, inequalities in representation might not be too serious. But in Arizona, with only 14 counties and a highly clustered population, this method produced striking inequalities that worsened over time. The authors of the constitution had made a modest accommodation to population differences in 1912 by allotting one senate seat to each county and a second to the five largest counties. Over the years, population growth, mainly in the Phoenix and Tucson areas, made this system increasingly unrepresentative. In 1953 the legislature proposed a constitutional revision in representation, which voters narrowly accepted. It did resolve the problem facing the House by limiting it to 80 seats, but this step was linked to a change for the Senate—defended as "simplifying" the system—that granted two Senate seats to every county, making representation even more unequal.

As a result, the tripling of Arizona's population from 1945 to 1965 affected the legislature in several ways. In the House, population growth boosted Republican votes, which produced more Republican representatives, especially from Maricopa County but also from Pima County. So, while Democrats maintained a majority in that chamber, Republicans now constituted an appreciable minority. By contrast, the partisan distribution of representation in the 28-member Senate remained virtually unchanged in these years, with only one or two Republicans winning in each election. Thus, while the urban areas of Maricopa and Pima counties burgeoned from half to three-quarters of the state's population, their representation in the Senate remained fixed at only one-quarter of that chamber.

Rapid population growth, economic development, and shifting policy priorities pushed voters in one direction, mainly toward the GOP, but they also forged the legislature into a unique political environment. Conservative Democratic voters in the state could, and readily did, alter their voting preference and eventually their party registration to the GOP. But conservative Democratic officeholders, the Pinto Democrats, were much more reluctant to change parties, particularly if their constituencies, mostly rural, experienced less population growth, and if maintaining traditional loyalties promised institutional rewards. Thus, the composition and behavior of the House became more complex, with Pinto Democrats playing off urban Republicans and moderate to liberal Democrats in pursuit of their own goals.

The Senate remained firmly controlled by conservative, rural interests and determined to prevent change. Burton Barr put it simply: "The rural counties, they were in charge, *they were in charge*." Ranchers made up part of this conservative bloc within the Senate, but the most powerful and implacable foes of change were connected with corporations such as railroad, utilities, and, most of all, copper mining companies. J. Morris Richards, a legislator himself, described the power of these lawmakers in his detailed legislative history. He noted, for example, that in 1945 Representative James Sharpe of Cochise County actively opposed "expenditures that might hurt big taxpayers such as the copper companies." He likewise described Senator William F. Kimball of Pima County, a candidate in the 1954 Democratic gubernatorial primary, as a lifelong conservative, who was "often being accused of being a tool of the large corporations in matters of legislation." To explain the efforts in 1963 by the House Appropriations Committee to slash state expenditures, he cited Lester Inskeep of the *Arizona Daily Star*, who described the chairman as "an employee of Phelps Dodge [the mining corporation] . . . which always objects to any increase in the state tax rate."[11]

Political Factions, Power, and Legislative Organization

Legislative organization and power resulted not simply from which party had the majority and from standard rules, but rather from personal connections, factional alignments, and decisions made anew at the beginning of every legislature. Reactions against this system would affect legislative structure and policy after 1965. Pinto Democrats held only a minority of House seats from 1953 to 1965, but they exercised considerable influence, winning the very powerful post of Speaker in every legislature during this era except for 1955–1956. None of these years saw a "normal" contest with all Democrats voting for their candidate, all Republicans voting for theirs, and the majority party's nominee being elected. Instead, Democrats split their votes for the House leadership post in every election except for 1957, when all members of both parties supported the Democratic caucus candidate for Speaker (see table 2). The most striking elections came in 1953, 1963, and 1965, when a coalition of all or nearly all Republicans and a minority of Democrats elected the Speaker.

The Speaker's election, often paired with the selection of the majority leader, essentially decided how the legislature in that session would be organized. Unlike the familiar practices in the twentieth-century U.S. Congress, where committee seniority determined chairmanships, committee

Table 2. Minority influence on Arizona House Speaker elections, 1953–1965

Year	*For the Speaker*	*Against*	*Election*
1953	Dem 22 Rep 25	Dem 28 Rep. 2	Coalition
1955	Dem 48 Rep 1	Dem 12 Rep 19	Democratic split
1957	Dem 58 Rep 22	None	Democratic consensus
1959	Dem 40 Rep 24	Dem 15 Rep 0	Democratic split
1961	Dem 41 Rep. 2	Dem 11 Rep 25	Democratic split
1963	Dem 16 Rep 32	Dem 32 Rep 0	Coalition
1965	Dem 18 Rep 35	Dem 26 Rep 0	Coalition

Source: Roderick Andrew Jacobsen, "Election of the Speaker in the Arizona House of Representatives during the Era of Coalition," (master's thesis, Arizona State University, 1967).

memberships were relatively stable, and the distribution of seats by party was uniform for all committees, in the Arizona House, as in many state legislatures, the Speaker appointed committee chairs and decided committee membership, including the distribution of committee seats. The Speaker made these choices based on personal political arrangements and factional interests, although coalitions negotiated some of those decisions. Chairmanships provide the clearest evidence of shifting power. Pinto Democrats held no chairmanships in the clear Democratic majority years of 1955 and 1961; Pintos and regular Democrats split the chairmanships in 1957 and 1959; but in the coalition years of 1953, 1963, and 1965, regular Democrats were completely excluded from these positions. The consequences of forging these coalitions are even clearer in that Republicans received nearly half of the chairmanships in the latter years.

This factional conflict produced major turnover in chairmanships: anywhere from half to all chairs in one session were replaced in the next, and new chairs often had no experience on the committees they ran. The most important committee was the Rules Committee, chaired by the chamber's presiding officer; the minority group never received seats on this committee, and it generally had only a few on the other major committees, like Appropriations and Judiciary. Committee membership was also volatile from year to year, partly because there was no standard division of seats by party or faction. In 1955 Pintos and Republicans were allotted a few seats on each committee, but Pintos received no major committee seats in 1957. In 1959 Republicans got five seats per committee, but in 1961 Pintos and Republicans received seats on only a few of the less important committees. The coalition legislatures of 1963 and 1965 changed this practice, however, and in a move to standardize legislative organization, they distributed seats in rough proportion to a faction's overall numbers.

Figure 7. Arizona legislative committee meeting, 1959. History and Archives Division, Arizona State Library, Archives and Public Records.

Chairmanships and committee composition were crucial because legislative rules gave committees and chairs almost life-and-death power over proposed legislation. Committees functioned as "sifting devices" in dealing with bills referred to them. Measures that the leadership or the committee chair disliked simply died in committee. In 1947 Robert H. Forbes complained about the "practice for committee chairmen to hold bills in their committees, thereby preventing open discussion on them," but his plea for openness had no effect.[12] Of course, committees killed bills for many different reasons as part of the normal, efficient operation of this or any legislature. Arizona's method differed because so many bills were disposed of this way, because chairs would act unilaterally, and because inaction often thwarted debate on major proposals. In 1955 and 1957, for example, the chair of the Senate Revenue and Finance Committee simply refused to convene his committee to consider an important gas tax proposal.

Rule changes adopted by the House in 1963 reduced the power of chairmen and opened the system to some extent. Refusal to hold meetings required approval by the Rules Committee, and committee members could require a chairman to bring up a bill for discussion if two-thirds of them signed a petition requesting this. Doing so was no simple matter, however, as Representative Harry Bandouveris found out when a chairman threatened retaliation against signers of a Bandouveris petition, striking "panic in the hearts of those who had signed the petition, and they immediately asked to have their names removed." But the Senate did not liberalize its rules, as evidenced by its treatment in 1963 of a House bill to create a long-sought budget director position. As J. Morris Richards explained, the bill "was referred immediately to four standing committees. It was not reported out by any of them, indicating that the Senate leadership did not favor the measure."[13]

Legislative action was also hindered by a lack of facilities and support, a condition common to most state legislatures at the time. Jack A. Brown,

Figure 8. Arizona Senate, 1950s. History and Archives Division, Arizona State Library, Archives and Public Records.

who first served in the House and later in the Senate, noted that when he first arrived as a freshman representative in 1963, "We had no offices for anyone except the leadership positions. The office was your desk." Lawmakers had limited telephone access: they received messages of phone calls, and to respond they could use one of "about six phones booths—they looked just like a phone booth on the street." More generally, he explained, "We didn't have hardly any staff—a chief clerk's office and very, very few others—to help us." For assistance with their correspondence, they could call for a secretary, who "sat by your desk and recorded or dictated your letters, and they went back to the secretarial pool to write them up and bring them back, and you would sign them."[14] The House staff numbered around 18 in the 1940s and rose to 45 in the 1950s, but this included everyone from the chief clerk, to pages, doormen, and mimeograph operators—and this for a chamber of 80 members. The Senate was a smaller body, but it had much less support: seven total staff in the 1940s and only 14 in the 1950s.

Partly because chairmen ran their committees like czars, committees operated in strict order and relative secrecy. Freshman lawmakers were advised to "trade in your mouth for another pair of ears," and bring concerns to the chair privately, rather than voice them in meetings. Longtime lobbyist Jack DeBolske explained that getting into a committee required

> an invitation by some member of the committee . . . because the meeting was behind closed doors. And when you went into the room after you got an invitation, you could then give your spiel, and they'd ask you the pros and cons of the bill, and you'd answer, and then they would ask you to leave, and then they would vote. And of course it was kind of unethical in those days for anybody to divulge how anybody else voted.

This situation improved in 1963, when the new House coalition changed the rules and opened committee meetings to the press and the public.[15]

Legislative Inaction, Conflict, and Leadership

Legislative inaction often resulted from differences between the two chambers, a problem for every bicameral legislature, but unresolved conflicts were more serious in Arizona and worsened during this era. The second session of the 25th legislature, which met in 1962, was a case in point. J. Morris Richards noted, "Neither branch would act on the measure of the other. All of the time spent in study, conversations, bargaining, and all else that went on in an attempt to create a program for equalizing property taxes," a vital issue, was wasted. Representative Nelson Brayton blamed the Senate not only for this but also for a host of failures, claiming that many bills "were overridden by the Senate, about 60 of them."[16]

Another cause of inaction was that particular groups or agencies sometimes acted defensively, to protect themselves and their power. J. Morris Richards observed that in the mid-1950s, for example, "The State Highway Commission, long entrenched and using its influence in many instances for political and sectional purposes, was able to fend off even the most beneficial legislation if it threatened the status quo." Partisan and political calculations also played a role, as when Democrat William R. Mathews opposed Republican Governor Paul Fannin's 1962 legislative program by labeling it an effort at "building his own political machine." Other objections to specific proposals often represented a broad, deep-seated resistance to virtually any changes in government. By the 1960s this opposition came especially from the Senate, and specifically from the duo of Senate President Clarence Carpenter and Majority Leader Harold Giss, who held their positions from 1955 to 1967. J. Morris Richards spoke for many observers when he claimed that they refused to accept "any change that would take from them the absolute power to determine the health or fate of any State agency or institution." Senator Alfredo Gutierrez (1973–1986) agreed, saying that Giss "liked things as they were and didn't want them changed much."[17]

Carpenter held the more prominent position, but Giss dominated this partnership. While presiding officers managed chamber proceedings, a majority leader worked the floor, interacting closely with members. According to Jack Debolske, Giss was "*The* legislator at that time." Burton Barr said, "Giss ran everything," while a common, puckish description referred to the Senate "as a large body of men surrounded by Harold Giss." By any account, he was one of the most powerful legislators in Arizona's history. Born in Minneapolis in 1906, he grew up in Los Angeles, and in 1938 moved to Yuma, where he owned a department store and a men's clothing store. A dapper dresser who often sported a boutonniere, Giss ran successfully for a House seat in 1948, and in 1950 he moved to the Senate, where he served until his death in 1973. Giss became Senate majority leader in 1954 and retained that position until 1966, when he became minority leader. His overall success as a leader came firstly because of his intelligence and hard work. DeBolske said, "He was one of the smartest guys I've ever run into," and Alfredo Gutierrez reported that he had "an encyclopedic kind of brain." Diligently reading the voluminous materials he received from lobbyists and other advocates for special interests and causes,

Figure 9. Senator Harold Giss and Senate President Clarence Carpenter. History and Archives Division, Arizona State Library, Archives and Public Records.

he became exceptionally knowledgeable about Arizona and its statutes. A second characteristic that both shaped reactions to him and influenced how the legislature operated was his courtesy. His colleagues on both sides of the aisle described him as a "gentleman," as someone who "played fair," a man who acted with a sense of decency and respect for his colleagues.[18]

Besides these personal qualities, Giss's success as a legislative leader depended on his mastery of legislative rules and procedures, a mastery based on his reverence for them. He used this expertise effectively not only in managing business in the Senate, but also in dealing with the House; Richards observed, "Seldom has Giss ever lost out when it came to a head to head battle against the House." Gutierrez admired his skills but believed that Giss used these to "muck up the works, put everyone on the defensive," for he seemed to "love process more than substance." Giss's legislative success was also due to his control of the flow of legislation, as he evaluated and supervised all proposed laws. This process started with his executive assistant, a retired judge, who read every proposal and gave Giss his recommendation. Giss then carefully examined the screened proposals. Barr later described the process, "If the Judge said no, [it was] goodbye. If the Judge said, 'Well, there's a chance,' it then went to Giss, and if Giss said no, forget it. It never surfaced." But if Giss approved a bill, it was virtually guaranteed to pass, for he knew how to assemble support for measures.[19]

The final and most crucial reason for Giss's success was his control of committees. Stan Turley, who served as presiding officer in both houses, explained, "He had Rules, he had Appropriations, he had Judiciary, and he had Finance, those four committees. He had about the same people on them, they would rotate around, there's your control. There's your control of every meaningful thing that goes on in those four committees."[20] But along with placing allies on these committees, Giss himself served continuously on Rules, Judiciary, and Finance, so as to keep a very close eye on things. Thus, he used Senate committees to control legislation through the Senate, and he screened bills, cleverly used parliamentary procedure, and negotiated not only over bills within the Senate but also over measures adopted by the House.

Giss achieved such success because the Senate was small and an idiosyncratic environment. Reflecting on this years later, Barr explained that Giss "got his power and strength because he out-worked everybody in the Senate, and they were content, more than content, these people, to let it happen." At a time when the composition of Arizona and the House were changing rapidly, representatives from rural counties remained in control of the Senate, and "They were glad to have Mr. Giss do all the work."[21] But while senators may have been content, many in the House and elsewhere in state government, and Arizonans concerned about conditions in the state, felt increasingly unhappy. While the legislature passed some measures during the first two postwar decades, including increasing school funding, raising unemployment compensation, and creating a regulatory code for savings and loan associations, many of the most pressing issues were largely ignored. In general, these years were a repeated story of both Democratic and Republican governors strongly recommending critical proposals to the legislature and then having that body take little or no action, even in special legislative sessions called to address only those topics.

One vital matter the legislature refused to tackle was restructuring the government. The 1940s saw a nationwide push for government reorganization to achieve greater efficiency. The 1949 Hoover Report presented reform recommendations for the federal government, many of which were adopted and which served as a blueprint for states to imitate.[22] Arizona, like many states, hired a consulting firm to study state government, and in December 1949 Griffenhagen & Associates submitted its report. During the 1950s the legislature adopted several of the firm's recommendations for restructuring its own operations, which mirrored actions taken by other states, including shifting to annual sessions, reducing the number of committees, and creating a Legislative Council with staff to help in drafting bills. The report was more critical of the executive branch, which it saw as a mishmash of different offices, agencies, boards, and commissions, many of which the governor did not control, and some of which no longer had any real function. In general, the report criticized an overly wide "dispersion of authority and responsibility," "illogical groups of functions," and "complexity and inconsistency in the forms," and it recommended many changes.[23] Despite emphatic gubernatorial requests to pass some of the proposed reforms, the legislature was unmoved. By the 1960s Governor Fannin focused his efforts on the most vital need and the key capacity other governors had possessed since the 1920s: creating a budget bureau.

The second crucial issue was equalizing tax assessments throughout the state. Arizona law required that property be assessed at full value, but beginning in the 1940s economic growth and political pressures produced major, growing inequalities between the 14 counties, as their standards for assessing residential property, for example, ranged between 5.5 and 21.1 percent of full value. Despite mounting problems and repeated gubernatorial requests, the legislature responded only by considering measures that called for studying or gathering information. The question of taxation was fraught, to be sure, since it would produce both winners and losers, but it was critical because it was an integral part of solving other pressing issues, like school funding. In 1963 Governor Fannin devoted his entire annual message to the issue of equalizing taxation, but circumstances, not Fannin's oratory and logic, finally moved the legislature to some action. The Southern Pacific Railroad had recently sued the state over its tax assessment, and the court decided that unless the legislature created different assessment percentages and property classifications, the court would mandate that all property, from residential to industrial, be placed in the same category and taxed at full assessment value. Facing such a potentially disastrous outcome, the legislature finally acted to authorize an appraisal, but the decision on classifications and rates was left to the future.

By the 1960s the legislature's failure to actively engage and resolve major issues had become a fundamental problem of governance, and one rooted in the legislature's culture and structure. The state's growing urban population was bringing changes to the House, especially in the election of

Republicans. Their coalition with Pinto Democrats helped push rule changes, but fundamentally it rested on common opposition to the regular Democrats rather than basic agreement on policy. The Senate posed the more serious problem, for the domination by rural legislators, some of whom were beholden to mining interests, created a culture of resistance to change. But this attitude grew out of a traditional legislative culture described by political scientist David Berman as they existed in the 1940s to the 1960s.

> Conservative Democrats from around the state stayed at the Adams [Hotel] during the legislative session. Lobbyists for the mining and agricultural interests made the Adams their power center as they wined and dined legislators—the principle means of influence were said to be the "three B's" of beefsteaks, blondes, and booze.[24]

Senator Alfredo Gutierrez confirmed this assessment, describing it as a culture of "corruption," meaning not necessarily an explicit quid pro quo trading of favors for votes, but referring to essentially unprofessional behavior by legislators that involved relationships of dependence on lobbyists for the mines, railroads, and major land interests. The mining association had a suite at the Adams Hotel, he explained, with an open bar and "attractive ladies always hanging around," and where "lobbyists brought cases of booze." Both farmers and mining companies had professional lobbyists, and the mining lobby was especially well funded and well run, but legislators were also contacted by farmers themselves, who "showed up in Levis and big hats, and palled around with everybody, and took everybody to dinner."[25] The Flying Farmers also took legislators on free airplane tours of the state.

In subsequent years, of course, legislative scandals on both the national and state levels would greatly heighten sensitivity to questions of influence and ethics, but in the 1960s, as Gutierrez emphasized, this "was the culture, it was what was done," and it had been done for 50 years. This arrangement was based on personal relationships and tradition, but it persisted also because lobbyists had information and expertise. Without a finance department, for example, the state depended on corporations for key economic data for making budget decisions. In addition, legislators in Arizona, as in many states, had very little support, and lobbyists provided some. With few staff members and virtually no one with subject or legislative expertise, Gutierrez noted, "lobbyists were expected to draft your bills. You took them to Legislative Council for format, but the world depended on lobbyists."[26] But despite the strength of this tradition, public debate about the role of lobbyists grew in the early 1960s, as did public charges of corruption and bribery, and then in 1965 a scandal broke over bribes paid to legislators for helping people acquire liquor licenses. The reputation of the institution was coming under increasing attack, and some legislators were determined to address this and make reforms.

Reapportionment

Besides sidestepping government reform and equalizing tax assessments, the legislature had also fumbled the issue of reapportionment. Given the scope and consequences of this task, inaction here is less surprising than other failures, but the issue could not be avoided. The result would transform the legislature and be a watershed event in Arizona political history, as it was in the history of a number of states. By providing equitable representation to the majority of citizens, it democratized state government, changed the partisan balance in the legislature, and helped create more responsible parties. It also prompted many states to strengthen state governments, transforming how policy was made and the kinds of policies that could be adopted.

Legislative apportionment had been a growing problem in many states for decades, but the Supreme Court had sidestepped the matter, ruling it a political question that could only by resolved by state legislatures. The difficulty, naturally, was getting malapportioned legislatures to reapportion themselves. In *Baker v. Carr* (1962), a case about the malapportionment of the Tennessee state legislature, the Court reversed its earlier decision and ruled that courts could decide cases of legislative apportionment. In February 1964 the Court addressed the substance of apportionment in *Wesberry v. Sanders*, declaring that congressional districts must be equal in population and establishing the principle of "one person, one vote." Up to this point, Arizona leaders knew about the issue but said little, and neither political party attempted to follow up on the implications of this case. That calm ended on April 27, 1964, when a University of Arizona law student, Gary Peter Klahr, filed a suit in federal court claiming that the malapportionment of the Arizona legislature and congressional districts denied him equal protection under the law. The context for this case changed pointedly in June 1964 when the Supreme Court's *Reynolds v. Sims* ruling specifically extended the equal representation standard to state legislatures. Since neither house of the Arizona legislature met this test (the Senate was the third-worst malapportioned legislative chamber in the nation), the issue seemed one of when and how, not *if* the legislature would have to change.

At a preliminary hearing on Klahr's case in June 1964, a three-judge panel decided to delay action until after the next legislature, meeting in spring 1965, had a chance to act. When the legislature did meet, it failed to adopt a plan, although, like some other states with malapportioned legislatures, it passed a resolution asking for a constitutional convention to overturn the Supreme Court's ruling. Finally, in a fourth special session in October, the legislature passed a plan. Since this was also discriminatory, the federal District Court quickly struck it down and put in place its own districting plan for the 1966 election, a plan that created a baseline for all subsequent districting efforts. The Court's plan increased the Senate from 28 to 30 members, while reducing the House from 80 to 60; it had candidates for House and Senate run from the same districts; it attempted to use county boundaries, combining smaller counties; and it invited the two parties to propose methods for creating districts within Maricopa and Pima counties.

Over the next seven years the legislature continued to pass new plans, prompting partisan and legal objections and rejections by the court. Unlike the reluctant proposals in 1965, these alternative plans did not seek malapportionment to benefit rural areas. Instead, these legislative proposals failed for other reasons, such as, for example, attempting to protect the districts of incumbents. A second difference was that the original court ruling on using population as a basis was enhanced by the 1965 Voting Rights Act, which banned the use of methods to restrict voting, such as literacy tests. The court also struck down gerrymandering strategies that would have reduced the influence of Indians, notably in Apache and Navajo counties. Finally, in December 1974 the court accepted a legislative plan without restriction, ending the conditional status of the state's districting system.

But while the fundamental principle of districting was shifted from geography to population, and while the principle of equal access was established, redistricting would remain a contentious task. The one virtue of the pre-1966 apportionment was its simplicity; the new system offered both partisan and personal opportunities, for creating advantageous districts and for ignoring issues of equality. The *Arizona Republic*'s Bernie Wynn reacted with shock to the Republican proposal pushed through the legislature in 1967, denouncing "the shrewd maneuvering of a handful of greedy legislators hungering for power."[27] Although subsequent plans might be less egregious, all would be complicated by political motives and calculations.

As serious as these problems were and would remain, the 1966 reapportionment created a new political world in Arizona. First, Maricopa County's representation in the Senate went from 14 to 50 percent, and Pima

County's representation added another 20 percent, meaning that the two urban counties now controlled both houses of the legislature. Second, the partisan balance of power changed to the Republicans, who controlled the House 33–27 and the Senate 16–14 after the 1966 election. The question was how this shift would affect what the legislature did.

Barr Enters the Legislature

Burton Barr began his legislative service in 1965, the last session before reapportionment, when a coalition still controlled the House and when that chamber was increasingly at odds with the Senate. As in the previous legislature, a coalition of Pinto Democrats and all the Republicans formed a majority that organized and ran the House. They chose Jack Gilbert, a Democrat from Cochise County, as Speaker and John Haugh, a Tucson Republican, as the majority leader. Gilbert and Haugh then gave a slight majority of committee chairmanships and major committee memberships to Pinto Democrats, but Republicans received significant representation, and caucus meetings were held to decide positions on legislative proposals.

As a freshman without prior political experience, Barr was only appointed to four committees of mid-level importance and had limited prospects for having any impact. As he later reminisced, "In those days the leadership never spoke to a freshman," except to say "don't bother them, don't talk to them." Barr was not alone in this position, for roughly one-third of the representatives were new, but the 1965 freshmen class included some very talented men. Seven of them, including Stan Turley, Bill Jacquin, Delos Ellsworth, and Barr, gathered weekly to discuss their ideas and agendas. Calling themselves the "dirty Seven," they dreamed of what they would do if they could run the state.[28] This group helped Barr learn about legislative issues and gave him the kind of camaraderie he had cherished in the military.

Barr's initial legislative work was quite modest, as he joined with colleagues to cosponsor certain minor bills, only a few of which passed. However, as a member of the Public Health and Welfare Committee, he cosponsored a notable health-care bill. In 1960 the U.S. Congress had passed the Kerr-Mills Act, creating a program of medical assistance for the elderly and providing matching funds for states that participated in the program, and Barr's bill proposed to establish Arizona's program. Seeing some support in the House, Speaker Gilbert told him to consult Senator Giss. After Giss reviewed the bill and pronounced it acceptable, Barr sought approval by the House and learned a prime lesson in lawmaking. When the bill came up, the majority leader told Barr, "'Just stand up, and move the bill, and don't say anything, and sit down.' So I stood up, I moved the bill, I sat down, and it passed. And that was . . . how it worked in those days."[29]

Barr's prospects received an unexpected boost in 1965 when four conservative Republicans quit the coalition, including the chairman of the State Government Committee, and Speaker Gilbert made Barr the committee's new chair. While it dealt mostly with minor matters, its jurisdiction included the proposal to establish the long-sought state finance department and budget director. Barr's committee endorsed the bill, which easily passed the House in February 1966. A positive step, but not necessarily auspicious: the House had voted for a similar bill in 1963 that the Senate killed, and since Senator Giss remained opposed, the bill's prospects seemed dim. Governor Goddard encouraged Barr to push for passage, but Goddard had only minimal influence on Giss, and Barr had none.

In March, Giss proposed a greatly weakened version of the bill, angering Goddard but moving Barr to use some unusual leverage. The State Government Committee had jurisdiction over legislative expenditures, and when a bill providing supplemental appropriations for Senate operations—normally a routine matter—came to his committee, Barr held it. A surprised Giss met with the freshman chairman to explain that such an action was inappropriate, but Barr announced that he would not budge until Giss acted on the budget bill. In the ensuing weeks, the Senate got its appropriation, Barr went head-to-head with Giss to craft a compromise bill, and eventually both houses passed a measure close to the original House proposal. After two decades of recommendations and efforts, the state was finally able to engage in responsible financial analysis and budgeting. The era of government reform had begun.

With the conclusion of the unusually lengthy session, Barr and his colleagues faced the challenge of running for election in newly defined districts. Barr won reelection handily and returned to the legislature as part of a new Republican majority in both houses of the legislature. This enabled the GOP to organize each chamber on a party rather than coalition basis, electing their leaders, selecting committee chairs, determining committee assignments, and pushing an agenda. But, as Stan Turley later explained, "We, the Republicans, didn't know what to do. We had never been a majority before."[30] This unprecedented situation resulted in greater competition for leadership positions, especially for Speaker.

The early frontrunner for the post was John Pritzlaff, a wealthy businessman who had already served three terms and been a leader in the previous legislature.[31] But personal circumstances intervened. Pritzlaff had not supported former Majority Leader John Haugh's bid for the Republican gubernatorial nomination, and partly in response to this, Haugh supported Barr. The caucus meeting stretched late into the night, and finally, after multiple ballots failed to produce a majority, causing a stalemate, the members recessed for a while. During the break, representatives held many discussions, including a key one between Barr and Turley. When the caucus reconvened, Barr withdrew his candidacy for Speaker and threw his support behind Turley, who won handily. Barr was then elected majority leader, and Turley named Pritzlaff chairman of the powerful Appropriations Committee. The three other members of the "dirty Seven" who had returned to the legislature also won leadership posts: Ellsworth was House Whip, while Bill Jacquin and Chet Allen, who had moved to the Senate, received leadership posts there. The group's dreams of running things had suddenly become real.

Barr's success surprised some observers. A reporter for the *Arizona Republic* wrote "For a man who clowned his way through his first two legislative years in 1965 and 1966, such a responsible post might be questioned." But the paper also noted that Barr had done well in handling the health care and budget issues and quoted him as saying, "the fun is gone. But I accept the responsibility."[32] Given Barr's lively personality and his penchant for humorous interactions throughout his career, his prediction about fun was far off the mark, but it does show that he recognized and accepted the challenge of leadership. His experience in crafting legislation and negotiating with other legislators, his exposure to debates about government organization and public policies, and the close relationship he forged with his group of six colleagues made him begin to think about leadership in a new arena.

CHAPTER FOUR

Legislative Leadership

"Burt [was] the most effective political figure that I know of in the history of Arizona, certainly in the state legislature."

—JON KYL[1]

"Time after time, he demonstrated his total mastery of the fine art of leadership—wheedling, cajoling, twisting, pushing, pulling, and eyebrow-arching his way to completion on the bills that really counted."

—JOHN KOLBE[2]

"Four governors of Arizona served under Burt Barr. I'm proud to be one of them."

—BRUCE BABBITT[3]

Burton Barr was at the center—and to some extent, he *was* the center—of the transformation of Arizona government and public policy from the 1960s to the 1980s. And he followed a unique path to become the state's dominant legislative leader. An able, ambitious majority leader like Barr might have been expected to seek the Speakership again, but he did not, and until 1986 he resisted requests, even party pleas, that he pursue statewide office. Instead, he remained as majority leader. In that office, he discovered the perfect place for his talents, and for that reason, and because of the circumstances of Arizona politics during these years, he was ideally situated to affect the transformation of Arizona government.

His impact grew quickly. After just a few terms in his post, journalists found him a compelling subject, yet they struggled for the right words to describe him, piling on metaphors in an effort to capture this enigma. "Burton Barr is many things," wrote John Kolbe, columnist for the *Phoenix Gazette*. "A tornado . . . leaving everything in its wake in a state of unsettled turmoil. A juggler, smoothly keeping five balls in the air and never batting an eye at an occasional fumble. A long distance runner . . . growing stronger and more exhilarated with each passing mile."[4] Kolbe's colleague at the

Arizona Republic, Bernie Wynn, an even more sober-minded reporter, asked, "Who soars like an eagle, works like a beaver, thinks like lightning, waggles his eyebrows like Groucho Marx and fixes his wife's and children's breakfast on Sundays? Rep. Burton S. Barr, R-Phoenix, is indeed a riddle."[5] While trying to explain Barr, these commentators, and virtually every observer, agreed that he was an undisputed master of the legislative process. Arguing against a Barr-supported proposal to increase the gasoline tax, conservative Republican Representative Jim Skelly referred to Barr as "Professor Harold Hill," the engaging con man in *The Music Man.* But after the House voted for the measure, Skelly shook his head and remarked ruefully to the press, "What are you gonna do? Barr always gets his way."[6]

Burton Barr's success as a leader and his legislative accomplishments advanced year by year, but looking at these chronologically would be repetitive and inexact; the major sources on his leadership are interviews taken a decade or more after he left office, and they focus more on characteristics and specific events, rather than a chronological pattern. Rather, it is better to assess how Barr used and embraced the elements of leadership, by examining his overall leadership style. Viewing Barr's leadership over the entire period is also most appropriate because the fundamentals of his style, techniques, and values were already largely shaped when he first became majority leader in 1966. Of course, he did adapt and learn as particular situations developed—conflict over health care, changes in the composition of the legislature, or a new Speaker or governor—but these were responses to specific conditions, not revisions of his basic approach.

Although Barr occasionally articulated some of his ideas about leadership, his modesty and self-deprecating style kept him from revealing his deeper insights. Equally important, he was essentially intuitive, not philosophical; he was pragmatic, not ideological. To appreciate his views of leadership, one must scrutinize what he did, more than what he said. Barr's approach to leadership started from his personality more than a specific set of ideas, and it grew directly from his experiences in the war and subsequently in business.

The vast literature on leadership identifies different characteristics of successful leaders, and influential leadership scholars like Bernard Bass and Peter Northouse have created categories for analyzing them. James MacGregor Burns summarizes these categories into two elements: the traits of the leaders and the situations in which they operate. He also notes the limitations of focusing on only one element; exclusive attention to traits can lead to a "Great Man" interpretation, while a purely situational analysis can yield a largely deterministic view of the past. The challenge is finding the accurate and nuanced blend of those factors for individual leaders. Certainly in the case of Burton Barr, both aspects were essential ingredients in making him such an outstanding leader.

This chapter begins, then, by examining his *traits*: his personality, skills, and interests.[7] Barr's personal characteristics guided his behavior and his relationships with people. As a legislator he followed that same approach, but he adapted it to legislative situations, evolving tactics for working with other lawmakers and seeking to gain their support for proposals. These techniques fit within his larger strategies about legislative and political behavior, about how to practice leadership, the importance of planning and teamwork, and the ways to create compromise and win agreement. Finally, Barr's leadership reflected his basic values, such as patriotism and citizenship, his love of Arizona, his ideas about the importance of party and party loyalty, and his focus on problem solving.

But while Barr's notions about how to behave as a legislative leader were personal, they were also influenced by his *situation*: the specific legislative structure at that particular time. "The institutional structure of the legislature, including its constitutional framework" and the rules governing its leadership, provided general constraints within which legislative leaders like Barr operated.[8] This meant working as part of a legislative leadership team, dealing with Republicans and Democrats, interacting and competing with Senate leaders, and vying with the governor. This complexity and the numerous participants made the legislature the ideal venue for his combination of personality, skills, and experiences. Finally, Barr was a man for this time—a time when partisan loyalties in Arizona were changing, when both parties were relatively competitive, and when economic and demographic growth made action necessary and possible.

The Traits of Leadership

Burton Barr's Character and Skills

"All politics is personal," runs a common adage, and if being interesting and engaging is generally important for politicians, the best of them are especially personable. Keven Ann Willey described Barr as having a "magical personality," and this quality was central to his being and to his success as a leader. At his core, Barr loved people. His wife Louise commented that he "never met a stranger," and he evidenced this in manifold ways. Traveling locally, across the country, or around the world, Barr would talk with people he encountered. His eagerness to converse brought friendships and enjoyment. On one trip to London he became so engaged with the patrons of a pub, sharing stories with them, that everyone stayed for hours after closing time. On summer vacations on Coronado Island near San Diego, he would strike up conversations with people walking the shore, prompting residents to jokingly suggest that Louise "keep him off the beach." His sociability was legendary. After a long day at work or the legislature, Burt loved to relax with friends, coworkers at the Maverick Company, and legislative colleagues. During legislative sessions, people came to his house every night; it was "Barr's Bar," Louise observed. His friendliness was not a strategic calculation; it was a core element of his personality. Some people need time alone, but being with people recharged Barr. While he did some gardening, and he faithfully read the newspaper, *TIME*, and *Sports Illustrated*, his relaxation and his vitality came from being with family and friends.[9]

People who met Barr, including political opponents, remarked on his "very engaging, charming personality." He was persistently positive, truthfully claiming, "I'm *always* enthusiastic" and "I'm *always* optimistic." He was joyful, explaining that he "always saw the fun of it," and that sense of fun was infectious, something "people wanted a part of." Humor was a central part of his attraction. He "always had a smile and a laugh," remembered Peter Burns, who had worked as a House staff member for Barr. He believed, "One should always get some humor out of life; otherwise life can get too grim." And things were funny not just to Burt. Jim Skelly remembered his "tremendous, tremendous sense of humor. I mean, that was his forte."[10]

He used stories, typically humorous and often self-deprecating, to engage people. While Barr pulled interesting and witty stories from all facets of his adult life, he drew especially on a vast array of tales from his military experience in World War II. He described, for example, an arrest he made in Austria of someone he was sure was a field marshal, since the uniformed man had many medals and an iron cross, only to discover that he was a Vienna trolley car conductor. Burns noted that Barr "would tell these stories to entertain people because he was an entertainer. I mean, he *really* was an entertainer. And I've never seen a public speaker—except an outright comedian—that could entertain an audience for an hour . . . and just going a mile a minute."[11]

A second part of Barr's appeal was his recognizable interest in and concern about people's circumstances. Phoenix Mayor Terry Goddard described him as "compassionate," a person who would call someone "to know how things were going . . . and really care," and a person whose concern "transcended any political agenda." Jim Bush, a veteran lobbyist and friend, observed that "Burt had a compelling desire to help," that he "always was willing to help. And not just me. I don't know of anyone that Burt" wouldn't help, and "not just on legislative things—personal matters." Jim Skelly agreed, "Burt helped people that no one ever knew about; helped them get jobs; helped them with problems. He was an extremely kind individual." Charlie Stevens, also a friend and a lobbyist, believed that Barr's eagerness to talk with and listen to people made him keenly aware of other people's problems, problems he would then try to help solve. He was so well-known for finding jobs for friends and their children that when Arizona passed a law licensing employment bureaus, Stevens joked that Barr would need to get a license to keep providing that service. Jim Kolbe concluded that he "was not only a kind man—I think he was generally kind to most people—but very generous."[12]

Barr's relationships were tied to his ability to pay attention. He listened, he showed sensitivity and insight, and he understood. Keven Ann Willey said, "He knew what made people tick." And John Kolbe claimed, "He had a way of knowing people . . . he was an absolute master at figuring people out." Louise saw Burt's capacity for insight in his relationships with her and their children, and she recognized this same sensitivity in his dealings with legislators: "He would look at them and almost know what they were thinking, or what they wanted and how to appease them, or how to get them something for what he was going to get from them." Barr used his insights to cultivate reciprocal relationships; he did not view people as pawns. His war experience had taught him to treat people respectfully, as individuals with value. Everyone, he said frequently, had a useful contribution to make.[13]

A striking characteristic of his personal interactions was rarely displaying anger. He almost never showed this toward his family. He did not argue loudly with Louise, and the children worried not about his wrath, but only about disappointing him or having to explain themselves. Barr's public behavior was similarly restrained. He could become angry, but the occasions were rare and brief. Peter Burns said he had seen Barr angry only about five times in eight years, and John Kolbe joked that his anger never lasted more than five minutes. His staff sometimes saw him irate, though more often it was brusque impatience, and they noted that he quickly calmed down. And in those cases, "He would go back to that person and try to mend fences. He was very contrite."[14]

While some politicians keep score or seek to even it, Jack DeBolske, a lobbyist for Arizona cities, felt that "one of Burt's strong points" was that "he could forgive and forget." Reporter Shawn Hubler cited Barr's "reputation of being unable to hold a grudge longer than he can hold his breath." Barr did not respond to personal provocation, but "touch Barr's family," Hubler observed, "and his friendly hustle turns to ice." This included Barr's relations with the press.[15] A more consequential exception to Barr's "no grudge" policy (except for his family) had to do with his political conflicts and competition with Governor Bruce Babbitt. On several occasions, Barr became furious with Babbitt and refused to speak with him. Once, after Babbitt had vetoed one of Barr's favorite bills, Barr had security guards throw the governor's lobbyist, Fred DuVal, out of the chamber. As he left, DuVal heard Barr "roar" that "This is MY HOUSE."[16]

But such displays of anger and personal pique were rare. More importantly, even if he occasionally got angry or in a few instances stubbornly avoided someone, Barr never sought to cause harm or to implement some form of payback. "I've never know him to do anything vindictive or mean-spirited to anybody," Charlie Stevens asserted, and Jim Bush concurred. People all around him understood and agreed that Barr did not carry grudges—a lesson he had learned from Eisenhower. Whatever the incident, it was in the past, because, as Alfredo Gutierrez explained, Barr was already too busy working on the next issue.

Of course, some of Barr's critics, while agreeing that he was not vindictive, felt that his forgiveness was limited, even deficient on some issues. For example, Tony West believed that Barr never fully forgave him for his role in working to repeal an auto emissions program. But West also remarked, "You never felt Burt had to get even. I never saw Burt get even with anybody."[17] Honesty and loyalty are desirable attributes for any legislator, but they are essential for any successful leader, and they were the acknowledged basis of Barr's relationships and the respect he received. Art Hamilton, the Democratic representative and longtime House minority leader, lauded Barr as someone who understood how to use power but "who abhorred using it in a way that hurt people, even if that might be to his benefit."[18]

Barr's interest in and treatment of people earned him friends and appreciation, but his successes also rested on his intelligence—and that people recognize it. His insightful evaluations of people demonstrated an emotional intelligence that he refined throughout his life. His prodigious memory was another facet of his broad intelligence. Like his business partner Richard Kaplan, his political associates often noted this, partly because he did not take notes or keep files. Nikki Corral reported, "He would come back from those meetings and tell you just exactly what he wanted from them, and quote people verbatim, but he never took a note." Barr was a very fast learner, impressing people with his capacity for quickly assessing the core of complex subjects. Rick Collins, a research staffer for the House, described how Barr could "take hours and hours of words of information and facts and figures, and listen to it and within minutes sound like he had done the research and put together all the information himself." Even more striking was his ability to "master a dozen complicated subjects at the same time." Barr could be receiving a briefing on a complicated topic and holding several conversations simultaneously, and at the conclusion, he would demonstrate a thorough understanding of what he had been told. Stan Turley was fond of saying that Barr was the only man who could talk and listen at the same time. Barr's intelligence was also evident when he harnessed it to the practical tasks of legislative leadership. Alfredo Gutierrez reported, "Burt could figure out a deal while Babbitt and I were still grappling with the politics of the issue."[19]

Finally, Barr had a great capacity for work. Charlie Stevens observed that Barr needed only four hours of sleep a night and that "he would work you right into the ground." People commonly described him as hardworking and tireless. Jon Kyl, who lobbied at the Arizona legislature before

Figure 10. Barr in a rare quiet moment. Burton Barr Public Library, Phoenix, Arizona.

serving in the U.S. House of Representatives (1987–1995) and then the U.S. Senate (1995–2013), said, "His office was always total pandemonium. He was always juggling a hundred things at once; he never had more than a minute or two to listen to what you had to say." Barr's dedication to work and his high level of energy were what some observers described as "extraordinary," and these were evident not just in how long he worked but in how he functioned. Peter Burns described Barr as "a perpetual motion machine. He never slowed down; I don't think he sat down." On the House floor, Barr was constant action, talking to different legislators, waving his arms as he spoke to someone, his eyebrows bobbing, peripatetically working the floor, scanning the House and the press table. Even off the floor, Barr was busy. Stevens said, "Burt could never sit still . . . he'd be waltzing, he'd be looking at the walls, he'd open the door and look out there. He was always on the move." He was, Louise confirmed, "just a dynamo, moving all the time."[20]

The Techniques of Legislative Leadership: Personal and Performance

Barr's character and personality—his sensitivity and interest in people, his humor and storytelling talent, his generosity and honesty, his intelligence and energy—served him well in politics. His political techniques were an extension of his personal skills, an adaptation to the environment in which he worked. Barr's legislative activities, like his life generally, started with "getting personal." Alfredo Gutierrez observed with admiration, "He knew every member. He knew every member's kids, he knew where they were going to school, he knew what mattered to them." And this attentiveness began early in the legislative cycle. Keven Ann Willey claimed that ten minutes after a freshman was elected, "he got a phone call from Burton Barr to get acquainted with him." He soon knew these new lawmakers "better than they knew themselves. He'd learn the names of spouses and kids, parents and friends." And he remained attentive, available, and accessible during sessions, despite the huge demands on his time. Not wanting to cut off anyone, he rarely left the House before 7:00 p.m.[21]

His relationship with his colleagues also rested on respect. Burns observed, "He treated every member, whether they were good guys, bad guys, or whatever, as if they were the 31st vote; that he needed them." Joe Lane, a Republican representative from Wilcox who later served as Speaker, commented more colloquially that Barr "made it nice. I never saw him kick anybody or cuss anybody." When legislators ill-treated him, Barr refused to take offense or let criticism rile him. Reflecting both his personal values and his political pragmatism, Barr noted, "I take a lot of guff, but I still love them when it's over." While Barr strove to build personal relationships, he did not take or make the occasional rough-and-tumble of legislative politics personally. Barr also treated members' legislative proposals with courtesy. "If he's going to back off a bill or make any changes, he always goes first to the bill's sponsor." Likewise, he dealt respectfully with disagreements over issues. Before a crucial vote on a tax proposal in 1982, he told the House, "Nobody is more virtuous than anybody else here. And nobody is more honest than anybody else."[22]

A final feature of his personal relationship with legislators was mentorship. In one sense, Barr mentored nearly every legislator, encouraging everyone to be actively engaged in legislative business, and Rick Collins noted the "long list" of people whom Barr had mentored, but with certain people, he developed a special relationship. When Alfredo Gutierrez entered the Senate in 1973, he presented a striking contrast to Barr. A Democrat, allegedly a "hot-blooded liberal," whose activism had started with leading student protests at Arizona State University and extended to community organizing with Chicanos Por La Causa in Phoenix, Gutierrez was just 25 and had served as a private in the army, he later noted, while Barr, almost 60, had been an officer and a war hero. But Barr ignored all of these differences, and so, too, did Gutierrez. "In the course of that first session," he recounted, "he came to see me and just started to talk to me about this and that and the other, and it became a habit of his when he came into the Senate, he would stop by and find me, and we would talk a while." After only a few years Gutierrez won a Senate leadership position, and he was soon working closely with Barr, though always, he hastened to note, with himself as the student and Barr as the mentor.[23]

When Joe Lane came to the legislature in 1978, he "could see real quick that Burt was *the* legislature," and he decided to "stick around this guy, because this is where the action takes place." Barr responded positively. "He liked me for some reason. He always called me 'kid'" (Barr commonly used that label). "He'd say, 'Kid, come over, I want to tell you something.'"[24] And Barr would mention something or give him a task. In 1985, after serving three sessions, Lane became majority whip, and two years later he was elected Speaker. While longevity in office was a necessary condition for his success, Lane's association with Barr and the knowledge he gleaned from it gave him a boost.

Both Gutierrez and Lane benefited from Barr's help, but his closest and most deliberate mentorship was with Art Hamilton. An African American protégé of Clovis Campbell, Hamilton resembled Gutierrez in being an activist, a Democrat, and first elected in 1972, although he could not take his House seat until he turned 25 on January 19, 1973. Quickly frustrated with the institution, Hamilton was surprised when Barr invited him to his office to talk. There, Barr "spent about an hour of what I'd later understood was incredibly valuable time, just trying to find out who I was, where I came from, who's your dad, what does your mom do, what do you care about." Barr then told him, "Kid, let me give you some good advice. If you want to be helpful, and you want to be a part of solving problems . . . I'll help you. But if all you want to do is whine about what's wrong with the world and what you can't change, go whine someplace else. I don't have time for that." Hamilton considered Barr's extraordinary offer "to make you a part of the process" and wisely jumped at the chance.[25]

This meant that Hamilton spent "an inordinate amount of time watching Burton Barr, because Burton was an incredible teacher of the process." Barr would sometimes tell Hamilton what he was doing, but most often he simply let him watch. "I tried very hard to ingratiate myself to Burton, even as a partisan. I behaved a good deal like a somewhat difficult, but nonetheless dutiful son, and, frankly, he treated me most of the time like that, and it gave me time to watch him do his thing up close and personal. It is probably still the greatest gift I received in this process." Barr's single most important piece of advice was "to learn the rules of the House. He always pointed out that he didn't need the rules because he had 31 votes to do what he wanted to do," but Hamilton could use parliamentary procedure to influence the legislative process.[26] And, on key occasions, he did.

Barr also recognized that legislative success required some level of performance, or playacting—sometimes dramatic, and sometimes comedic. The most visible evidence of this was Barr's appearance. He owned innumerable hats of all sorts, and wore them or twirled them on his finger. His ensembles were more eye-catching. Joe Lane described Barr's coming to the legislature wearing "the darnedest outfit you have ever seen. And some of the ladies would say, 'Burt why don't you wear a coat that matches? Your tie doesn't match anything.'" Barr responded, "When I get up in the morning, I just reach in the closet, and whatever is handy is what I put on." James Sossaman reported his surprise seeing Barr for the first time, "dressed as he usually is, in a jacket that a baby had spit up on, and no tie, and a hat on." Even in a legislature with members dressed in a range of styles, Barr stood out, and he was far too clever not to realize that *not* being well-dressed was an advantage for someone whose work was persuasion.[27]

Parts of Barr's behavior were essentially theatrical, but none more so than his role as negotiator with Governor Babbitt. Clearly, their interactions centered on serious matters, and Barr could be genuinely angry with Babbitt. Keven Ann Willey reported Barr's "dramatic" complaint that if it weren't against the law to hit a juvenile, he would punch Babbitt. But Barr played most of his best anti-Babbitt scenes directly for a legislative audience. Representative Chris Herstam described how Barr would "play the caucus like a fiddle." After letting "the caucus scream and yell about the evil Democrat, Bruce Babbitt," he would announce, " 'I'm going to go up and give him a piece of your mind.' And we all knew that he would go up there and say, 'Oh, they're mad at you [about] this now, and how do we solve the problem?' " After negotiating, Barr would then return and claim "I ripped his head off" and got him to compromise. "And half the caucus would shake their head and say, 'Oh, okay.' And Burt would go ahead and get the bill passed." The drama satisfied some and entertained others, but as James Sossaman also noted, Barr's real role was acting as a mediator.[28]

Barr loved humor and used it effectively in his performances. Barr's mirth was often spontaneous, but some was calculated. He opened caucus meetings with three or four minutes of witty comments, setting the mood, and then got to business. When discussions got tense, he would interject jokes or light comments. Al Kluender remembered when Barr eased tensions in a meeting with the ironic quip, "Well, that's why I get paid the big bucks." Jim Skelly described vying with Barr "over an environmental bill on the floor. Well, by the time he was finished with me, I couldn't catch my breath even. I couldn't even ask him another question, I was laughing so hard." Jack Brown, the Democratic minority leader, described the effectiveness of Barr's humor. "He was fun to spar with on the floor, verbally, and he always had a comeback. He always had some joke, some comment to make, to lighten things when they got a little too heavy." On another occasion, after some wrangling, Barr had gotten the caucus to approve a spending measure, when a page told him that Senate Majority Leader Sandra Day O'Connor needed to talk with him about some proposal. Barr "came back about ten minutes later and the eyebrows lit, you know, and he looked at us and he said, 'Now if you think *that* was a good program, wait till I tell you about *this* one.' And then he sold us something that Sandra wanted instead of the [measure they had previously approved]." Barr's humor was winning because he used it carefully, to lighten the moment, and because it was a gentle, often self-deprecating humor.[29]

Winning Friends and Influencing People: Techniques for Getting Support

In *Heavy Lifting: The Job of the American Legislature,* political scientist Alan Rosenthal distinguishes two aspects of passing legislation: the substantive part of fashioning the measure and the strategic part of enacting it.[30] It is a useful distinction, and this study of Burton Barr deals separately with those two segments of his lawmaking efforts. This chapter focuses on his technical and strategic approach to enacting legislation, while chapter 5 analyzes how he shaped the substance of major proposals and programs. This division is analytically helpful and practically necessary, given the length of his career and how many issues he addressed, but one must remember that Barr practiced lawmaking as a dynamic, interactive process. Creating laws meant shaping and reshaping the heart of measures to account for diverse reactions; passing laws involved forging different patterns of support depending on the characteristics of the measure. This was apparent, for example, when Barr had used staff to craft proposals on controversial topics. If he was unsure how the caucus would react, he would have staffers make a presentation and watch the reaction. If it was positive, he would move to the front of the room; if it was negative, he would move toward the back, eventually stepping in and shifting the discussion. More commonly, Barr would anticipate how individuals would react to proposals, as Alfredo Gutierrez observed. "He could hear a briefing and know, 'That'll give me a vote.' Or, 'I'll never get that guy because that's in it.' I mean, he had this amazing ability to synthesize all this."[31]

Barr's flexibility—his ability to listen, reflect, and learn—was a generally valuable quality, but it was especially notable and useful in how he handled proposals. Rick Collins recalled that "He would think through things over night. There were many occasions where we would make a recommendation to him and he would say, 'No, no way am I going to go there.'" But the next day he would support what he had opposed "because he was able to distance himself from the situation for a moment, reevaluate, and figure out a game plan." Sometimes his reevaluation occurred more quickly. Peter Burns described a break in a negotiating session with the Senate in which staffers explained that something was unconstitutional. Barr responded abruptly with, "Don't tell *me* what's unconstitutional!—16 and 31 [majority votes in the Senate and House] is constitutional, and we're going to get this thing, because that's what they need." So the staffers dropped their objection, but a short time later, when negotiations resumed and the contested point was raised, Barr responded, "Don't you know that's unconstitutional?"[32]

Barr's ability to change his mind, and to talk and listen at the same time, is illustrated by the debate over repealing the sales tax on food. The proposal had support from Democrats, but Republicans and city leaders opposed yielding the tax revenues, while grocers complained that this would mean extra work and expense for them. Democrat legislators were too few in number to push this through the legislature, but citizens placed the issue as an initiative on the fall ballot. According to Art Hamilton, Barr knew that simply opposing this would be politically unwise, but "Republicans needed to figure out some other way to position themselves." Barr's initial solution was to retain the tax but let people claim a tax credit for those expenditures. Hamilton explained, however, that "after about a day and a half of trying to do his best pitch work, Burton became convinced that this was not a good idea, and he jettisoned it like a bad headache," and so he swung over to champion the repeal of the sales tax on food. To win support for this, he arranged a sales tax credit for merchants to buy barcode-scanning equipment, and cities got the option of maintaining their local tax on food. Barr had spoken, listened, changed his position, and solved the problem.[33]

Joe Lane portrayed Barr's considerable flexibility as central to his leadership style. "I have seen him go 180 degrees on an issue within a day or two, depending on what was going on, where the votes were and everything else." Rather than adamantly adhering to his personal views, Barr listened to his colleagues. Lane likened him to a billy goat leading his herd up a mountain.

> But you'll notice also, once in a while, that old billy goat looking back over his shoulder, making sure that he's not going here and the herd is going off over there. And that was Burt. Burt was always taking the temperature of the caucus and determined where his members were, and in that way he would get over there in the lead of the caucus.[34]

Barr considered this pragmatic approach to be reasonable self-control. "I have to be big enough to accept the fact that my own personal view can't be paramount so as to destroy the work of everyone [every Republican] who has come to the legislature."[35]

His flexibility, then, served the larger task of leadership: finding consensual solutions. Peter Burns concluded, "The big thing about Burt is that he would bring everybody to consensus. He would ride the horse until it died." John McCain noted Barr's accomplishment of creating consensus among Republicans and then reaching across the aisle to Democrats. Art

Hamilton praised Barr's remarkable effectiveness in connecting "disparate groups," and one of his predecessors as minority leader, Jack Brown, said with admiration that Barr "knew how to bring the sides together, even though they were fighting pretty bad." Barr himself spoke clearly about the central requirement for building agreement: "It takes leadership to bring together the ultra-conservatives, the moderates, and the others, and to weld them into one unified force."[36]

Barr's main tactic was persuasion, and he excelled at it. Jane Hull, a conservative colleague from his district, who later was elected Speaker and then became governor, marveled at "his ability to come in and talk for 15 minutes, [and] he could talk you into jumping off this ledge." Alfredo Gutierrez remembered the time Barr was talking with Senator Bob Usdane, who "kept saying, 'No, no, no.' And Burt said, 'If you're going to say no, that's okay, but I would like you to nod while you are saying no—okay? This will make you feel better when you ultimately say yes.' And, of course, he did." Persuasive skills are necessary for many occupations, but none more so than for sales. James Sossaman described Barr as an excellent salesman and said that he used those skills effectively in the legislature. "Burt was very bright," he noted. "Burt was always three steps ahead of his caucus, because if they wouldn't buy this program, he'd already thought up two more to sell."[37]

Some of Barr's efforts at persuasion invoked a sense of duty. Believing that legislators wanted to do "good," he urged them to think not of themselves but of larger goals, and he would sometimes recount his experiences during World War II in horrific battles like Anzio. But inspirational calls to duty have limited effectiveness. While many male representatives like Joe Lane found his war examples compelling, other legislators did not. Jane Hull, for example, explained that she would "mumble to [fellow conservative Representative] Pat [Wright], 'We're going to storm Anzio again, and the taxpayers are going to get screwed.'" Consequently, personal appeals were often a smarter strategy, and Barr's worked partly because of his knowledge of his colleagues. He knew that "It is important that I work with them and be with them and get to know them, their family, themselves as friends, not as opponents."[38]

Art Hamilton explained Barr's effectiveness as his "ability to find your soft spot, your special spot, and to move you toward it." Alfredo Gutierrez was even more specific. "He understood the precise human nature of the membership: how much they wanted a particular deal, how far they would go, how courageous they were, how loyal they would remain." Terry Goddard said, "He knew people almost better than they knew themselves. He knew what they wanted, he knew what they liked."[39] Barr said he was simply trying to "figure out the bottom line. . . . What will a person be willing to give to get what he or she is after? I distill the differences and come up with a product that can be sold. That's my forte, my contribution."[40]

But for all of his labors to find consensus through persuasion and personal connections, Barr also knew that legislative leadership sometimes needed a hard edge. "You can't operate [just] by consensus," he explained. "I have to get 31 people to come together. I have to be the guy that hammers and hammers until we get the vote." Charlie Stevens argued that Barr preferred to use the carrot, but if necessary, he would use the stick. Seeking support on a difficult vote, he summoned a recalcitrant legislator into his office. He "pulled from his desk drawer the politician's pet bill," asked him how much he liked it, dropped the bill back in the drawer, and shut it. Jon Kyl summed it up: "Burt cajoled, threatened, pushed, pulled, threatened some more; whatever it took to get people into an agreement, he did it." Al Kluender, who served as chairman of the House Education Committee in the late 1960s, recalled how "Barr severely chastised me, yes, even browbeat me, to get a certain education bill out of my committee."[41]

Sometimes Barr parlayed circumstance to his advantage. At the end of a legislative session, as legislators pushed to finish up before the deadline, the chambers often held all-night sessions. On those occasions, Barr operated at a distinct advantage, since he could go for a week on only two hours of sleep a night. So, during the night, Charlie Stevens recalled, "He would wake people up . . . and say, 'Look, here's the conference committee report, I need your signature.' He was awake, he was functioning, and they were tired and sleepy; and they would get up and sign the conference committee report, and he would go off marching away." As majority leader, Barr led the vote-gathering process, but on certain occasions the Speaker participated in the efforts. On a contested budget vote in 1975, Republican legislators were summoned to meet with Barr and Speaker Stan Akers. "One by one the members disappeared into the Speaker's inner sanctum, and one by one they emerged," John Kolbe reported. " 'They're really good at it,' marveled a freshman who had just undergone his first 'persuasion' session. 'Back and forth, just like a script. In fact, I just voted no so I could see how it's done.' "[42]

But while Barr did sometimes hammer and browbeat legislators, he typically used milder persuasive methods, for he recognized what political scientist Alan Rosenthal shows to be the case for legislatures generally: that "threats and intimidation are rarely employed" because they seldom work and can be counterproductive.[43] Instead, leaders must build relationships and create mutually satisfying arrangements. Keven Ann Willey described how Barr commonly operated: "He didn't call a legislator in and arm-wrestle him to the ground on a vote. He called the legislator in to ask about his family and his kids, and what was important to him, and what piece of legislation he would like to have passed, and 'Oh, by the way, would you please vote for my bill too?'"[44]

Alfredo Gutierrez recounted another aspect of seeking votes, the quid-pro-quo exchange in which some legislator said, "'I need a culvert.' So, you got to give him a culvert, man. And the guy up there needs a bridge. Or he's trying to get reelected, and some guy wants a building named after him." Such trades were common, he argued, but not disruptive to legislative decision-making: "The good part about those members, they had little buckets. You put the little thing in it, and they would go away happy." In some cases, the matters were not very material and the trade not so explicit. Jim Skelly sponsored a minor election bill that Barr got enacted. The next day he asked for Skelly's support on a bill. Skelly disliked the proposal but agreed to vote for it, because "You have an obligation to a guy who just worked his ass off to get my bill through, and he had no interest in it at all."[45]

Sometimes Barr used surrogates to round up votes. One evening Barr was toiling to get votes for a tax bill. He told Joe Lane to explain to his friend Mike Morales, a Tucson representative, "exactly how this dang place works, and then when you come back, we'll have that vote." So Lane took Morales out for "a couple of margaritas, we talked, and when we came back over, he voted for it. Burt came over and slapped me on the back and said, 'That's the way to go, kid.'"[46] Barr also asked lobbyists for help. On one occasion, when pushing a "Bill of Rights for Mentally Retarded Persons," he called Charlie Stevens into his office and asked him to get the votes of three representatives. Stevens initially resisted, saying that he did not know the bill that well, but when Barr persisted, Stevens carried out the assignment and obtained support from two of the legislators, and Barr won the vote.

Increasingly, after the mid-1970s, people criticized Barr for raising and distributing campaign funds to Republican legislative candidates, alleging that money was the basis of his legislative victories. "Money for your campaign?" wrote Shawn Hubler, accusingly. "Barr's coffers seem bottomless." Although later prohibited by state law, during these years this method was legal and not unusual. Barr was sometimes approached by donors, interests of one sort or another, and other times he requested contributions—commonly for candidates, but also for initiative campaigns and for charitable causes. Barr critics, from reporters like Tom Fitzpatrick to various legislators, opposed this practice as creating a system of obligations. A few suggested that Barr was indebted to those who contributed to his fund; more often people criticized his use of that fund as constraining the recipients. Senator Peter Kay, who prided himself on "never taking any of Barr's money," asked rhetorically if any legislators receiving money "are going to say no" when later asked for their vote. Tony West charged that such legislators "were always beholden to him. And we always thought Burt ran around with at least 15 or 16 sure votes in his hip pocket that he could produce on almost any given subject." Even Jim Skelly, also conservative but a friend, suggested, "You feel an obligation to somebody who was nice enough to give you campaign dough."[47]

The reality was far more complex than these accusations suggested, particularly because of changes in political campaigns. Barr defended his activity by citing the dramatic increase in the cost of campaigns for state legislature—from the $750 he had spent on his first campaign in 1964 to races costing $50,000 by the early 1980s—and emphasizing the severe burden on individual candidates. While certainly assisting those individuals, his efforts further increased the role and impact of money in politics, but the situation was neither simple nor one-sided. The initial increase in campaign spending came from economic and business interests such as mining corporations, but as Alfredo Gutierrez notes, the list of interests grew and diversified considerably over time to include groups like the state's taxpayers association, right-to-life groups, and trial lawyers. For them, donating to a party leader was far easier than trying to determine which individual candidates to support. And, as Hamilton and Gutierrez acknowledged, Democrats used the same system of raising and dispensing campaign funds. As a consequence, the use of political action committees (PACs) increased dramatically: between 1974 and 1982 the number of Arizona PACs quintupled. With Barr's support, Arizona responded to these changes with legislation in 1974 and 1978 that required detailed lists of contributors and the reporting of any contribution of $25 or more.

Barr's method of distributing money was fairly simple. For example, a friend of Joe Lane's asked if he needed money for his first legislative campaign and then arranged a meeting with Barr and another first-time candidate. After a 15-minute conversation about campaign activities, Barr wrote Lane a check for $5,000. The only obligation Barr ever suggested to Lane or any other candidate was to be the best legislator they could be. John Kolbe, who was quite politically savvy, argued, "The money raising has been greatly exaggerated by the people who analyze his power and skills, because he did so with a willy-nilly for everybody—he did it for people who beat the shit out of him all the time." In 1984, when he made headlines by raising $100,000, Barr provided $26,569 to his district running mates, Tony West and Jane Hull, both conservatives who strongly criticized him. Barr also contributed substantially to legislators like Senator Jeff Hill of Tucson, who Kolbe called "an ideologue who has called Barr nearly every name in the book." Barr also never used money to oppose an incumbent Republican. Indeed, the only standard he seems to have used in giving money was financial need and a competitive race. Noting that Barr contributed to all Republicans, Chris Herstam said, "I do not know of any instances where Burt would ever lean on people to vote for a bill or to support him in an effort because he had given money to their cause." However, Barr certainly gained good will from his contributions, and his contributions to prospective new legislators enable him to meet them under favorable circumstances. Jon Kyl offered the most balanced assessment, arguing that money probably helped Barr "build alliances," but that other factors played greater roles in shaping Barr's success.[48]

Strategy and Leadership

Barr's emphasis on planning was one of those other factors that made him successful. He first learned this value in the military, starting with his work on the invasion of North Africa in 1942. He mentioned that experience repeatedly to justify the need for planning. Referring to the landing, Barr would wryly observe, "Sure, we missed the beach by 29 miles, but we had a plan. And *a* plan will beat *no* plan nine times out of ten. So you've got to have a plan." When a session ended, Barr would work with House staffers to decide which issues to advance during the next session. Chris Herstam explained, "Burt just kept coming in every year [asking,] 'Okay, what're the major problems? What are the three or four big issues we've got to solve?' He would never spread himself too thin. He'd let politicians of less strength deal with the smaller issues, but he would always keep his eye on the three or four big issues of the session." While certainly attentive to whether a problem could be resolved, Barr started by gauging its importance. To manage an agenda defined by the importance of issues, not by his interests or expertise, Barr would focus on one item, Art Hamilton observed, "for a week, two weeks, three weeks, master as much of that stuff as he needed to master to be able to sell his solution, sell it, and then move on to something else."[49]

When asked if Barr could be considered a "policy wonk," Alfredo Gutierrez joked, "I don't think he ever read a bill in his life," but he also stressed

Barr's "amazing ability to synthesize" masses of material.[50] He could do this because he was a quick study, he listened to what advocates said, and because he used his staff effectively, having Nikki Corral read every bill and "be able to tell him what it was about, who represented the interests, who the interests were that were promoting the bill." But while Barr understood the value of details, he also perceived that success meant focusing on the main features of a plan and not "overselling." He schooled staffers to think about the broad topic and not the details by humorously comparing the selling of a legislative proposal to his business sales: "When I go in to see Clyde Smith to sell him a freezer, do I tell him that this freezer keeps everything at minus 32 [degrees], and it has a compressor that is four-and-a-half horsepower, and that it's on a three-phase watt, and it does all this? I just say, 'Clyde, do you want the red one or do you want the blue one?'"[51]

Chris Herstam expressed the common and insightful understanding that Barr "was committed to solving problems; that's why he ran for the legislature in the first place." Barr knew that not everyone came to the legislature with the same sense of its possibilities, that some people viewed their duties more philosophically, while others were drawn to ephemeral political calculations that would favor inaction and gridlock. Barr's outlook was simple. "I believe we're not here just as a jury to pass judgment on the time, we're here to get on to the problems and try to solve them. That takes time, that takes sweat, that takes work, that takes creativity." His good friend Eddie Basha described Barr's legislative strategy as mirroring his military one. "Burt had a philosophy: 'You take the hill.' And Burt knew how to take the hill."[52]

To succeed meant crafting a proposal and getting the majority to vote for it. He referred to this with the tag "31–16–1," meaning the majority of votes in each house, plus the governor's approval. With his emphasis on planning and achieving solutions, he rarely let bills go to the floor unless he already had the necessary 31 votes committed. Usually this meant starting with one commitment of support and building to 31, but that method was sometimes problematic, so Barr used a range of strategies in asking legislators for their votes. Promises of support became harder to obtain as he got past 22 or 23 pledges, especially on more controversial issues, so he would often build his coalitions "backward." He would tell someone, "I know that you are having difficulties [supporting the bill], but if I need a 30th vote, would you be the 31st vote?" And many people, not wanting to be obstructionist, would say, "Well, if you can get 30, I'll be your 31st." He could then go to another person and say, "Look, I've got my 31st vote, but some of these folks are shaky, will you be my 30th vote?" Understanding that some commitments really did waver, Barr often built in some insurance.

For a vote on an important budget bill, for example, he had seven commitments for his 31st vote; for a vote on a gas tax, he had commitments from ten people to be either his 30th or his 31st vote.[53] Depending on the situation he would change how he built his majorities. Peter Burns described alternative strategies: "I saw him work to get his votes—start with one and build to 31. I saw him start with 31 and build down, and I saw him start with 33 and build down. 'If you won't be my 31st vote, will you be my 33rd vote? Well, I've already got a 33rd vote, so will you be my 32nd vote?' "[54]

Beyond independent agreement on the merits of a measure, Barr obtained some promises of support because of an explicit or implicit exchange of favors, which reflected the personal relationships that he formed, but these exchanges also represented an assessment of contingency by Barr and the legislator. On one occasion, after Barr had worked hard to pass a bill that Jim Skelly wanted but in which Barr had no real interest, he asked for Skelly's support on a measure to distribute some state sales tax money to cities. Skelly disliked the proposal, but recognizing Barr's help to him, he agreed to be the 31st vote, believing that Barr would never get enough votes to pass the bill. In the initial deliberations, the bill had the support of only 17 legislators, but then, Skelly reported, "They brought one guy in from the hospital, Horace Owens; they got the drunks out of the bar, you know what I mean? It was 25. I still wasn't worried. Got up to 27. I started getting real worried. Went to 28; went to 29; they never got 30." Skelly later learned that Barr had gotten commitments from four legislators to be the 31st vote, but he couldn't get the 30th vote. "It was one of the few times I remember Burt losing anything on the floor."[55]

Vote-gathering negotiations most often occurred with individuals in private, but Barr also sought votes more publicly in caucus meetings. This setting encouraged different or additional tactics, since some general appeals, like invoking Anzio, did not work with every legislator. One of Barr's strategies was group pressure. On one occasion, Barr was seeking votes for a bill involving some regulation of hospitals and was slowly building support, using a variety of appeals. The tally eventually reached 30 supporters, and the tension rose as Barr looked deliberately at the still-uncommitted caucus members. Finally, another member entered the room. Barr asked pointedly, " 'You a yes?' and the guy says, 'Yeah.' And he [Barr] says, 'Good. Let's get out of here,' with a big smile on his face."[56]

Senator John McCain explained that Barr's focus on results accounted for his political victories. "He had a unique ability to take a complex issue, to crystallize it into simple terms and figure out what the options were, select the most viable option and then build a coalition around it." Barr also recognized other dimensions and requirements of being a leader. Practicing consensus politics involved trying to ensure that "nobody bore the full expense or went out of the room a total loser." Generosity was vital. More than just personally thanking people for their support, which he did, he also publicly touted the value of shared effort. "You can't do it alone. You've got to have a good Speaker, and from there on it is a team effort." Drawn from his military and business experiences, this perspective characterized his earliest legislative efforts. In 1966, after winning adoption of the Finance Department, he publicly praised the Speaker and majority leader, acknowledging that "without their support these measures would never have passed," as well as thanking past governors, many legislators, and citizen specialists. Throughout his career, Barr continued to value teamwork and praise others, and he sometimes did not accept the credit he deserved. Charlie Stevens noted, "He did not want accolades or anything. I watched him pass around bills of importance to other legislators so they could get credit." It was, naturally, both generous and strategic, since it reduced somewhat the perception of Barr's dominance in lawmaking, and it expanded the level of participation by others, which he sought to encourage.[57]

This attitude also shaped other decisions that Barr made. For example, he did not try to over-manage the chamber, allowing members the leeway to pursue other issues of concern to them that did not conflict with his agenda or disrupt the chamber. He also relied on committee chairs to resolve some things without his intervention. So, when city annexations suddenly became a major issue in 1985, Barr accepted assurances from the committee chair, Chris Herstam, about finding a solution, and he spoke reassuringly to the press. He also believed that one aim of leadership should be in fostering leadership in others, and his relationships with Art Hamilton, Joe Lane, Chris Herstam, and others realized that strategy. Eddie Basha articulated the connection between leadership and mentoring when he claimed, "Burt was a leader. You know, he knew how to mold people; he knew how to lead."[58]

Barr fully and happily embraced the opportunities and responsibilities of leadership. He referred laughingly to a wartime friend whose goal had been learning to be a follower. That was not Barr's desire: "I wanted to be out front where the bullets are flying, where I could take the heat and the responsibility." He believed that leadership made a difference, that outcomes were not the inevitable result of larger forces. Leadership was crucial for devising good and workable proposals, in gauging the timing of "when to fight, when to run, when to compromise," and in being able to bring diverse factions together into a common effort. Strategy, generosity, and teamwork were central in how Barr functioned, but he was also competitive and admitted, "I *like* to win, it's always been my goal."[59]

Art Hamilton noted, "He understood power and how to use it," and his experience brought cumulative advantages. "He was in the position for so long," Rick Collins observed, that "he almost was larger than life" for new members. Having already received advice and financial assistance toward their campaigns, when they entered the legislature, they were often overwhelmed by his personality and greatly impressed by his mastery of the process and the institution. Barr was "the hub of the wheel, for outsiders, for staff, for legislators." For information, directions, solutions—for any situation that developed—people would go to him. Everyone knew he had power. He won so often that they expected it, as evidenced in Jim Skelly's comment, "Barr always gets his way." And expectations reinforced and added to the reality.[60]

But leadership and power also had a price, which Barr fully understood. His relationships with the media were friendly, but always with an edge, said John Kolbe. The normal process of accomplishing legislative business also created conflicts. James Sossaman remembered when he "really got mad at Burt" over an issue and "had a knock-down, drag-out [fight], and I totally lost it." Only long after the event did he realize that "Burt was just trying to get the session over with," and that Sossaman's issue was just an ordinary casualty in the legislative process.[61] The larger problem was winning, for if Barr always won, then others always lost, even if he tried to structure results that gave them some solace. Typically, legislative leaders are constantly seeking support, but if some members instinctively oppose them, then legislating becomes that much harder. Barr tried to respond to this problem by treating those members with friendliness and humor, and by finding occasions for cooperation.

Barr explained the price of leadership to his two Democratic counterparts. While crossing the capitol mall one day, he encountered Alfredo Gutierrez heading in the opposite direction; each of them was seeking votes in the other's chamber. Gutierrez must have looked downcast, and Barr laughingly asked, "They hate you, don't they?" As consolation he told Gutierrez that his members hated him as well, but he added: "Don't worry. If they hate you, you're [doing] good." Art Hamilton reported similar sentiments and a longer conversation with Barr. When he was elected minority leader, Barr warned him, "If you want their affection, you ran for the wrong job." Stressing the importance of finding internal satisfaction, he said, "Son, on the day you do your best work, on the day you do things as

Figure 11. Barr and the press. Burton S. Barr Collection.

well as you have ever done them, you get people to vote to how they should vote, you demand that they pass what you think they ought to pass, you require your people to be responsible and do their job, you won't have a friend in the caucus." And he added, "They won't like you for it, but they will respect you for it, and they expect it from you."[62]

Leadership, Values, and Conflict

Barr's activities as majority leader also reflected his basic values. And these started with family. This, everyone recognized, was his own top priority, but he also advised others to think of their families and their lives outside the legislature. After Peter Burns expressed anxiety over a policy question, Barr offered him some perspective, saying, "This is not important; your family's important, your health is important, your life's important." While intensely serious about legislative business, he did not live his life for the legislature. He was also intensely patriotic: "I've always had a strong personal belief in this country and everything it represents." He considered citizenship "the greatest thing I have," and he felt that everyone should contribute to their community and should be part of the political process. These deeply held beliefs were the product of Barr's life experiences, beginning with his father's ideas of assimilation and citizenship. His years of service in the military had fostered his appreciation of camaraderie and a conviction that everyone could make some useful contribution. And his second marriage and children had given him a sense of perspective and balance.[63]

Barr loved Arizona, the place and the people. A postwar migrant to Phoenix, he was enamored of the growth he saw around him and the possibilities for the future. But as he entered the legislature, it was clear to him that the state's political system, its structure of government, and its policies were controlled by traditional rural interests—ranching, mining, farming, and utilities—and that they were preventing the state from meeting modern challenges and providing the quality of life that Arizonans should have. Barr believed in the ideal of public service, and he was devoted to serving the interests of Arizonans.

A pragmatic focus on solving problems won Barr admiration and respect in many quarters, but not from some Republicans. Jane Hull remarked, "I came from the Republican Party. Burt was not really involved with the Republican Party," while Tony West complained, "Party registration . . . was so secondary to Burt; he didn't care." According to Jon Kyl, "Burt always had a somewhat uneasy relationship with 'the Republican Party,'" partly because his beliefs did not mesh with those of some members, but also because "you rarely saw Burt at Republican Party activities." Joe Lane agreed that Barr ignored the party a bit, asking Lane to make speeches to the party faithful, but he defended Barr by noting, "Sometimes the Republican Party gets a little misguided in going off over here on certain principles and doing certain things, when a lot of time a more pragmatic approach works better." Chris Herstam went further, arguing that partisanship "often becomes an impediment toward good public policy making. Burt never let that happen."[64]

That policy-oriented approach faced challenges within the GOP. Tony West alleged that "a lot of Republicans resented" Barr's willingness to seek bipartisan support for policies. More than that, the *Arizona Republic* concluded, Republicans resented his pragmatism on strictly partisan grounds: "His refusal to engage in purely political standoffs has prompted Barr's Republican colleagues to accuse him of 'selling out' to Babbitt and Gutierrez, or allowing them to look good by claiming credit for programs passed by what has become a GOP-controlled legislature."[65]

But Barr was neither ideological nor very partisan, and he responded to such criticisms without apology. "It may appear to some of my contemporaries that I'm not the good-old, rock-ribbed Republican conservative, but that's tough. I'm not going to live in the image that they'd like me to have." He believed in bipartisanship because, as Stevens explained, "He believed in Republicans and Democrats working for the good of the state."

For Barr, patriotism trumped partisanship: "I believe in this country and I *always* believe a new president is going to do well, Democrat or Republican." He spoke little about party identification per se, but reflecting on conditions when the Republicans took over the legislature in 1966, he concluded, "The Democrats didn't do anything—nothing—it was status quo. We came in and had to start building the state, coping with the burgeoning population growth that hit us in the 1950s and 1960s."[66]

Chris Herstam understood how that Arizona experience had shaped Barr's identification as a Republican, but added, "I think his business background and his own military background made him feel more comfortable in the Republican Party." Eddie Basha agreed and emphasized that Barr was "a true supporter of business. He was an entrepreneur in his own right; he was a small businessman. He understood, I think, how oppressive a government can be on business." But parties always contain a constantly changing array of interests, and this was especially the case in Arizona during these years. Charlie Stevens described Barr as "a different type of Republican," one who was focused on finding ways to help people. Jon Kyl effectively summarized Barr's viewpoint: "While Burt did not have a strong political ideology, he had a set of views on things, and they were generally pro-business and pro-growth, and he believed in activist government." Barr's ideas of federalism, which were practical rather than ideological, were a core part of this. He shared the general Republican opposition to an expanded federal government, not because he favored inaction, but because he believed that state governments should solve problems, with federal intervention only as a last resort. "I believe we can do it better than the feds," he insisted.[67]

While Barr was widely lauded and respected for his leadership style, the praise was not universal. Some critics felt that he tried to do too much, that this made him less accessible, harder to talk to, and (too often) late to meetings. Charlie Stevens's complaint was that "Burt could never leave a problem alone; he had to solve it," and Stevens believed this solution-oriented approach could sometimes cause difficulties. Tony West also objected to Barr's focus on solutions, alleging that a Barr policy "may or may not be in the best interests of Arizona, but he wanted to accomplish the mission, close the deal, and if it happened to be in the best interests of Arizona—and in most cases it was okay—then fine."[68] Of course, Barr believed that serving Arizona was a primary goal, so this better reflects criticism of policy content, not the leadership per se.

Another criticism involves Barr's flexibility and willingness to compromise. Some argued that Barr took the path of least resistance, believing that sometimes other, preferable options were politically possible. While possible for specific cases, this counterfactual assessment is generally unconvincing, since it is contradicted by nearly all contemporary testimony and by numerous cases where policies passed only because of a flexible approach. Winning a legislative majority does not necessarily mean that an alternative proposal, more conservative or more liberal, could have passed by an only slightly smaller margin. "What's really true," argues Gutierrez, is that Barr "*created* the path of least resistance. He made that happen, he didn't wait for it to occur and then walk through it."[69]

Barr's most severe critics believed that these tactics constituted his only principles. Republican Senator Stephen Davis denounced Barr as a "philosophical prostitute," and John Kolbe believed "Burt was virtually without any serious principles." Tony West contrasted Barr's behavior with that of "Most of us" who "think we have a little bit of principle. You kind of stay glued to your principle." To a large extent, such stark assessments reflect a conservative frustration with legislative outcomes during this period. Barr clearly had principles, beliefs, and preferences—but not an ideology. He followed not a catechism but a map of a larger world of issues. His range of acceptable solutions was wider than that of conservatives, but not internally inconsistent. He described his approach to compromise by saying, "The secret in legislating is to bend without losing your original objective," and arguing, "It isn't necessary to compromise yourself."[70]

Conservatives were less dismayed by compromises where Barr won only "half a loaf" (or just a slice) than by the occasions when Barr made severe changes in course, the 180-degree turns to which Joe Lane and Tony West referred. A case in point is the repeal of the sales tax on food described earlier. Barr shifted his position in this instance because of the merits of the case and because he saw the policy would be changed, if not by the legislature then by voter initiative. He could have remained unmoving and lost the vote; instead, he bowed to political reality and cushioned the change by passing two additional, offsetting measures. In a second instance, which Tony West considered highly telling, Speaker Akers decided not to support one of Barr's proposals, and Barr reversed his position. Since Barr was part of the House leadership team and subordinate to the Speaker, the decision seemed politically necessary, if a little uncomfortable.

A final case is the state's adoption and then repeal of the Medicare policy over several sessions in the 1970s (see chapter 5). Barr had pushed the initial adoption of the policy, together with other Republican leaders, but rising cost estimates for the program, plus growing GOP opposition, forced Barr to argue for repeal. It was, obviously, quite unusual for a leader to support repealing a measure for which he had previously labored so hard. However, in this case Barr faced two real considerations: the unanticipated financial difficulties and the revolt of his caucus. He decided, in these circumstances, to adopt the pragmatic course. Barr's response at the time was simple: "You can be in the middle of a stream and drowning with a gurgle, 'I was right,' but I want to be around again so I can come back with another idea, issue, or program."[71]

A final set of criticisms came from both legislators and newspapers, and they involved purported conflicts of interest. A perennial source of dispute in legislative politics, sensitivity to it grew in the 1970s and 1980s, boosted by an onslaught of scandals, starting with Watergate, and the major increase in the amount of money in politics. These led to discussions about the behavior of legislators and other officeholders, and periodically led the legislature to reevaluate its standards. In October 1973, Barr headed a bipartisan committee of both houses to strengthen its current ethics standard, adopted in 1968. He observed that some people complained that the press coverage of Watergate was overly critical, but he believed the scrutiny was good. As a powerful legislative leader, Barr could help reform the rules, but his power also made him a target of allegations. After a newspaper story in December 1973 reported that he had favored a bill to relax the quotas on liquor licenses, and alleged that he would personally gain from this, Barr explained that restricted quotas had boosted the license cost to ten times the official price, clear evidence of a bad licensing system, and he defended his support of the bill by explaining that passage would not earn him any money. But during an interview in which he explained these points, he recognized that the appearance of conflict was harmful, so he publicly withdrew his support for the bill.

In February 1974, after a newspaper exposé, the state's consumer protection agency charged two supermarket chains and three dairies with using inaccurate weights. Barr publicly defended the grocers, claiming the problem was unintentional error and not fraud, since the machines weighed both high and low. He also placed an angry call to the assistant attorney general in charge of the agency, asking whether the businesses had been warned about the problem before charges were filed. Barr quickly cooled off and, recognizing that his inappropriate call might seem an attempt to influence the investigation, explained that "no pressure was intended" by it.[72]

He also moved to rectify several problems that the incident had revealed. First, the legislature passed a standardized weights and measures code (Arizona was the only state without one) and created a lab for implementing it. In addition, while the investigation of fraud remained with the attorney general's office, a new weights and measures agency was created within the state's Department of Administration. Thus, after Barr's initial instinctive and angry action had prompted assertions that he was trying to influence the case, he acknowledged the problem and quickly shifted into his problem-solving mode.

The following year another grocer-related controversy arose, this time over a cost-per-unit pricing system created in 1974 but never implemented. Senator Manuel Peña accused Barr of having a conflict of interest, since his firm did business with this industry. Barr indignantly denied the allegation, saying that he had no pecuniary gain from the system, and that he had no more conflict of interest than did Peña, an insurance man, had in dealing with insurance companies. In reality, the charges pointed to a general dilemma for legislators: when did knowledge and connection with the subject of legislation pose a conflict of interest—for legislators who worked as realtors, educators, health-care workers, or virtually any employed person? The allegations rose again in 1980, with the debate over repealing the sales tax on food (noted above), and specifically over Barr's support for a tax credit for grocers who bought new product-scanning equipment. Critics alleged a payoff; supporters defended this as a normal protection against economic harm, and said it was needed to pass the tax repeal. Despite Barr's denying that he was acting as an agent of his business associates and friends, some people felt that he had used his influence inappropriately.

In March 1983, Tom Fitzpatrick, columnist for the *Arizona Republic*, published more serious allegations aimed directly at Barr. In several acerbic columns, Fitzpatrick accused Barr of raising campaign funds and using them to "intimidate" legislators; of owning condominiums in Mexico and California, plus other substantial properties; and of being connected to a lawyer for the Arizona Licensed Beverage Association, which lobbied against raising the drinking age to 21, and who Fitzpatrick felt had suspiciously won two liquor licenses in a lottery. Finally, he alleged that Louise Barr was benefiting financially from ownership and/or management of various businesses. Fitzpatrick's articles were dismissed by those who knew Barr, particularly because they relied heavily on innuendo and on simply piling up accusations, and also because they included numerous errors regarding Barr's property ownership, the misuse of campaign funds, and the allegations that Louise had a financial stake in businesses, when she was merely listed as an officer because she was their CPA.[73]

At first, Barr had not imagined someone could misconstrue his behavior and position; after the articles were published, he was furious with the columnist for attacking his wife and stopped talking with him. But the articles, and letters published by Fitzpatrick encouraging his attacks, damaged Barr's reputation and revealed an undercurrent of suspicion toward people in public office and about connections between legislators and special interests. Barr responded some weeks later by proposing to expand the financial disclosure requirements for public officials. To objections from some of his colleagues, Barr answered that the public had "a right to know such information about its officials." He added, "I have a business, that, by the way, has become famous lately. If I feel that this is an imposition, then I shouldn't be in public office."[74] Despite opposition, he won legislative approval for the bill. Barr encouraged widespread and private contributions to political campaigns, and he frequently admonished members of the public to contribute, but he did not see a fundamental problem in the connection between contributions and political influence, and he believed that public disclosure of contributions would eliminate the danger.

Assessing Leadership and the Legislature

A premier scholar of leadership studies, Bernard Bass, surveyed the substantial literature on the specific traits of effective leaders and summarized them in four clusters: cognitive ability (notably intelligence, decisiveness, vision, articulateness, and imagination), social competency (including interpersonal skills, tact, and empathy), emotional competency (especially self-confidence and optimism), and character (integrity, honesty, and discipline).[75] The preceding analysis of Barr's leadership shows how clearly he displayed all of those traits and helps to explain his success as a legislative leader.

But, as noted earlier, effective leadership has a second dimension, and that is the situation. Where and when a leader works significantly shapes the challenges and possibilities for leadership. The institutional setting that Barr faced—the Arizona House of Representatives, the Senate, the governor, and the executive branch—played critical roles in shaping the actual constraints and challenges that Barr confronted.[76] And the economic and political conditions in the state were the other critical factors. As discussed earlier, by the mid-1960s urban population growth and new economic development generated increasing political pressures, and the reapportionment of 1966 opened the door for new forces to transform the legislature, a complex process that would continue for nearly two decades. The result was the creation of a much larger, more efficient, and more professional government in all branches. This was, quite simply, an extraordinary opportunity for leadership. It was one for which Burton Barr was ideally suited, but it also enabled him to act and learn in ways that would otherwise not have been possible.

The Impact of Situation on Leadership

Legislators and the Challenge of Legislative Service

The initial postwar assessments of many state governments included a doleful view of state legislatures and especially some legislators. If governors and the executive branch were chastised for their failings, the legislative branch drew even greater fire for being inefficient, lacking resources and capacities to work cooperatively with governors, and attracting too many members without adequate skills or preparation.[77] By the late 1970s conditions had improved considerably in nearly every state. Arizona also registered this sort of seismic shift in government, but with its own unique features. Barr's career spanned this era of reform, so he faced multiple changing leadership challenges, first in the inadequate legislature, then while he pushed for modernization, and finally in a reformed institution.

The quality and training of Arizona state legislators was a legitimate cause of concern. Although Stan Turley felt that Arizona had "a lot of good legislators" in the 1960s, and that rural counties sent "their more prominent citizens," other observers were more critical. According to Senator Pat Conner, half the senators "were either drunk at the Westward Ho or didn't know what the shit was goin' on." When Louis Gonzalez first came to the legislature, he "felt completely lost and out of place," unaware of how the assembly functioned or exactly what to do there. Surveyed by the *Arizona Republic*, one freshman legislator complained about "the mediocrity of intelligence—the inability of certain legislators to admit their own lack of knowledge," while another claimed that "the majority of the legislators don't know what's going on." That lack of knowledge was sometimes quite visible. Stan Turley gently recounted an instance when, after being questioned about a bill he favored, a legislator rose and said, "'Boy howdy, man alive, goodnight Ada, when you have a bill like this, vote for it,' and he sat down and they voted for it." Another time, when a lawmaker "was being questioned, he got flustered and ended up shouting, 'I don't know anything about this bill, but it's good for Tucson and that's all I care.'"[78]

Of course, legislative service was not necessarily attractive to everyone. Through the 1960s legislators received only $1,800 a year, and even after salaries were increased several times by the 1980s, Barr quipped, "For $15,000 what do you expect, Winston Churchill?" But beyond that, the state legislature was a demanding environment. Steeped in tradition, these institutions operated under complex rules and unwritten norms of behavior: a study of four legislatures in the 1950s identified 42 informal rules of conduct. Pat Conner confessed that when he came to the legislature, he found it an "awesome place," and the "procedure and rules of the house—you knew nothing about that." Even Stan Turley, who served as both Speaker and Senate president, confessed, "I never could figure out of those procedures up there, if you didn't have that dope sheet to go by, telling you what to do next." New legislators had often held some prior office, but many county and municipal boards and councils used only the simplest rules of order, and experience there provided no training for legislators.[79] Typically, a handful of members had the knowledge and experience that gave them a significant advantage over others. Barr's ability to make quick sense of things enabled him to move quickly into that group and become an effective legislative leader.

Besides difficulties with rules and norms, legislators struggled with knotty and contested subjects. The increasing complexity of policy-making from the 1960s to the 1980s made legislative service even more challenging, partly reflecting Barr's impact on the institution. An assessment in 1979 explained that legislators increasingly depended "on experts they trust to be well-informed on a particular issue," for no one, however able or aided by non-expert staffers, "can be fully knowledgeable about every bill's implications." The 1983 survey of freshmen legislators also reported their surprise at the "volume of information legislators are expected to absorb" and how much research was needed to prepare a bill, and they were "overwhelmed by the amount of paper work." Joe Lane voiced his surprise, when he shifted from lobbying the legislature over single issues to serving as a legislator, at the "total complexity of the issues you deal with," and how often "you've got ten different issues coming in the front door at the same time."[80]

Barr's ability to handle multiple issues simultaneously enabled him to maintain leadership in an increasingly demanding legislature. His work ethic and strategy also provided the example for Lane's primary advice to new legislators: "do your homework [and] study the issues," and his hyperbolic claim that in one legislative term "you learn more than you learn in four years of college." Lane also described the value of finding a mentor. He and other legislators had established that relationship with Barr, but this was common and useful, for in an institution of few members, personal ties were crucial, and they could develop variously. Senator Leo Corbet had grown up in Yuma, so when he first came to the Senate, he sought out Harold Giss.

Although from different parties, Giss counseled Corbet, telling him "whose ox was being gored" by particular pieces of legislation. Senator Louis Gonzalez connected with Manuel Peña, who "took time to talk to me about certain things and certain expectations, and how to do certain things."[81]

The most important norm for legislators personally involved honesty and trust, two of Barr's core values. In the words of one lawmaker, "The one dictum everybody agrees with is that all you have in the legislative process is your word." A central institutional norm involved the role of freshmen, who, as Joe Lane reported it, were told, "You kept your mouth shut and sat in the back. You didn't do anything until you were told to do something." Art Hamilton described his freshman experience as, first being appointed to the Insurance and Transportation Committees, "where a lot of freshmen got put, because that was a place you put freshmen." Then, in an early committee meeting, the chair first ignored his efforts to question someone testifying before the committee, and then chastised him for asking an "impertinent" question.[82]

Complaints about treatment of freshmen rose over time, perhaps influenced by the highly publicized behavior of active post-Watergate freshmen congressmen in 1975. In 1979 Representative Diane McCarthy challenged the tradition and appealed directly to freshmen to support her bid for a leadership position. Claiming that Barr and Speaker Frank Kelley "are of the old school," she asserted that in the previous "two years, freshmen haven't observed this rule," and argued that they had come with "definite ideas and want to be heard." House members viewed her as "bright, ambitious, strong," but longtime *Arizona Republic* columnist Bernie Wynn reported some legislators "don't trust her, saying she is devious and doesn't keep her word." And some criticized her overt appeal to freshmen and for alleging "how bad the leaders are."[83] In the end, the norms regarding trust and freshmen held, and McCarthy was not elected to the leadership.

It is possible that McCarthy's loss may also reflect another legislative norm regarding gender. Polly Rosenbaum described the legislature as, "A man's world, very much, very much so. Women were intruders." While women in Arizona held far more legislative seats, became committee chairs, and attained leadership positions before women in other states, gender inequality remained one of the legislature's norms. Jane Hull alleged that Barr was "uncomfortable" with women lawmakers, and that he even felt they should not be in the legislature. The charge is serious, but it is also somewhat extreme, particularly given the position women had achieved in the legislature. Moreover, Hull fought with Barr on issues of managing the legislature, and as a conservative, she frequently opposed him on policy issues, so her allegation may have stemmed more from personality and ideological conflict than from gender differences. Barr's relationship with other women legislators may be a better guide, most notably his close friendship with Sandra O'Connor, whom he described as "an extraordinary woman" and whom he touted on multiple occasions for governor.[84]

The Importance of Legislative Structure

When Republicans won majorities in both houses in 1966, they set about revising certain features of the legislature, but they also had to work within an institutional culture and characteristics determined by the larger process of governance. Keenly aware of the legislature's image of ineffectiveness, the new leadership, including Barr, wanted to pass major pieces of legislation and in shorter annual sessions. They achieved both aims in 1967, adjourning after 64 days with an impressive roster of new laws, earning notice from *TIME* magazine as the "Gung-Ho legislature." But such brevity did not last. Sessions doubled in length in 1970–1974, rose higher thereafter, and declined back to around 110 days after 1979. But legislative workload and output are better measures of leadership efficiency. As shown in figure 12, Barr's legislatures faced increasing demands, with the number of bills introduced into the House increased dramatically,

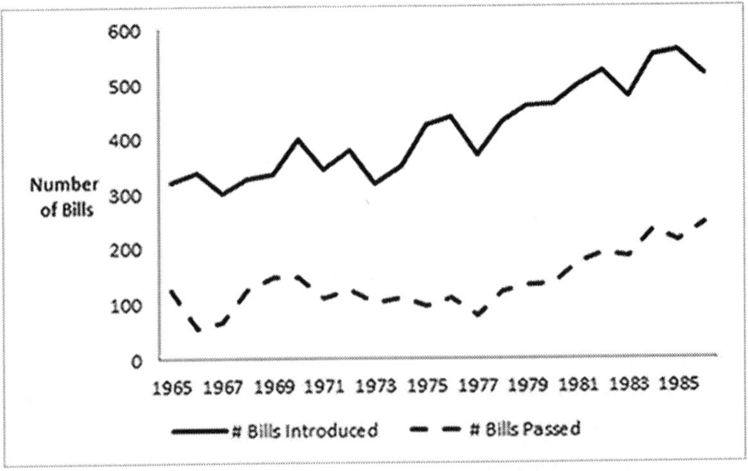

Figure 12. Legislative action by the Arizona House, 1965–1985. *Journal of the House of Representatives*, 1965–1986.

from 322 to 518. Even more importantly, the number of bills passed jumped from 124 to 246.

Barr's legislative service was exclusively in the House, a distinctive aspect of his career. From 1966 to 2000, a total of 73 House members shifted to the Senate, while no senators changed houses. This may relate to Stan Turley's observation that the Senate "seems to have a little more power as a group than the House," but the reason is unclear, since both Arizona houses had the same authority, districts, and two-year term of office. Perhaps that stemmed from belief in the "little federalism" comparison with the U.S. Congress, or the traditional reference to the "upper house" (although John Kolbe remarked that the only "upper" about the Senate was the elevation of their noses). The smaller size of the Senate may have played a role, or perhaps its usual success under Harold Giss's direction. Whatever the source, in politics perception is often reality, and both can be enhanced and the basis for action. Louis Gonzalez related that Senate protocol was "to be better dressed than our counterparts in the House." Senator Ben Arnold of Pinal County jibed, "Why would you want to waddle around with the ducks in the House, when you can fly with the eagles in the Senate?"[85] Burton Barr faced these expectations when he came to the legislature, and while members still shifted to the Senate, as majority leader, he clearly altered the balance of power between the chambers.

Being majority leader put Barr in the middle of the biennial competition to control the House. The prime organizing decision was the House majority caucus's selection of a Speaker, for Speakers determined personnel and process: as noted in chapter 3, they influenced the selection of the floor leader and whip, appointed committee chairs and all committee members, and assigned bills to committees, including the crucial conference committees. They also handled the administration of the House, and as chair when the House was in session, they managed the floor debate. In Arizona, as in many states, the selection process started well before the session opened, and while the decision could sometimes be harmonious, at least on the surface, contests for this position can reveal competing political forces as well as alternative notions about leadership and how the chamber should operate.

Unlike the decisions in 1966 and the 1950s, changes in House leadership thereafter were uneventful, but 1976 saw a return to conflict. Stan Akers, elected Speaker in 1972 and 1974 as a "tough, often dictatorial, no-nonsense leader," anticipated a challenge in 1975 from Frank Kelley, who was identified as "peddling increased caucus democracy." Akers responded by loosening caucus restrictions on members, giving them better information, and even being reasonable toward Democrats, but this was too little, too late, so Akers pulled out of the race. Eight years later, Kelley faced a revolt. Although members extolled "his attention to detail, procedural streamlining, and evenhandedness," they faulted him for being aloof and rarely available. But political factors also determined this contest, as newer lawmakers, eager for leadership posts, pushed to displace Kelley. It is all the more surprising, then, John Kolbe observed, that Barr's position as majority leader was not in jeopardy. "Call it force of personality," he suggested, "call it stamina, call it political footwork, call it unparalleled success," but the notion of replacing "the nation's senior legislative leader" was not "seriously entertained."[86]

Kolbe identified major strengths that kept Barr continuously in office, but other factors were also at play. On a few previous occasions, rumors about replacing Barr had wafted through the House, but in each instance Barr had effectively dispelled any challenge. His extraordinary longevity in office was also because, as Nikki Corral explained it, "He *loved* being where he was."[87] Barr's unwavering commitment to his position was common knowledge, as was his lack of interest in being Speaker. It was a shrewd decision not to pursue this role. First, it removed him from the most serious conflicts over visible prestige and appointment power, while enabling him to influence the selection of Speakers and their decisions. Second, being Speaker required doing administrative work, which Barr disliked; and he had no wish to chair the House meetings. Serving as majority leader, however, let him introduce issues and devise policies. It allowed him to work the floor, pulling together compromises, assessing members' opinions, and getting their votes. Speakers focused on administering House business and parliamentary floor management, enabling Barr to focus on major programs.[88]

While the Speakership was nominally the top post, Barr expanded the scope and authority of the majority leader, making it the most powerful leadership position. As Jim Skelly put it, "Burton's ideas overwhelmed everything." That did not mean, however, that Speakers were simply figureheads or that Barr treated them that way. Jim Skelly observed, "Burt was always smart enough to realize that the Speaker came first," and Art Hamilton emphasized that Barr always showed "proper deference" to the Speaker. He knew the Speaker had prerogatives, "and rather than trying to push his agenda past the Speaker, he would always sit down with the Speakers" and seek to persuade them. Speakers could, and each occasionally did, say no to Barr's plans or to how decisions were being shaped during a session, and he dutifully changed direction. He did so because he believed in teamwork, and because Speakers were his political allies and his friends. Moreover, he understood a broader political reality that, as Art Hamilton explained, "He had to have a strong Speaker. And Mr. Barr was at his best when he had that."[89]

Managing Legislative Business

Throughout this period, Barr became an increasingly central part of Arizona's legislative modernization and its adoption of creative public policies. Efforts at managing the legislature were nominal before 1967, but the new Republican leadership in that year determined to be more efficient and established a procedure of weekly meetings for Speaker Turley, Senate President Marty Humphrey, and Governor Jack Williams to share information and coordinate activities. Two years later, this arrangement was modified, when Speaker Jack Haugh hosted the weekly meeting with Governor Williams and included other legislative leaders, notably Barr, but also lawmakers working on particular topics. Interchamber planning meetings were held less regularly thereafter, and meetings with the governor changed drastically after 1974, when Democrats reclaimed the gubernatorial office, but leaders in each chamber made coordination of some sort a continuing priority. Within the House, the leaders coordinated their plans and met periodically with committee chairs, irregularly in some sessions, and in other years on a weekly basis. The caucus usually met weekly during the session and a few times when the legislature was not meeting, and, depending on the wishes of the Speaker and the willingness of the members, would designate a few or many bills as "policy bills" requiring party support. Barr's centrality in this planning grew measurably, as he labored before and during each session to determine which proposals the legislature should address, worked to coordinate the House leadership, and came to play the primary role in negotiating settlements between the houses and with the governor.

Lobbyists were crucial cogs in the operation of the Arizona House and, along with representatives of the media, constituted an auxiliary part of the legislative world, but their role changed over time, because state government expanded and because of Barr's decisions. Stan Turley explained, "The legislature really is rather dependent upon the lobbyists. Good lobbyists can be a great help to legislators," and in many ways, that was true. Many legislators described highly productive relationships with lobbyists, who were informed, dependable, and helpful. Chris Herstam said he had "learned a lot watching Jack DeBolske and talking to him about issues," and lawmakers commonly touted Alan Stanton as a model lobbyist. Pat Conner mentioned the value of their information and the bills they drafted. Yet lobbyists focus not on the general public good, but on obtaining specific benefits for their clients. Representative John Kromko was one voice denouncing the dangers of lobbyists, claiming that lobbying created an unhealthy relationship in which "legislators are more loyal to the lobbyists than to their constituents," and arguing that lobbyist-written bills often included obscure passages that gave their clients major benefits that lawmakers had not intended. A symbol of the unacknowledged but intermingling of personal interests was lobbyists' contributions to a fund-raising dinner for Harold Giss after he went bankrupt in 1965.[90]

As majority leader, Barr interacted constantly with lobbyists, working with them on key policy questions, since they were crucial players in the successful adoption of key legislation, and he became good friends with some, like Charlie Stevens. But while Barr considered them legitimate participants in the legislative process, he abhorred the traditional system of influence and favors that operated out of the Adams Hotel.

Very soon after his initial election as majority leader, Barr took the first step in changing this system. "I issued a little dictum out of my office," he said, "that there would be no meetings at the Adams Hotel, goodbye and I'll see you later, and that I wasn't going to go there, and so long. That meant that those people had to come to the legislature. Well, that was the last thing they wanted." One of the lobbyists "lectured" Barr, as he reported it later, saying, "Now, listen kiddo, here's how it works." Barr said okay and then ignored the lecture. The second phase occurred the following year, when Barr pushed through a long-overdue, major revision of the state property tax system, to the consternation of the major economic powers. Although this impaired Barr's relationship with those forces for a decade, he considered it a vital strategic advance. "We taught the establishment powers one thing," Barr said. "We taught them the legislature met at the Capitol and not at the Adams Hotel."[91] And he followed this up in 1970 by pushing for improved registration and regulation of lobbyists.

Despite these changes, lobbyists continued to offer legislators "hospitality" and benefits, and to operate a suite at the Adams Hotel. As a freshman legislator, Alfredo Gutierrez went there several times, and the flattery and attention made for a heady experience. His perspective changed, however, because of a phone call. It was Barr, who told him he had an important decision to make: "Who runs this joint, you know; the lobbyists down there or you? You want something done, they come to your office." He cautioned him further, "[Y]ou'd better be in charge, not them, or you're going to be just like them whores, Kid." And then Barr hung up on him. Gutierrez took the warning to heart and later reflected that he avoided being "seduced" by their praise and these offers "because Burt was there saying 'don't believe that crap—you're not that smart.'"[92]

Barr's objections to this system were not its illegality nor because of serious public criticism. Instead, he objected to what Jon Kyl described as "the good old boy network" with "not all decisions being based on the merits." Kyl touted the changes Barr made as creating "a real reform era," noting that "Burt was a very honest man, a very direct man, and business was conducted in a very straightforward way at the Arizona legislature while Burt was there."[93] In this instance, the values of one person in authority were instrumental in effecting change. But Barr's success also built on prior criticism of this system by other legislators and was enabled by support from new colleagues. Reforming the lobbying culture was only part of a much larger transformation, and Barr was at the forefront of these efforts.

The first steps, taken in 1967, included establishing a Legislative Budget Office and a Legislative Budget Committee, on which Barr served, to enable the legislature to share decision-making with the newly created budget office under the governor's control. The legislature also revamped its committee system and launched interim committees, which would meet after a legislative session ended to prepare for the next one, and Barr typically chaired one of the most important of them. It adopted several procedural reforms, such as, in 1968, extending the deadline for introducing bills from the 15th to the 36th day of the session and, in 1970, establishing a consent calendar for handling noncontroversial bills.

Providing additional staff support was crucial to improving the quality of legislation and liberating legislators from an unhealthy dependence on lobbyists. Barr and his Senate counterparts Sandra O'Connor and Alfredo Gutierrez pushed hard for adding staffers. In 1969 they expanded the Legislative Council, which had a bill-drafting service, by providing funding for a research division, with more professionals hired for each division. During the next decade, staff support for each house and for committees increased appreciably, and in the mid-1970s legislators in both houses received individual offices. Finally, the legislature moved to raise legislative salaries from their paltry level. In 1968 the legislature proposed and voters approved a salary of $6,000, along with travel and living expenses (this was raised to $15,000 in 1980). Although still modest, this figure meant that fewer people were excluded from legislative service because of financial hardship.

Determining the quality of the legislature when Barr was a leader is a difficult task, but a national study done early in his career presents a rough comparative assessment. The Citizens Conference on State Legislatures began collecting data in early 1969 for their study, which appeared in 1971. While this reflects some changes accomplished at the beginning of Arizona's reform process, it is a fairly good indication of how poor the legislature was at the beginning of Barr's leadership.[94]

Among all the states, Arizona ranked 43 in the overall quality of its legislature , far behind its neighbors, Nevada (13), Utah (15), New Mexico (11), and Colorado (28). Of the five assessment categories, Arizona did well in Function (11), which measured a general ability to conduct basic business; and in Independence (17), meaning relations with the executive branch, legislative oversight, controlling lobbyists, and minimizing conflicts of interest. It ranked below average in being Informed (38), which covered the capacity to collect, process, and use information. The worst rankings were being Accountable (47), meaning that access to and comprehensibility of authority was weak for both legislators and the public; and Arizona ranked dead last on being Representative (50), a measure of unclear connections between representatives and constituents; inadequate compensation, diversity of membership, and access to resources; and poor treatment of minority party members.

The better rankings in Function and Independence were achieved because of some of the changes made by 1969, and the other rankings show how far Arizona needed to go. Along with the changes (cited above) that the legislature would make after this study, it also revised its internal proceedings, notably opening committee meetings and making more information generally available. Although some movement for change had begun earlier, reapportionment was the turning point. It had brought a swing group of new people to the legislature, people with successful careers in business and professions, urban Republicans and some Democrats, who had no interest maintaining incapacitating traditions. Barr was central to this group, but other legislative leaders—like Bill Jacquin, Stan Turley, and Delos Elsworth, from the "dirty Seven" group, as well as Tim Barrow, Bill Jenkins, and Sandra O'Connor—shared the credit for establishing professional standards for how the legislature should function. Their goals echoed a transformation of state legislatures across the country and showed their awareness of those actions and the recommendations of national associations, like the National Conference of State Legislative Leaders. While the old guard regarded these as associations of "over-educated fools," the new leaders viewed them as the source for standards and ideas.[95]

An essential part of legislative professionalization and of Barr's ability to achieve results was the staff he built, a group answerable primarily to him, rather than to the committee chairs for whom they nominally worked. In the late 1960s Barr hired a lawyer and a university economist to work on finance and education issues, and he slowly added more specialists, with the noteworthy additions in the mid-1970s. In 1974 he recruited Nikki Corral from the Speaker's office to chart legislation for him, among other tasks; in 1975 he recruited Don Isaacson from being Rules Committee to being majority counsel, where he functioned as Barr's chief of staff and then became director of research; and in 1976 he hired Peter Burns, who was nominally a staffer for the Ways and Means Committee.

By 1980 he had assembled an impressive group that he used quite skillfully. A Tucson journalist claimed they gave Barr a decisive edge in accomplishing things: "If he wants statistics on the number of yaks in Tibet, the staff turns almost as one to find what he wants, and then writes legislation about the yaks." Jon Kyl observed, "He commanded most of the information of the House of Representatives," and, "Everybody worked for Burt, either de jure or de facto, and when you control the information, you can control a lot of policy."[96] But more important than having them gather information was Barr's involving them in the larger planning exercises. After each session, he would formalize a majority program for the upcoming session, and have the staff prepare research reports of the topics, and this would become at least the main part of the legislative agenda for the next session.

Legislative Partners: Conservatives, Democrats, and Senators

Barr's role as majority leader and his ability to accomplish his goals were heavily influenced by the composition of the legislature and who was governor. While Republicans controlled the House after 1966, the size of their majority varied, and that affected the behavior of both majority and minority members (see table 3). Democrats in the Senate, with a majority from 1974 to 1978 and a large minority in the next four years, also affected legislative politics and strategy. Finally, while Republicans regained the governorship in 1966, Democrats won back the office in 1974 and kept it until 1986. Majority status and the size of a majority influenced everything from the chamber's rules and committee assignments to the psychology of members. Having a governor of the same or different party could

Table 3. Political parties and Arizona government, 1964–1984

	House Seats		*Senate Seats*		*Governor*	
Year	*Rep.*	*Dem.*	*Rep.*	*Dem.*	*Name*	*Party*
1964	35	**45**	2	**26**	Goddard	Dem.
1966	**33**	27	**16**	14	Williams	Rep.
1968	**34**	26	**17**	13	Williams	Rep.
1970	**34**	26	**18**	12	Williams	Rep.
1972	**38**	22	**18**	12	Williams	Rep.
1974	**33**	27	12	**18**	Castro	Dem.
1976	**38**	22	14	**16**	Castro/Bolin/ Babbitt	Dem.
1978	**42**	18	**16**	14	Babbitt	Dem.
1980	**43**	17	**16**	14	Babbitt	Dem.
1982	**39**	21	**18**	12	Babbitt	Dem.
1984	**38**	22	**18**	12	Babbitt	Dem.

Note: Bold indicates majority party.

Source: *Arizona Capitol Times*, February 6, 2004, 13.

influence not only basic policies, but how the governor interpreted the powers of the office.

Barr's primary concern was having a Republican majority in the House, and that determined his strategy of dispersing funds to all candidates, especially those in close races. For all but one of the sessions until 1976, House Republicans had a modest majority, which placed a premium on party discipline. Despite the perception born of Barry Goldwater's prominence, the Arizona Republican Party was relative diverse in its political views, and representatives of its different factions served in the legislature. Jack DeBolske identified a lot of "middle of the roaders" and said the urban Republicans "were basically more liberal" than the Pinto Democrats. That GOP group supported modernization, expanded government, economic development, creation of urban institutions, improved education, and social benefit programs. This was, Charlie Stevens explained, "a different era" and Barr was "a different type of Republican," noting that he "worried about people, poor people, sick people, education for children; those were high priorities."[97] Within the GOP, some shared those priorities, but others did not.

In every House session the Republican caucus contained some very conservative members who objected to Barr's pragmatism and his limited partisan loyalties. Jim Skelly referred to a "group of conservatives" who disagreed with Barr, including himself, Pete Corpstein, Donna Carlson, and Carl Kunasek, all of whom served in the House between 1974 and 1982; Jane Hull described a "dissident cabal" of herself, Pat Wright, Lilian

Jordan, and others, whose legislative service clustered in the years from 1976 to 1985. Many of them operated from a general ideological position based simply on reducing the size of government. In some cases, their opposition stemmed from a strict legal interpretation of an issue, as was often true for Jim Skelly, and in others, their resistance rested on a moral objection. But most commonly the immediate if not the underlying cause of dispute came down to money. Jane Hull felt, "Certainly in those early years, that everything Burt did cost money."[98]

Whether it was tax rebates or tax increases, cutting programs or creating new ones, Barr always sought to win the support of some of these members, if he could, not by talking about ideology, but by trying to persuade them on the merits of the measure. Getting their backing was easier if he had a good personal relationship, as he did with Skelly. It was harder if the personal tie was weak, as it was with Jane Hull, who disliked his need for responses of "three sentences," or having only "30 seconds" to make a presentation. He had better success when people valued him as a floor leader and believed that party loyalty required their support, but stressing party responsibility could be problematic, for some of these lawmakers resented his lack of partisan zeal and his very limited campaigning. With some members, he had very little common ground. When Tony West was asked about the issues on which he supported Barr's views, he said "not many" and named none. Many of these conservatives opposed him not only on firm ideological grounds, but also because they considered his efforts at compromise to be essentially unprincipled. For the most part, this involved a general rejection of conciliation as a desirable or necessary part of the legislative process, but some people, at some times, believed that concessions were short-sighted and unnecessary; they favored brinkmanship.[99]

The difficulties that Barr faced in the House stemmed from broader political conditions in the state. In his historical analysis of Arizona politics. David Berman observed, "From the 1950s to the mid-1970s, the Republican Party was relatively unified and centrally directed." Barry Goldwater, Paul Fannin, Congressman John Rhodes and their supporters maintained control, but they faced a "deep-seated enmity on the part of one wing of the party identified . . . with Publisher Evan Mecham" that periodically boiled over. As the party grew in size and diversity, however, and as former leaders dropped out, that central direction disappeared, so that by the mid-1970s "sharp ideological divisions" became more common and more visible.[100] That trend was also evident in the legislature, where the number of conservative members increased. The impact of their gains was minimized, however, because Republicans increased their overall numbers in the House starting in 1976, giving Barr leeway in finding his majorities.

Democrats, in the state and in the legislature, were also divided. Rural conservatives, urban liberals, labor supporters, and minorities competed to chart the party's direction in a time of great upheaval. Reapportionment had seriously reduced their power, and suburban growth bolstered Republican strength, but protecting the voting rights of minority groups and their greater turnout provided some counterbalance. Barr felt Democrats were in disarray in 1966 because they had held power for so long, and Arizona "was changing to a total urban climate. The issues that we were addressing weren't issues that they had ever been involved in." But by the mid-1970s Democrats had recognized the shift in political fortunes and had begun adopting a more centrist and pragmatic approach.[101]

Perhaps the experience of Republican-Democratic House coalitions before 1966 initially predisposed Republicans to a relatively evenhanded treatment of Democrats, the new minority, but that attitude soon dissipated. In 1974 Speaker Akers announced, "We've got the responsibility for

Figure 13. Barr and district colleagues: Reps. Tony West and Jane Hull. Burton S. Barr Collection.

running this thing, and by God, we're going to run it."[102] He then unilaterally assigned Democrats to committees and allotted them far fewer seats than their proportion of the House membership. Two years later, however, with Frank Kelley as Speaker, Republicans chose to give Democrats their proportionate share of most committee seats. Later, when Art Hamilton was minority leader, Democrats functionally assigned their own members to committees. Barr was generally evenhanded in dealing with the opposition. His solution-oriented approach to governing enabled him to cooperate with Democrats in either house. Jack Brown, the House minority leader for two terms, sat behind Barr on the floor, deciding about "what we were going to do." He explained, "We worked together on a lot of things, and on a bipartisan basis were able to get some things done."[103] Barr's connection with Art Hamilton, as noted earlier, was even closer, and in both cases the relationship was cooperative but competitive.

Barr's bipartisanship caused problems. Besides some Republican "resentment" over his use of or "reliance" on Democratic votes, some Democrats also objected. Meetings with Art Hamilton occurred at Barr's office because Barr "always thought that he made Democrats crazy when he showed up on our turf." Barr's relationship with Alfredo Gutierrez was the most consequential, because Democrats controlled the chamber for two sessions and thereafter remained a relative strong minority—and because of Gutierrez. Nikki Corral said, "They were marvelous together. They were like frick and frack. They enjoyed each other. They played off each other. They fought amiably. And they seemed to complement each other intellectually."[104]

Gutierrez referred to their early discussions as "a conspiracy, because his caucus viewed me as evil," so instead of holding conversations on the floor of either house, "it was prudent that we do them privately." But while the content of individual conversations was private, their relationship, their partnership, was not. As Mr. Magic and Captain Chaos, Barr and Gutierrez played the legislative halls, crafting compromises, looking for votes, and passing legislation. Given the division among the Democrats—Gutierrez described Democratic Senate President Bob Stump (1974–1976) as "narrowly, narrowly conservative" and "contemptuous of the urban liberals"—Gutierrez quickly abandoned the notion of pursuing party-line votes: "If we did that, nothing would have happened." Fiscal policy was a primary reason for the triumph of this bipartisan partnership. If conservative Republicans rejected the leadership's budget, particularly if this action came later in a session, passage would require Democratic votes, and those were not free. Republican critics called it "shopping at Alfredo's store," because in exchange for supporting the budget, Gutierrez demanded the adoption of some policies that he favored.[105]

Barr's relations with the Senate combined the difficulties of working with conservative Republicans, negotiating with Democrats, and dealing with leaders of another chamber. The House-Senate conflict in Arizona resembled that in other state legislatures, but it was aggravated by the Arizona Senate's "upper house" syndrome rooted in the pre-Barr era, when Harold Giss won virtually every battle. For two decades, Barr almost completely reversed this pattern. After one House battle, Jim Skelly reflected a common verdict, saying, "The Senate doesn't have a chance with Burton Barr." Jon Kyl noted judiciously, "In the Senate, Burt was sometimes, somewhat resented," while Joe Lane was blunt: "The Senate hated Burt. I mean absolute hatred. They were so jealous of what he did." And some of the conflict was personal. One major senator, Lane noted, "could not stand Burt because Burt made him look like an idiot. But Burt was a doer, and people were very jealous of him."[106]

Barr's drive for action created tensions with the Senate from the start. He acknowledged this before the 1970 session, announcing, "We will be sure everybody, including the senators, knows just what we are doing." Conflicts built over the decade, as Barr recorded victory after victory over the Senate, and by 1980 journalist John DeWitt wrote, "Barr's reputation is so awesome that the Senate is showing distinct signs of paranoia." John Kolbe agreed, citing a "particularly virulent strain of paranoia which has infected the Senate's Republican majority—or, more accurately, a couple of its key members" and which had stalled any progress on education and tax programs. "So fearful were those key senators that House tornado Burton Barr is scheming some nefarious coup to overthrow their best-laid plans, they have become paralyzed from effective negotiating." But "trying to anticipate his plot" was foolish, Kolbe observed, since Barr was so flexible that he would adjust and win, however the Senators acted—and he did.[107]

In 1983 opposition to Barr became even more visible, as newspaper headlines announced, "GOP Senators Gunning for House Leader." Senate President Bob Usdane tried to explain the conflict by noting that senators were "a little jealous of Barr, who "has been a bone of contention in the throats of many people because of his effectiveness . . . his ability to solve problems and collect votes." He dropped that objectivity, however, by adding, "I guess it'd be kind of fun to win one over on him." Senate Majority Leader John Mawhinney tried to claim that competition between chambers was healthy and would lead to better programs, but he also criticized some senators who "think their primary function in life is to joust with

Barr." This was not, he suggested, "the best way to legislate . . . having lost so many battles with him in the past."

Conservative Senator Jeff Hill was particularly vocal and public in his criticism, demanding "No more of this unicameral legislature with Barr as majority leader, governor, committee chairman and everything else." Two weeks later the budget issue was resolved, and while Hill claimed some satisfaction, the newspaper headline announced: "Barr Biggest Winner in Debate over Budget." The following year, in response to another debacle, Senate President Stan Turley referred somewhat sadly to Senate Republicans as "a majority that thinks like a minority." The conflict had various dimensions: one was conservative frustration with Barr's policies; another was differences within the Senate; but another was Senate conflict with a united House, for as Art Hamilton explained, "Republican senators' conflict with Barr during the 1980s was accentuated because Barr and I worked so closely together, in many cases we worked out our differences and had a united position against the Senate."[108]

The Struggle for Leadership: Barr versus Babbitt

Even more consequential than intensified conflict between the two houses was the dramatic change in Barr's relationship with the governor. Provisions in the state constitution, political expectations, and the behavior of the state's governors had combined to produce a fairly weak governorship that was essentially dominated by the legislature. The postwar chief executives were able men who identified problems and requested legislative action, but they had relatively limited impact, in contrast with their counterparts in nearly all other states. The election of Sam Goddard in 1964 marked a slight shift, but mainly for how he perceived the role and his efforts to address significant topics, rather than for his ability to spur the legislature to act. His successor, Jack Williams, "was available for consultations and for resolving rifts, but he did not take strong positions and, in effect, let the legislative leaders work out their problems for themselves." Raul Castro, who was elected in 1974 but resigned after two years to accept a diplomatic appointment, never proposed an agenda to legislative leaders. He concluded that the legislature had greater power, so, he explained, "I worked more as an administrator than as a leader in formulating and executing public policy."[109] Secretary of State Wesley Bolin succeeded him but died after only four months, and he was replaced by the state's attorney general, Bruce Babbitt.[110]

Barr felt a commitment to anyone holding the office, regardless of party, and claimed, "My goal as a majority leader was to help them." This was a relatively simple task with Williams, who was cooperative but not assertive, and with Castro, who had a similar approach to the office. Thus, Barr's experience with governors up to 1978 taught him that the office was weak; in 1972 he had stated publicly, "The governor doesn't have any power." But this assessment was wrong. Governors had the veto power, they could summon the legislature into special session, they could command public attention—the bully pulpit—and, by the mid-1970s they had authority over an enhanced executive branch. What was lacking was a governor willing to use those powers and with the political savvy and ambition to do so.[111]

When Babbitt suddenly became governor in 1978, his political résumé was slim. A member of the well-known Babbitt family from the Flagstaff area, he graduated from Notre Dame, earned a master's degree in geophysics in England, and earned a law degree from Harvard. After working for the director of Volunteers in Service to America, he came to Phoenix and practiced law, and he won election as attorney general in 1974. His relationship with Barr started after Ted Babbitt, his cousin and Barr's close friend, asked Barr to help Bruce in his new office. For that reason, along with his inclination to aid new officeholders, Barr pushed the legislature to pass a statewide grand jury bill, Babbitt's top legislative priority, but not an issue on Barr's own agenda.

Prospects for future cooperation seemed promising when, the day after being sworn in as governor, Babbitt showed up unannounced at Barr's house wanting to chat. Troubled by a sore back, Babbitt asked if he could lie on the floor and talk from there, and Barr, amused, agreed. To an extent, this symbolized Barr's initial view of their relationship, with himself dominant and Babbitt in a subordinate position. After all, Babbitt's only political experience was one term as attorney general; Barr was 20 years older, he had been majority leader for 11 years, and he had been setting the direction for state government for some time.

Barr's immediate strategy was to help Babbitt, to suggest actions, and to make the governor a valued part of Barr's operation. But Babbitt had other ideas. Smart and politically ambitious, he was a centrist Democrat who avoided simple liberal and conservative labels. He had his own agenda, and soon showed his intention to be active and independent. He was, Alfredo Gutierrez claimed, "the most aggressive, assertive, ambitious, Governor we've ever had. He made things happen. He pushed, cajoled, laughed, irritated, preached, but he really got to understand the levers of state government."[112]

His most important power, Babbitt realized, was his veto, and he used it as previous governors had never done, or even thought about (see table 4).

Table 4. Gubernatorial vetoes, 1959–1986

Governor	*Years*	*# Vetoes*	*# Vetoes per Session*
Fannin	1959–64	11	1.8
Goddard	1965–66	10	5
Williams	1967–1974	12	1.5
Castro	1975–77	10	3.3
Bolin	1977–78	0	0
Babbitt	1978–1986	114	12.6

Source: Toni McClory, *Understanding the Arizona Constitution* (Tucson: University of Arizona Press, 2010), 124.

He started immediately, issuing 5 vetoes after taking office in 1978, and 21 in 1979. He used vetoes to direct the legislature regarding key items on his agenda, to push greater support for social services, and to prevent the legislature from reducing the powers of the executive branch. Particularly during Babbitt's first term, Barr was surprised and sometimes felt aggrieved when, instead of negotiating with Barr until they formally agreed on a measure, Babbitt would keep his own counsel and publicly veto a measure. Part of the problem, Peter Burns explained, was that "Burt loved the legislature, and Babbitt was the first Governor he'd ever known, probably, that could finesse the legislature." Babbitt could move more quickly, and he "had the intellect and the political acumen to do it," so legislative-executive relationship became "a little bit more competitive."[113]

Although Barr's anger was typically very brief, with Babbitt he made an exception. After a series of vetoes and political disputes in 1979, Barr stopped speaking to the governor for months, relying instead on intermediaries. Barr's excessive response brought an editorial rebuke from the *Arizona Republic.* On another occasion, when Babbitt outmaneuvered GOP politicking about a prison site, placing it in the heavily Republican district of the Senate majority leader and vetoing Republican efforts to change that decision, Barr and other Republicans were furious. More often than not, it was Babbitt who facilitated an end to these spats, often showing up at Barr's door with the morning newspaper. In one case, after Barr refused to speak with Babbitt for weeks after the governor had helped torpedo Barr's initiatives to control hospital costs, Babbitt arrived at Barr's Flagstaff cabin with his young son, and Barr relented.

The governor's power had grown in part because the state government had modernized and expanded. So, seeking to reduce that power, in 1981 the legislature passed a bill requiring legislative approval of any rule or regulation that would increase costs. Babbitt felt the measure wrongly handicapped the administration and vetoed it. John Kolbe reported that "Barr came unglued, purpling the air with expletives not often reserved for a personal as well as political friend." He threatened retaliation against the governor's agenda and then added the vetoed measure to an urban state lands bill, "daring the governor to veto a proposal dear to his heart."[114] Babbitt did not blink. He said he would veto the bill, and so Barr dropped his effort, killing for a time the urban lands bill, which he himself had worked for and supported. One Republican lawmaker described Barr's behavior as irrational, and few thought the regulation measure was so important as to warrant his reaction. The dispute had to do in part with ego and political advantage; Barr was troubled because Babbitt was proving to be a skilled politician, and one close observer claimed, "He has won, or appeared to have won, nearly every battle they've gotten into."[115]

The rivalry also resulted from differences in their positions and political styles. Magic was not enough for an executive leader. Babbitt had to operate and lead in public, not only in private negotiations. Besides working with the legislature, as governor he needed to explain his actions and to persuade the public; his ability to do so was vital to his political success. This differed from the accountability of individual legislators, even legislative leaders. But while Barr's style, his pride, and the executive-legislative differences help explain the collisions of these two men, Babbitt bore some responsibility. He came to the office thinking like a lawyer, negotiating on an individual case basis. He failed to realize that dealing with the same negotiating partners over many cases formed a history, and that in the long term, success required that he both respect the legislative negotiators and demonstrate a level of mutuality and sensitivity to their needs.

Various commentators have said that Barr and Babbitt had a love-hate relationship, but theirs was more like a fondness-fury connection. Their basic association was friendly but not close; and while each at some times felt anger toward the other, neither man ever exhibited fundamental hostility or hatred. Nor were their reactions the same: Barr became angry, uncharacteristically so, but Babbitt usually remained relatively detached. Despite their disputes and differences, however, they shared a mutual respect, a sincere regard for the other's political skills, ability, and vision for the state. This enabled them to cooperate very effectively on many major items, and this cooperation was crucial to the considerable success that each man experienced. Political calculation did color their relationship, as Barr often chided Babbitt for being ambitious and believed that led him into making mistakes.

A far more important political dimension to their relationship was the basic hostility that some Republicans, notably legislators, felt toward the governor. Barr felt some of that anger directed at him for working with the governor, even though he often tried to mask his efforts from the caucus. Despite occasional deviations on his part, Barr was clear about his basic goals: "Some people here would like me to be continuously at war with" Babbitt, but he refused to let important policies fail "just to make him look bad."[116]

Burton Barr and Legislative Leadership

Barr came to the legislature with a personality, skills, and values that made him well suited for leadership, and the unique character of that institution gave him special opportunities.

The length of Barr's leadership career gave him time to build a long list of accomplishments, but it also meant there was more risk of resentment and conflict. In several sessions, notably in 1975 and 1979, his House colleagues voiced considerable unhappiness with him, and some talked of replacing him. In one sense, these moments reveal his weakness, but they are better evidence of the complex reality in which he worked, a world of ambition, power, vision, and change. Successful leadership involves a blend of acceptance and challenge, continuity and change. Barr dealt with the challenges posed by the various elements of his legislative world and surmounted them.

Leadership comes in different forms. While certain traits are generally useful, the situation determines which of them are most necessary for success.[117] Barr's opportunity for leadership came at a particular point in history, a time when the state—particularly its urban elements—had grown dramatically, when the parties were changing, and when the need and direction for change were visible. Serving then, during Arizona's "modernizing moment," gave Barr a unique prospect for leading the legislature and the state.

Barr's success started with the traditional power of the Arizona legislative branch and expanded because reapportionment provided an impetus for change, as it did in other states. His support of legislative professionalization through reforming rules and creating a support system appreciably increased his effectiveness as a leader. These efforts paralleled but exceeded progress in other states, as Arizona moved from a low position in 1965 to near the top tier of effective state legislatures by the mid-1980s. But in three respects the Arizona situation and Barr's position were unlike those in other states. Barr's leadership grew because of lower, not greater, partisan polarization, highlighting the special character of this historical era and Barr's bipartisan disposition. Barr's effectiveness also came despite the reform of the executive branch and the governor's increased power. Finally, Barr was even more unlike nearly all other leaders because his preeminent power came not from holding the formal top position in a chamber, but from combining his personal strength with what was formally the second position; as noted earlier, his leadership was both personal and situational.

Many leadership studies identify transactional leadership as the dominant form of legislative leadership, and Malcolm Edwin Jewell and Marcia Lynn Whicker explain the central values of "bargaining, reciprocity, and payoff, guided by the values of fairness, tolerance, and trust."[118] They also distinguish a number of possible roles for legislative leaders, which can be summarized as: affecting policy output as gatekeepers, coalition builders, or negotiators; presenting and guiding policy as state, public, or party leaders; shaping participation and influence in the legislative process; and mentoring legislators or training themselves for higher office.

Barr excelled as a transactional leader, as Mr. Magic, successfully negotiating and building coalitions, guided by the essential values for legislation of integrity and fairness. He also made distinct choices about the leadership roles he filled. Unlike Harold Giss, he rarely functioned as a gatekeeper on policy, seeking instead to revise and modify proposals. He encouraged and rewarded participation, and he frequently mentored other legislators. Although Barr necessarily had a public role of sorts, speaking to the media about legislative matters and occasionally at public events, he left most of these responsibilities to others, preferring to be home with his family. And, for the same reason, he spent little time at party events, dinners, or the like. He understood that speculation about his seeking higher office could benefit him and occasionally considered the possibility, but he never viewed the legislature as a stepping stone to higher office.

Legislative leaders can sometimes reach beyond this, to what James MacGregor Burns first called "transformational leadership," by inspiring active followers, making leaders, and creating a vision. While this role is best suited to grassroots participation in politics and applies less well to a legislature, given its constraints and purposes, Barr did fulfill the central expectations of transformational leaders. Moving people beyond passive acceptance into followership and then leadership requires leaders to be role models, encourage initiative by their followers, and develop interactive relationships with them. Barr sought in several ways to inspire leadership, such as by being a mentor, but Barr went beyond an acceptance of that role to working actively to foster mentoring, even to his partisan opponents, Art Hamilton and Alfredo Gutierrez. Garry Wills argues that a *real* leader mobilizes followers not just for self-interest, but for a shared goal that they believe is *right.* At its best, Barr's leadership went beyond persuasion to become inspiration, convincing legislators of their shared goals and the need to act, even if not everyone agreed with the particulars.

CHAPTER FIVE

Burton Barr and Policy-Making in Arizona

"Burton Barr 'wrote the legislative history of this state for 20 years. There is hardly anything that got done that he didn't have his fingers on.'"

—JOHN KOLBE[1]

"He brought the state kicking and screaming into the twentieth century."

—ALFREDO GUTIERREZ[2]

"Whether it was water quality, freeway construction, child care, health care for the poor, shelter for the homeless and countless other issues, Barr was the taskmaster who made the system work."

—PATRICK CANTELME[3]

Postwar growth fundamentally recontoured Arizona, making it larger, urban, and high-tech, and posing new and thorny problems for Arizona's lawmakers. Much of the state's huge population increase was urban: by 1970 more than three-quarters of Arizona residents lived in cities. Phoenix and Tucson grew exponentially, but the population of old and new suburbs also exploded. Every city faced huge demands for added and expanded infrastructure, from streets and highways to schools and parks—not to mention the need for new types of facilities—and the speed of this change greatly increased the burden on cities. The awareness of growth and a sense of the newness of these communities forged an enthusiasm for change, and the many immigrants from other places brought new ideas and expectations.

Transformation of the state's economy occurred at a similar pace and scale. While prewar Arizona had produced raw materials, postwar expansion resulted from the deliberate and successful efforts to attract high-tech industries employing a more educated, better-paid workforce. The economy also benefited from federal policies that located defense manufacturing and military facilities in Sun Belt areas. These fundamental shifts involving urban life, manufacturing, and education defined the new and increasing needs of Arizona and the responsibilities of government.

Reapportionment of the state legislature in 1966 realigned the state's political representation with its new population and economic realities. Contemporaries viewed this very hopefully, and some observers, like Barr, would later describe it as the fundamental dividing point in the state's history, the demarcation between rural and urban dominance. But in 1966 the impact of that realignment was neither clear nor certain. Reapportionment did redistribute legislative seats to urban areas, but neither the use nor the form of that potential was inevitable. Describing actions or laws as "ideas whose time had come" can convey a false certainty to their passage, timing, and form; substituting hindsight for analysis can minimize the significance of what people accomplished. In 1966 Arizona's traditional forces remained within the legislature and the state, and they had experienced, able leaders who desired to maintain their authority.

But a growing array of Arizonans were eager to bring the state into a new era. In his 1966 Farewell Address to the legislature, Governor Sam Goddard summarized, "The needs that were not met this year were largely the needs of a highly industrialized, urbanized people and economy suffering rapid growing pains. This is the pattern of our society in Arizona now, and there is no turning back." After noting that "the old ways of meeting problems are gone," he concluded that "the promise of the new life" would be realized by "the young, new leadership of whom some fine examples are right here in this chamber today."[4] By the late 1970s the struggle for reform had shifted to include various Democratic legislative leaders and Governor Bruce Babbitt, but in the initial decade or so, urban Republicans provided the reform leadership. The new leaders like Bill Jacquin, Delos Ellsworth, and Sandra Day O'Connor—people with "big ideas," as Alfredo Gutierrez phrased it—led in defining issues and enacting them into law, but the largest figure in this entire group, the hub of the people and the process, was Burton Barr.

Understanding Barr's Policy Leadership

As the majority leader for two decades, Barr identified the major problems, forged politically workable solutions, and achieved their enactment into law. Jon Kyl said, "He had so much to do with so much during a tremendously dynamic period in the state's history."[5] Barr's vision was to modernize Arizona, Alfredo Gutierrez explained, and "He genuinely believed that this place could be a model for the nation."[6] Time after time, Barr was the agent who crystallized the elements of change. And legislative success had a cumulative effect, encouraging the adoption of additional laws and programs that responded to the new urban and economic realities.

One central part of this transformation, analyzed in the previous chapter, was Barr's role in revising the legislative culture so that it was geared toward solving problems through persuasion, compromise, and working across the aisle with Democrats. The second part, discussed here, was Barr's role in bringing about the policies that reformed and modernized the state. This is not a complete legislative history of the era. That would require assessing all the legislative battles, what bills passed and failed, and that would necessarily move too far away from Barr. The focus instead is on Barr's connection with all the major legislative accomplishments. Although he sometimes acted more behind the scenes, in most cases he was the catalyzing agent for success. As a consequence, some topics are covered and others are not. The general patterns of state spending are discussed, for example, but not detailed struggles over individual appropriations. Barr's role in tax policy, both increases and cuts, are highlighted because those were central to building the state's capacity and responding to popular pressures. Of course, judicial decisions, executive actions, and urban initiatives also influenced what happened, but the state legislature and Burton Barr confronted all of the issues central to Arizona's modernizing moment.

Barr entered the House with certain policy interests that he hoped might be enacted. His first priority was government efficiency, including reform of the tax system, and his second was health care, but becoming majority leader redirected his responsibilities and opportunities. Being on the chamber's two major committees, Rules, and Ways and Means, meant that he had direct committee responsibility for all major issues coming to the chamber. Barr's position also forced him to mesh his priorities in some way with those of House Republicans, but more often Barr was setting priorities for his colleagues. Sometimes his preferences triumphed, as John Kolbe phrased it, "almost entirely by sheer force of his energy and personality."[7]

Barr's instinctive approach to all situations, whether military, business, or political, was to plan, and this was an especially necessary tactic for dealing with the highly complex business of legislating. Besides the normal difficulties of working any measure from idea to law, good planning was crucial for legislative success because every legislative session could see new, unexpected proposals and some type of crisis or emergency. Barr did not simply react to last-minute proposals or the demands of individual legislators; he worked proactively, defining the top issues the legislature should handle during an upcoming session, setting his staff to work on these, and then often cosponsoring bills. He strongly supported and helped direct the legislative effort begun in 1967 to use interim committees to study questions and propose solutions. In 1970, for example, interim committees examined government reorganization, centralized licensing, uniform salaries for state officials, and a juvenile code, among other efforts to find systemic solutions.

Barr cared about and helped to draft proposals in many areas, but it is difficult to track his exact contribution in every case. Formal sponsorship of bills affords only a limited indicator of a lawmaker's ties with a measure. Barr often cosponsored bills, but major proposals typically had many cosponsors, and he less commonly appeared as the primary sponsor, especially after 1980. In part, this was strategic: he wished to spread credit and commitment to proposals, and he wanted the freedom to recast a bill to win passage. A greater obstacle to assessing his responsibility for legislation is that he touched virtually all of it and engaged actively with the major bills from an early stage through to their enactment into law. He helped generate or frame bills through his staff's intersession planning work, by serving on or chairing the main interim committees, through membership in advisory groups like the Council on the Organization of Arizona State Government, and by serving on the Legislative Council, which oversaw all interim committees. More importantly, as vice chair of the House Rules Committee, Barr touched every piece of legislation, affecting both the form and outcome. And as a member of conference committees and a negotiator with the Senate and the governor, Barr had a hand in every significant decision.

Barr's foremost continuing aim was the numerous measures for reforming government. Budget problems were constant and involved basic funding levels for various programs but especially K–12 education. For Barr and the Arizona legislature, taxes were an annual topic, especially cutting but also raising them, and these decisions yielded both political and policy consequences. Barr worked hard to modernize various social services, but he was deeply immersed in health-care problems on a continuing basis, and he was a central figure in fashioning the state's major health programs. Barr's participation was central to resolving disputes over water, most importantly, in the 1980 Groundwater Management Act. That truly landmark piece of legislation was produced by many hands, but legislative passage owes much to Barr's contribution.

Arizona's growing environmental problems, such as air quality and urban sprawl, attracted concerned participants, including Barr, and his political skills were essential in to the passage of related legislation. Meeting the state's escalating need to fund all levels of education required Barr's forceful leadership, as did the drive to build a highway system that met the needs of burgeoning urban areas. Finally, Barr led action on other items, from revising the criminal and juvenile codes, to the construction of correctional facilities.

Redesigning Government: The First Steps

Postwar Arizona state government was a mess. Small and decentralized at statehood in 1912, it had grown topsy-turvy over 50 years and become an ungainly, unstructured jumble. The 1949 Griffenhagen Report had laid out the basic problems. The state had too many elected officials exercising independent authority, while the governor's primary power was the initial appointment of (too many) officials, who then operated with impunity. State government mostly consisted of 115 loosely connected units. These operated under many undifferentiated labels, such as commission, board, and department; they were of random sizes; their selection reflected different requirements; they frequently performed mixed administrative, legislative, advisory, and/or judicial functions; and they often had overlapping jurisdictions and responsibilities, such as receiving fees, purchasing, or managing equipment. Especially problematic were commissions that operated basic services for counties and exercised excessive latitude in their decisions.

The Griffenhagen Report had landed on legislative desks with a dull thud, and for the next 17 years it gathered dust, but its principles and proposals attracted growing support in Arizona, bolstered by the example of other states and the encouragement of public associations. The first successful step occurred in 1966, when Barr won the establishment of a Budget Division, which was paired with the Joint Legislative Budget Committee and then a Legislative Budget Office. In the same year, a lesser measure but also following those same administrative principles reorganized the Parole and Pardons Board to focus on hearing cases while assigning the administrative functions to a full-time director. But major changes came in 1967, with the first reapportioned state legislature. Barr, whose initial campaign touted the need for a reliable "state tax base and responsible, orderly government at all levels," had led on the finance fight, and he now spearheaded the broader struggle for government reform.[8]

The state's tax system, like its financial system, had been a recognized failure for decades. Barr confronted the problems—and the forces resisting change—head on. Despite fierce opposition from major economic interests in the state, Barr and his supporters such as Stan Turley and John Pritzlaff held their ground. Relying on a statewide property survey previously mandated by the legislature, Barr led the successful fight for a state Property Valuation department, run by a director, that would make property assessments for county officials to send out, and a State Board of Property Tax Appeals. By reducing the powers of the county assessors and removing the State Tax Commission from dealing with property taxes (and setting it on the road to extinction), this law removed the inconsistencies and inefficiencies in the system, created basic equity in property taxes across the state, and thus provided an equitable basis for increased state revenues.

Other laws further demonstrated the legislature's use of the new principles of standardization, efficiency, and transparency. A scandal in 1966 over state liquor licenses had fueled a public uproar. In response, the legislature established a new State Liquor Board and superintendent for licensing, separated licensing and enforcement responsibilities, and shifted control of narcotics to the attorney general's office. Other government reforms that year were less dramatic but still meaningful, such as the reduction of administrative inefficiencies by adding a central purchasing division for the state's new finance department, a move Barr strongly supported. New areas of active responsibility were assigned to existing units: a division of consumer fraud was established in the attorney general's office (a measure Barr had cosponsored); the state Board of Health housed a new air pollution control agency. The legislature also formed advisory councils and other boards to meet assorted responsibilities. Notable characteristics of these new or reorganized entities were standard sizes, a shift from ill-defined commissions to boards with specific managerial authority, and use of staggered terms for members.

Critics of state government and its agencies, including Republicans not in power, newspapers, and businesses observing government, had often complained about political cronyism and that government employees were required to make political contributions. The legislature attacked those problems with a flurry of legislation that Barr cosponsored and worked for. A 1967 law prohibited bribery and corruption of public officers and employees, and a second statute banned public officers from being coerced into contributing funds for political activities. The legislature went further in 1968, creating a uniform merit system for state employees, with job classes and a prohibition on political influence affecting promotions. A law passed the following year added a further caveat, as public officers were explicitly enjoined from compelling political contributions from employees or other public officials. Barr also cosponsored two bills on ethics issues, one to establish a code of ethics for officials and employees, and another for a legislative code of ethics regarding bribery and corruption, but those did not pass at this time, nor did his proposal to register and regulate lobbyists.

Reorganization of existing agencies and venturing into new areas often went hand-in-hand. The specialized task of regulating insurance in the state was taken from the state's regulatory agency, the Arizona Corporation Commission, in 1968 and given to an appointed insurance commissioner, while a new Department of Mental Retardation in 1970 assumed the duties of a division of the state health department. Interest in promoting economic growth prompted the creation of an economic development advisory board. Recognizing the changing nature of the state's economy and dangers to its workforce, the 1968 legislature reformed the Arizona Industrial Commission. Expanded from three to five commissioners (now the generally preferred number for commissions), the commission was empowered to set safety standards and award workers' compensation, to hire a director to handle administration, and to designate hearing officers to hear cases. These actions mirrored Senate President Bill Jacquin's argument that "our state boards and commissions have got to be overhauled drastically, with modern business and enforcement powers so they can operate in today's modern society."[9]

Improving government also meant fixing conditions for government employees and officials. Recognizing that the woefully low salaries created hardship and reduced the pool of potential officeholders, in 1968 the legislature recommended that voters approve raising legislative compensation from a per diem amount limited to $1,800 for a regular session to an annual salary of $6,000, and raising travel allowances from $12 to $20 per day, and voters did approve this. At the same time, lawmakers raised salaries for state and county officials, boosted the pay of some county officials a few years later, and formed a state salary commission to remove the issue, as much as possible, from political squabbling. Steps were also taken to remedy other failings: the number of county supervisors was raised to five, a commission was created to determine judicial qualifications, and the term of office for state officials was extended, with voter approval, from two to four years. Finally, and most consequential, voters approved a legislative measure that eliminated the elective offices of state auditor and of state examiner, replacing the former with an appointed position of state finance commissioner.

These reforms triumphed over different types of opposition but typically involved the redistribution of power. The proposals to fashion a budget division and restructure the state property tax system prompted hard-fought battles with the state's ruling economic interests. Another modernization measure provoked the complaint that standardization removed the traditional discretionary authority exercised by boards or local authorities. Dissent was often based in an older political ideology, a Jeffersonian belief in local governance, and a suspicion of power. This philosophy had appeared in debates before reapportionment, but it was especially evident afterward because Republicans pushed for expanded state authority and standardization, while Democrats continued to champion the powers of local officials. Representative Jack Brown, the House minority leader for several sessions, opposed the state property tax reform bill in 1967 because "too much power was taken away from the assessors." Brown also dismissed arguments that centralizing state purchasing would be cost effective, labeling it "just a big-city bill designed to give Phoenix and Tucson all the profitable purchasing."[10]

Brown's objections reflected the partisan balance in the House, where 31 of 34 Republicans came from the two urban counties, while 15 of 26 Democrats represented the rural counties and agreed with Brown's Jeffersonian notions. Partisanship also tinted objections to eliminating the state auditor's office, for Jewel Jordan, who had held the office since 1950, was one of only two Democrats still holding a major statewide office. Republicans argued that partisanship had not inspired the proposal, and while they did not mind the partisan side benefit, the idea came from several nonpartisan studies and fit the structure of most other states.

Reconstructing State Government

The measures enacted from 1966 to 1971 followed the standards of efficiency, uniformity, and transparency. They placed government officials and employees in more protected and financially secure positions, and they reorganized agencies by separating administrative, advisory, and judicial responsibilities. But these changes had essentially provided examples for a more basic and much larger task of reorganizing state government. Serious preparation for this had been ongoing since 1967, with the creation of the Council on the Organization of Arizona State Government. The Council, with Barr as a member, had commissioned a report on state government, and its recommendations concerning the state auditor and examiner had been enacted in 1968, but the report also offered many additional suggestions for future implementation. In 1970 an interim House committee on state government organization picked up part of this challenge by a detailed study of particular topics, but in 1971 the House Governmental Affairs Committee, using Barr's House research staff, wrote a report recommending a dramatic, almost wholesale restructuring of state government.

After a decade of study and with a clear momentum for change, the legislature zoomed into action, and from 1972 to 1974 it enacted sweeping revisions in the structure and functioning of state government. While not every proposal was adopted as offered, the result closely resembled the committee's recommendations.[11] The desire for better overall management of the executive branch led to the formation of a Department of Administration, which included the newly created finance unit, encompassing the budget division, and the purchasing division, along with additional units like accounting and planning. The Department of Economic Security, proposed by an interim committee, combined eight state agencies dealing with employment issues and, most important, replaced county welfare commissions, which had operated using idiosyncratic standards. While funding would remain an issue in years to come, a clear and responsible structure now existed.

In a simpler and less dramatic shift, the Transportation Department combined the old Highway and Aeronautics Departments. A seemingly similar change—forming a Department of Revenue and eliminating the Tax Commission—had more far-reaching consequences, since this gave the governor more fiscal authority and standardized some features of the tax system. A final major improvement was fashioning the Department of Health Services from a hodgepodge of health-related commissions to assume responsibility for community, children's, behavioral, and mental health. In all of these developments, Barr was a moving force. Six months before the new health department was established, he detailed its structure, removing environmental health and including mental health. In explaining why the state health board would be eliminated, he articulated one of his guiding principles: "The governor should stand or fall on his record," and not be forced or able to blame a board. By contrast, Democrats continued to oppose reorganization for giving the governor too much authority and as adding "another whole layer of expensive, self-serving bureaucracy in state government."[12]

Subsequent years saw some further reforms following the principles established during this spate of reorganization measures. In 1975 the State Real Estate Department was reorganized, with the commission being relegated to serving as an advisory body. A sunset law for government agencies began in 1978, requiring that offices periodically justify their continued existence. The Atomic Energy Commission was altered in 1980 from a promotional to a regulatory body, and a Racing Department was created in 1983 with distinct regulatory functions. And in 1985, after years of discussion, the legislature established a Commerce Department as an administrative home for the state's array of programs promoting economic development.

Barr was deeply involved in these reorganizing and professionalizing decisions. In the initial stages he was an active and visible participant on particular measures, pushing through the finance system and the property tax reform, as well as sponsoring additional reform legislation. After he became majority leader, his contributions expanded to planning legislation, building public support, framing and revising proposals, and working for their adoption. But because Barr was a leader of the chamber and because these measures had so many visible supporters, the importance of his contributions was not always fully evident.

Barr's initial view of government reform as an effort to achieve greater efficiency prompted his support for improving state government and expanding its powers at the expense of local authorities, who seemed too likely to act in arbitrary and inequitable ways. But Barr also recognized the modernization, professionalization, and expansion of state governments and gubernatorial offices across the nation. He understood these as a necessary response to the increasing challenges of postwar society, and he increasingly believed that state government should be active in numerous policy areas. This perspective was also central to his views of federalism. Barr supported the notion of "New Federalism," articulated most prominently by President Richard Nixon but discussed widely at the state level, and he believed in a "competitive federalism." State governments, and notably the legislature, he felt, should be the "decision-maker on national issues such as health, welfare, environmental controls. It's up to us to formulate the state's posture and then—and only then—go to the feds."[13] Only a well-structured, well-managed state government could balance those responsibilities.

Fixing Taxes

Peter Burns claimed, "Besides just the art of politics, Burt had two passions in terms of what did he like to do in public policy. One was taxation, especially property taxation and school finance, and the other was health care."[14] Both were central problems during this period, but taxation politics and policy were always at or near the top of his agenda. His fascination dated back to his college education and business background, and it was sustained by his innate skillfulness with numbers. It was also a functional part of his leadership duties, since being majority leader put him on the Ways and Means Committee. But the primary reason for Barr's interest was his understanding that taxes were a trip wire for state politics and that tax policy determined revenues and thus limited what programs were possible. Arizona tax policy was particularly significant during Barr's era because of changing economic circumstances but also because it was tied to a virtual regime change, evident in the fundamental shift in power to urban, industrial forces, the reallocation of taxes, and the major restructuring of Arizona's system of government.

By 1961 Arizona relied primarily on various sales taxes (65 percent), state property tax (14 percent), and income tax (8 percent), as well as various fees, for its revenue.[15] Each tax presented possibilities and complications. In addition to the general sales tax, there were sales taxes on specific items, like gasoline taxes, whose revenues were restricted to designated purposes, plus others that targeted the state's winter visitors. State property taxes were linked to state taxation for and spending on education. Sales and income taxes had been initiated in the 1930s, and since then, taxation policy had included adjusting rates for the different types of taxes. In 1965, for example, the legislature increased the state gasoline tax, the cigarette tax, the sales tax on restaurants, and the rates of the state income tax. During Barr's era, and to a fair extent because of his choices, state policy was more focused. Initially, it centered on policies related to urban interests, by the early 1970s it dealt more with tackling inflation, and a decade later it changed to address several funding crises.

In 1967 Barr helped lead the Arizona legislature to resolve a taxation problem that had worsened and festered for over 25 years. The state's decentralized tax "system" allowed counties to determine property assessments and tax rates for different categories of property, and by the 1950s the inequities were producing growing criticism from all sides (as noted in chapter 3). Governor Fannin devoted his entire annual message in 1963 to the topic, but to no avail. What finally forced action was a lawsuit by the Southern Pacific Railroad, for the Arizona Supreme Court ruled that unless the legislature created an equitable system using different assessment percentages and property classifications, property of all types would have to be assessed at full value. In 1966 the legislature had mandated a statewide assessment of property but had not devised the system.

The newly apportioned 1967 legislature accomplished that task, with leadership from Barr, Speaker Stan Turley, and Senate President Marshall

Humphrey, and in doing so they fundamentally altered the state's entire tax system. As the *Arizona Republic* explained, "The legislature shifted a very substantial part of the tax load from the homeowners to other interests."[16] Its most important decision set different tax rates on the assessed value of different types of property: 60 percent for mines, railroads, and timber; 40 percent for utilities; 25 percent for other businesses; and 18 percent for farms and homes. This generally reduced residential property taxes but increased taxes for other property owners, notably utilities and railroads, and it generated what Barr called "extraordinary" opposition from interests who considered this proposal "the destruction of the state as they knew it."[17]

The bill's second major feature changed the funding of K–12 education, which had come mostly from local and state property taxes. The new measure substantially boosted state funding from $80 million to $143 million, but that came from revenues other than property taxes. This raise came with a proviso, however, restricting increases in local school taxes to 6 percent per year, unless voters approved more. Finally, the state explicitly recognized and sought to ameliorate some disparities in district resources by providing a $12 million equalization fund. To pay for the increased commitment to education and the property tax reduction, the legislature raised income taxes, plus taxes on cigarettes and liquor, and added new levies on equipment and rental property. Educational funding was not a problem that could be permanently solved, however. Increased population and school costs, differential levels of wealth in school districts, and the nature of property taxes periodically returned the problem to the top of the legislature's agenda. In 1974 and 1980 the legislature had to struggle again to establish new levels of spending, distribution, and control, but the 1967 legislation was fundamental, for it accepted the state's overall responsibility for education and its obligation to counter differences in districts' financial resources.

Rural forces and many major businesses vigorously opposed this plan, as did most Democratic lawmakers, but urban interests, supported notably by Eugene Pulliam, owner of the two Phoenix newspapers, and the votes of urban Republican legislators, produced a victory. By shifting some of the tax burden to the state's major economic interests, urban residents had established a more equitable basis for increased state revenues and taken a crucial step in adjusting the distribution of power and opportunity within the state. "It's better than I had ever hoped we would have," Barr said, voicing the sentiments of many.[18]

An additional tax policy affected by an urban-rural division was the state's gasoline tax. Those revenues had originally been apportioned to provide roads across the state, a reasonable decision given the state's population and its needs. By 1960, however, this allocation still benefited rural areas disproportionately and ignored the changed reality in which cities' needs for streets, bridges, and overpasses, not to mention highways, were growing exponentially. Efforts to improve this began in the early 1960s, increasing the tax to 7 cents, and, in 1965, with a designated share going to counties (17.6 percent) and to cities (8.7 percent). This added revenue was still very insufficient to deal with urban problems, however, so the drive to boost funding for cities continued. By 1973 Barr was the point man on this drive, chairing an interim committee on the subject, and in 1974 the tax was raised to 8 cents and the share to cities was doubled.

The Rise and Fall of Property Taxes

By 1973 the success of those efforts and the worsening problem of inflation pushed the legislature to begin shifting its modifications of tax policy from redressing urban grievances to reducing property taxes. During the 1970s one of the most visible impacts of inflation was the jump in property values. The resulting rise in property taxes affected everyone in some way, but it particularly burdened people on fixed incomes, and it was especially problematic because property taxes funded education. Barr began addressing the problem in 1973, and almost annually over the next dozen years he and his staff created tax plans directed at reducing property taxes through rebates, lowering the rates, or changing the assessment mechanism. Starting with the House Ways and Means Committee, of which he was the vice chair, Barr sought support for his plans, compromising where necessary, and winning legislative approval for most of what he had proposed. The end result was rather striking, for by 1986 the rate had been dropped from $1.75 per $100 of property value to $0.38.[19]

The planning and politics around property tax legislation meant deciding about how much to cut but also who should be helped. While all homeowners benefited from general cuts, during several years concern for people on fixed incomes yielded additional consideration for the elderly. Homeowners directly felt the impact of increased rates, but advocates for renters argued that they were also affected, since rents were being raised to cover increasing taxes on those properties. Consequently, in 1976 and 1978 the legislature gave tax breaks to renters. Legislators also deliberated over what kinds of tax relief to offer. In most years, they made permanent cuts through rates or assessment, but on occasion they offered one-time rebates on taxes paid.

A primary consideration in every case was making up for the lost revenues. In 1973 Barr had posed a broad view of tax policy, observing, "If the tax base was tipped more toward income or sales" it would "more reflect a person's ability to pay than on inflated [property] values."[20] In 1974 the legislature followed Barr's early analysis by raising sales and excise taxes to compensate for cutting property taxes, but that was the last attempt to adjust the balance between different types of taxes. Even the income tax was cut slightly in 1978 and 1981. A second approach was to reduce expenses, and Barr periodically spoke out about the need to lower government spending. In 1977, for example, he even claimed that education could be cut, that state universities "have gotten grandiose ideas," that K–12 education "should get back to basics too," and that the costs of special education needed to be closely examined.[21] Calls like these did hold down spending, but the problem was largely resolved because the state's population growth and general prosperity kept generating more revenue. Even with the various tax cuts, from 1970 to 1980 real revenues—that is, controlling for inflation—doubled.

But if this balance of tax cuts and revenue growth looks manageable in retrospect, it was less clear at the time. By the late 1970s tax revolts were spreading across the country, and passage of Proposition 13, which severely restricted property taxes in California, showed what voter frustration and fears could produce. Peter Burns remembered, "When Burt saw Prop 13 pass, he was sure that that was an issue here," and so he began thinking about how to respond should tax protests arise in Arizona. Barr's political instincts were right. Bill Heusler, a political gadfly from Tucson, spearheaded a drive that placed a voter initiative proposing severe tax restraints on the 1980 ballot.

An additional reason for adopting a broader approach to tax revision was that education faced growing constraints. Over the years, state support had fallen from over two-thirds to less than half of schools' budgets, while the seven-percent limit on increasing school budgets had handicapped many local districts. Moreover, sharp inequities in tax rates existed because districts with large industries received those tax revenues and thus could adopt substantially lower home property rates than other districts.

In November 1978, Governor Babbitt appointed a commission on taxation in preparation for a special legislative session in 1979, but as John Kolbe noted, this would not be effective since it was competing with "a clout-laden legislative committee" assisted by "some bright and experienced staffers" and "chaired by none other than Burton Barr."[22] By the following September, Barr had run basic training seminars for legislators and held hearings for citizens in preparation for the special session, which began in November 1979 and ran until April 1980. In the end, the legislature produced a complex combination of legislative measures and constitutional amendments that satisfied a wide range of interests.

Homeowner property taxes were restricted to 1 percent of their full property value, with limits on the increase in the annual assessment and the annual tax increase. The constraints on state government spending were clarified; holding down spending by local government and community college districts, but with allowance for voter-approved taxes; and the debt limits for local governments and school districts were raised. The state sales tax on food was abolished, which pleased liberals, but the loss of that revenue thwarted conservatives' desires to provide greater property tax reductions. The mining companies, which had complained about their higher assessment classification and had recently closed mines because of declining copper prices, benefited from a drop in their assessment from 60 percent to 40 percent, with additional reductions to follow.

A final element of the bill was improving the funding for education. The state established a clearer formula, defining a state-guaranteed basic support level and adding funding depending on student characteristics and local spending based on property taxes, which the state would restrict. The most important change was "recapture," whereby the substantial property tax revenue from major industries, which had been going only to subsidize the low tax rates of their local districts, would now be distributed statewide. It was, Art Hamilton later concluded, "a real testament to Burt's ability to bring incredibly disparate groups of people together and figure out how to get it done. And I think it is probably one of his greatest legacies."[23]

The entire package of legislation was very cleverly designed, offering something to many different interests. Barr, the chief architect, along with Senator Ray Rottas, immediately set out to win public support for these measures. He raised money for the campaign, and in the June special election, all ten of the proposed constitutional amendments passed by 4–1 margins. Next came the general election in November, where Heusler's Proposition 106 threatened a much severer restriction on taxation and government spending. Barr also led the public campaign against Proposition 106, raising money, speaking in public, and organizing other opponents. The election results were decisive, as 70 percent of Arizona voters rejected the proposal.

The 1980 legislation did not mark the end of property tax reductions: in 1981, 1984, and 1986 the legislature further lowered the basic rate. But the primary dynamic on taxes had shifted because of a decline in the state's economy, part of a national economic recession. By 1982 the economy had begun to slow, and in 1983 real revenue was roughly 20 percent below the 1980 level. The legislature responded by slashing spending, but vital needs required more revenue. This scenario was what critics of the 1980 cuts had warned about, but Barr had pushed for those cuts because he feared more severe cuts and a loss of flexibility. Now he waited until recognition of the crisis had overwhelmed House Republicans' earlier stand against a tax increase, and he won legislative approval for a one-cent increase in the sales tax for 13 months.

But in November, with the economy still in the doldrums, Barr realized that it might be necessary to extend that tax. Speaking to the Arizona Chamber of Commerce business roundtable, he outlined serious spending needs, such as flood repair (bridges and highways), more prisons, health care for the indigent, and education, and made a surprising comment: "I said it—that we will never let the sales tax (increase) continue. I don't know what it will taste like to eat those words, but if that's what it takes, we're going to have to do it."[24] By spring, when the legislature met, conditions were no better, and Barr moved into action. Speaking to the caucus, one reporter wrote, "He waved his arms, he wiggled his eyebrows, he slammed his fist on the podium and talked about the good of the state. He whipped out his overhead projectors and his Xeroxed copies. It was an oratorical fandango, a conga line of rationalizations."[25] In the end, the caucus agreed with Barr's reluctant assessment, and the legislature made the sales tax increase permanent.

A final tax problem confronting Barr was the recurring one of the gas tax. The 1974 law had increased the rate and cities' share of the revenues, but urban needs had continued to grow. Barr responded in 1981 by getting the legislature to boost the tax and allot a larger share to cities, but this prompted a petition drive by a diverse coalition of opponents, which prevented the implementation of the tax and threatened to repeal it when the vote was held. At a meeting that included Babbitt, whose election was imperiled by this issue, and Terry Goddard, a leader of the petition drive, Barr moved instantly to find a solution. "Where there had been this rather amorphous meeting of some very important people in the city," Goddard said, "when Barr got there, suddenly it had purpose, it had energy, and he asked some of the toughest, most directed questions about things that clearly hadn't been completely thought through by me or my supporters in this petition effort."[26] Barr decided to have the legislature pass a new measure—thus killing the initiative—which would include money for buses (a major concern of petitioners), and the tax would be raised over the next two years from 8 to 13 cents. Which is exactly what the legislature did in 1982.

This provided good, incremental improvement, but important leaders in Maricopa County argued that critical transportation needs in the

Figure 14. Floor work: Barr and Reps. Joe Lane, Mark Killian, Jim Ratliff, and Bob Denny. Photo by Mari Schaefer, *Tucson Citizen*, April 7, 1984.

Valley required the prompt construction of a highway system in the county. To provide the sizable funds this would require, they wanted to enact a half cent sales tax. They brought the proposal to Barr, who received it enthusiastically. The legislature proved unwilling to enact another tax or to allow the county to do it, but agreed to refer the issue to the voters. Jack DeBolske recounted, "Barr was in the forefront of that . . . campaign and everything else." The voters ultimately approved the measure and DeBolske concluded, "I don't think without him we would have probably made it."[27]

Caring for Health Care

Barr's second policy passion was health care, and he displayed his interest in this topic from the time he entered the legislature. While he did not talk about any personal reasons for his concern with health care, his experience of spending a year in the hospital and in recovery while in the army must have influenced him. He also had a private awareness of health costs, after his infant daughter spent 48 hours in the hospital in 1970 and the bill was $1,000. But beyond his personal reasons, he was interested because health care concerned everyone and was becoming one of the most troublesome public policy questions. Beginning as just one of various social propositions in the 1940s, it became linked with helping the elderly and indigent in the mid-1960s, but by 1970 it morphed into a major problem concerning the entire population.

While rising costs and decreased access constituted the essential difficulties, health care included many interrelated parts, each of which could seem more challenging at different times. Efforts to fix health care involved a fluid system, serious problems, and powerful interests. Given Barr's focus on identifying and solving problems, it is no wonder that he worked so hard on this one. His initial goals for health-care policy were extremely ambitious, and judged by that standard, his record was successful but incomplete. Yet recognizing the issue's enormous complexity, its shifting dimensions, and the divisions surrounding it, and comparing it with efforts on the national level, clarifies the import and value of what he accomplished.

Barr began working on health care in 1965, when he introduced legislation enabling Arizona to participate in the federal Kerr-Mills program. Created in 1960, this limited initiative provided some federal matching funds to cover "medically needy" elderly persons not receiving public assistance. (This program was surpassed in 1965 by the Medicaid Program, a much more comprehensive program discussed below.) In 1966 Barr cosponsored several other measures, including one to exempt from legal liability a physician who gave emergency aid.

Over the next five years, Barr's perspective on health care matured and expanded. While Medicare offered health care to the elderly, and Medicaid addressed health care problems for the indigent, the general population confronted rapidly rising costs and diminishing access. Health-care costs rose quickly in the 1960s, hospital costs most dramatically, but doctors' fees, and the cost of drugs, medical equipment, and tests also rose at alarming rates. Paying for "normal" health care was costly enough, but the danger of catastrophic events forced analysts to reconsider the relative roles of private insurance and government programs and to think about all of the factors affecting health care. Barr's position as majority leader expanded his initial awareness, given his responsibility and his opportunities such as chairing a special committee on hospital costs. He became more proactive in looking for solutions when he traveled to California to learn more about alternative health-care delivery systems, and to Washington,

DC, to speak with federal officials about using new approaches in connection with federally funded programs.

In 1970 he began offering legislation to deal with specific facets of health care, but in his discussions with reporters and his speeches before various groups in the early 1970s he displayed an insightful analysis of the breadth and long-term dimensions of health care in Arizona and the nation. With the backdrop of national discussions about possible national health-care reforms, with plans being offered by Senator Edward Kennedy and President Richard Nixon, Barr discussed actions at the state level. Describing Arizona's health-care industry as "a mess" and the system as "doomed," Barr said, "The cost of health care is way beyond the capacity of 85 to 90 percent of the population without a very comprehensive insurance plan," adding, "If the family is faced with a very serious illness of any kind, most policies would be inadequate."[28]

In Barr's efforts to structure a comprehensive insurance system, a reporter noted, Barr met in December 1970 "with federal officials about making the entire state a health maintenance organization (HMO) that would use state and federal funds to develop multiple health delivery and financing systems." With considerable insight, Barr argued against centering health care on "expensive hospital facilities," and instead promoted "low-cost preventive medicine designed to keep people out of hospitals, the use of out-patient clinics and para-medical personnel to assist physicians with more routine medical chores." He concluded that "the whole system is designed purely for crisis care," and that it put hospitals at the center: people could only get insurance payments if they went to hospitals, while people without insurance or those unable to pay, left their debt with the hospitals. Insurance companies, Barr argued, simply passed along their increased costs to the public as higher premiums, further reducing the number who could afford insurance. Medical specialization added to higher costs, while "the doctor bases his medical care on your insurance policy." Barr also faulted the leadership of the medical profession, saying that it had "resisted every change in the last 40 years."[29]

Barr also contemplated the future. Predicting that health care would become "the greatest single expense in this country's history," he anticipated a great increase in the number and variety of health-care-related jobs, and he predicted that nurses and physician assistants would come to assume more of doctors' responsibilities. In 1974 he asserted that some form of national health insurance was "a sure thing," but connected this with admonitions about the dangers of inaction. Allowing the existing problems with health care to worsen, he counseled, would result in "socialized medicine" and ultimately mean that doctors "will not be independent practitioners any longer." He repeatedly warned about the danger of unilateral federal action as a reason for taking private and state actions to deal with the problems. "In the long run," he said, "change is coming. We're just trying to work out our own changes in Arizona."[30]

In 1971 Barr introduced five bills relating to health care, all involving some planning and with a broad view about the direction for health-care reform. Two bills were ultimately enacted. One funded an effort by the Arizona Health Planning Authority to develop a total health plan for the state, a beginning step to craft an insurance plan and regulate costs. The second required hospitals to post their rates and get permission from the state health commissioner before starting any new construction. A third bill, which Barr had stressed but was not funded, would have started a health plan for state employees to be used as a model for the state. Over the next several years, Barr pushed additional legislation, with some success. He got the state to authorize the creation of health maintenance organizations (HMOs), to allow the licensing of physicians assistants and nurse practitioners, and to expand the state's involvement in health-care planning and control of hospital construction.

Barr frequently spoke about the problems of health care in Arizona and possible reforms. Concerned about the limited availability of doctors in rural areas, he urged the University of Arizona Medical School to encourage its graduates to practice for a short time in rural areas. To encourage compliance with this goal, he suggested that the school was accepting too few students and too many non-Arizonans, and that it was producing too many doctors interested in specializing. He also recommended that a two-year public service commitment by beginning doctors might help solve the problem, and said if private solutions did not emerge, that government would have to step in.

One partial solution to this problem, he believed, and a valuable improvement to health care generally, would be the expanded use of physician assistants to provide basic diagnoses and care. He had expected more results from the enabling legislation he had pushed through, and he strongly criticized as overly restrictive the licensing rules that the state medical association had successfully demanded. He dismissed their warning that physicians assistants would provide "second-class medicine," arguing, "If you haven't any medicine available at all, you are in trouble." Barr also spoke critically of hospitals for overbuilding. He recommended that they "become public utilities," and that a state commission should set their rates. While he supported hospital improvements, he argued, "The way we are going to reduce the cost is to keep people out of hospitals, not put people in them."[31]

Public discussion of health care shifted to a new worry in 1975, when the last insurance company providing medical malpractice insurance in Arizona announced it would stop writing policies in 1976. In response, the legislature formed a joint committee, chaired by Barr and Senate Majority Leader Alfredo Gutierrez. Meeting in the fall, the committee crafted a balanced bill with provisions for creating new insurance companies, providing malpractice tort reform, and strengthening the regulatory powers of medical examining boards. What Barr and Gutierrez managed to get through the legislature was rather different, for the law simply allowed the Arizona Medical Association to create a malpractice insurance company for Arizona doctors. Contending with doctors who wanted no increase in supervision, lawyers who resisted any changes in tort law, critics who disliked protecting doctors, and others who wanted to add an anti-abortion provision, the floor managers of the bill were compelled to eliminate key provisions of the original proposal. But for Barr, who recognized that having malpractice insurance available was essential for keeping physicians in the state, this was still a success.

From Medicaid to AHCCCS

Creating a health-care system for the indigent was a complex and torturous task that spanned Barr's entire legislative career. The Medicaid program proposed to replace a county-based program with one administered by the state and funded by the federal government. Constitutional and political considerations forced changes, delays, and repeal, but then new circumstances led to the adoption of a substantially different proposal. As a result, Barr pushed for this program, in one form or another, from the early 1970s until he left the legislature in 1986. Finally, divisions over the programs threatened Barr's leadership position, and prompted serious political divisions. On one level this was a struggle over providing health care for indigents, but as the previous analysis shows, Barr viewed the issue of indigent care as part of an overhaul of the entire health-care system, and he used this to push for broader changes.

The 1965 Medicaid law offered matching funds to states, helping them provide medical coverage to low-income people and people with certain disabilities. While the federal government defined general guidelines, the program was administered by states, which had considerable leeway in determining standards for eligibility and benefits. After implementation started in 1967, states began participating in the new system, and after Alaska finally signed up in 1972, Arizona became the lone holdout. The state remained outside the system for several reasons. Conservative objections to a federal program, which they considered socialized medicine, motivated many people, including the Arizona chapter of the American Medical Association. They preferred to retain the traditional county system. Others worried that expanding coverage would produce escalating costs, and the projections put forward by some critics, including one of Arizona's health commissioners, were frightening. Still others looked fearfully at a large bureaucracy and fretted about inefficiency and corruption.

But other forces, including social liberals and those critical of local government failures, argued for participating in this vital initiative. As the awareness and concern about poverty grew, the state's failure to assist its needy citizens increasingly seemed callous. The unwillingness to use available federal funds seemed fiscally imprudent. And criticism mounted of the county-operated system, funded primarily by property taxes, with its wide and growing disparities in eligibility, benefits, and facilities. One of the county problems that raised strong criticism was the Maricopa County Hospital. Describing it as "a disaster and a shameful thing," Alfred Gutierrez explained that Barr had tried unsuccessfully to get additional funds for it in the 1960s. By 1972, when Gutierrez campaigned for the senate and proposed replacing it with "a decent hospital through Medicaid," Barr was also pushing strongly for better options. Described by Athia Hardt as "a longtime critic of the county system," Barr proposed to replace it with a system in which the poor would be cared for in "private hospitals and have it paid for by the state and the federal government." Three months later, in February 1973, Barr advised county supervisors that hospitals would eventually be regulated like public utilities and urged them to wait before building five health clinics, because he expected Arizona would create a Medicaid program. He also argued that this program "should be handled through private insurance companies and by the contracting-out for services."[32]

Over the next year, Barr worked with other leaders, including Republicans Stan Akers, Bill Jacquin, and Sandra Day O'Connor, as well as Democrats Craig Daniels, Jones Osburn, and Alfredo Gutierrez, to build support for a proposal. In 1974 a House bill was bottled up in the Senate Appropriations Committee until Barr used a clever parliamentary maneuver: he attached the proposal to a minor Senate bill, thus forcing the measure to the Senate floor, where it passed, with the aid of Democratic votes. The product of various compromises, the bill attempted to avoid several perceived difficulties. It restricted benefits to groups covered by the Medicaid mandate; it used fixed payments to HMOs; it expended current county funds for indigent health care to match the new federal dollars; and it was scheduled to begin in October 1975. Problems appeared immediately, but the legislature resolved them in 1975. The revised measure restricted access to reduce the cost, it changed the county contribution from specific dollar amounts to a ratio, and since the matched funds had to come from the state, it allocated state monies but had counties reimburse the state for the cost. And, as a response to conservatives, it further delayed implementation until July 1, 1976.

By early 1976, however, fears were rising about the cost of the program, with stories appearing about other states, describing escalating costs as well as problems with fraud. Conservative Republicans, pushing for tax cuts and lower spending, demanded that implementation be stopped. Governor Raul Castro favored the state program but would not request state funds to support it. Nevertheless, Barr continued to defend the measure. Before the showdown caucus meeting on the subject he announced, "We are not coming out of this caucus until we fund Medicaid," but he emerged from a bruising meeting after three and a half hours, having lost the fight. He then announced to the gathered reporters, "There is absolutely no way this state will fund the Medicaid program as we know it on the books. It just doesn't work."[33] Bowing to the caucus decision, Barr subsequently led Republican efforts first to delay and then in 1977 and 1978 to repeal the measure.

Barr's complete reversal of his position disappointed his Democratic allies like Art Hamilton and provoked sarcastic jibes from conservatives, some of whom viewed this as damning evidence of a superficial attachment to principle. But Barr accepted "that my own personal view can't be paramount," that the majority had the right to decide policy, even if he disagreed, and that the current financial and political conditions did not favor the program. He also did not believe in resigning over a single policy loss, arguing, "I want to be around again so I can come back with another idea, issue, or program."[34] And he soon proceeded to do exactly that.

He was aided in his renewed efforts by Governor Babbitt's determination to make progress on the issue. In the spring of 1979 Babbitt proposed getting Medicaid money by creating a program for poor children. After promising Barr that he would keep a low profile, he then publicly labeled opponents of the proposal "redneck legislators," which effectively killed the proposal and infuriated Barr. But both men remained interested in moving ahead, and the next two years saw various proposals for some kind of Medicaid program. Conservatives still opposed this, but public concern for people without health care was increasing. The inequalities between counties had become even more egregious, but the most compelling factor was the ballooning economic burden of indigent care on counties. These costs had risen during the 1970s, but the 58 percent jump between 1978 and 1979 ($118 million) and 1980 and 1981 ($186 million) seemed catastrophic. While the legislature provided stop-gap funding for the overruns, a major overhaul of the program was desperately needed.

During 1981 legislative leaders and Governor Babbitt drafted a proposal enabling the state to receive federal money but also protecting it against rising costs. Working with new ideas about managed competition, combined with other notions about managing health care, Barr and other state leaders negotiated with federal officials to receive a waiver from existing Medicaid requirements. The Arizona Health Care Cost Containment System (AHCCCS), enacted in October, was unique because it included prepaid capitation financing instead of the traditional fee-for-service funding; it would be operated by a private firm chosen after competitive bidding; and physicians were the primary gatekeepers to hold down the demand for services.

This prepaid managed care network was an innovative approach to providing indigent health care, and while many people worked to develop the policy, Barr's involvement was critical. Don Isaacson, who was one of those who actually wrote the legislation, said bluntly, "AHCCCS wouldn't have happened without Burt Barr." John McCain saw the crucial importance of Barr's political skills in achieving passage of this program, arguing, "The AHCCCS program is an outstanding and shining example of the kind of things that Burt was able to achieve when he had built relationships with his political friends, but more importantly relationships with his political adversaries."[35]

But the saga of Medicaid and AHCCCS had one more chapter to be written. The program lacked a clear administrative structure, and the private company providing service was unable to operate within the budgeted amount. As a financial crisis developed in the spring of 1984 and the private contractor pulled out, a new solution was desperately needed, and soon. Working quickly, Babbitt and Barr recruited Dr. Donald Schaller to run AHCCCS, Babbitt called a special legislative session, and Barr pushed through a bill allowing the state to administer the program. While conservatives worried about the shift to a state-run system, they saw the value of greater accountability. As the changes were implemented and with a few months' perspective, Barr declared, "I believe the AHCCCS concept is right. I am satisfied with the Schaller administration. I believe that in six months, they'll have the program turned around. The dark days are over."[36] And despite discussions about the level of funding, the structure of the program proved to be sound. In the end, Barr deserved substantial credit: for developing the initial support, achieving legislative enactment of two bills, keeping a commitment to fashion an innovative program, and working with all parties to achieve a solution.

Water

Arizonans have always been concerned about water, and they have worked persistently to increase the supply. Patterns of water use by various parties were set in the years before statehood, with physical and legal systems designed to perpetuate these patterns. As a consequence, the state's political leaders pursued additional water sources, but they were almost entirely stymied by any proposals that involved usage. That conflict was vividly apparent in the postwar period, but Barr played a vital role in revising the state's water policy, helping to shift the pattern of usage to serve the burgeoning needs of urban users, and to assure the security of water sources.

From territorial days well into the twentieth century, agricultural boosters touted Arizona's soil and its water supply, especially after the creation of the Salt River Project and its storage capacity. Water was also necessary for mines, while the existence and expansion of cities depended on their ability to find water sources and to construct delivery systems. Since usage patterns were largely set in the early twentieth century, Arizonans focused on expanding the supply. This influenced that state's relationship with neighboring states, particularly from the 1920s to the 1960s, as it competed for Colorado River water, especially with California.

During the 1960s the state legislature determinedly asserted the state's intention to bring Colorado River water to central Arizona, and provided initial funding even before Congress authorized the Central Arizona Project (CAP) in 1968. The administrative mechanism was established in 1971, and construction of the expensive system of pumps, canals, and water storage began in 1973. State residents and leaders were overjoyed by this progress, coming after 50 years of conflict, but the need for this water had altered during the course of the struggle. With agriculture consuming 90 percent of the existing supply, and with seemingly little chance to revise that pattern, the burgeoning urban populations made cities the primary beneficiary for CAP water. A change in government highlighted this new reality. As part of the reform of Arizona government, the Arizona

Water Commission was reconstituted in 1971 from an older agency and given redefined responsibility for dam safety, managing watershed, and collecting hydrologic data. But two years later it received a different sort of task: reviewing the water plans for new subdivisions. Not only did this mandate explicitly involve the impact of urban development, it also moved from a focus on surface water to one on groundwater.

While the state had actively promoted acquiring surface water, legislative solutions for the problems of groundwater had been almost entirely ineffective. In 1948, after persistent pleas and with clear evidence that overdrafting of groundwater had substantially lowered the water table, the legislature had finally responded by prohibiting new wells in Critical Groundwater Areas, but it had placed no restrictions on drawing water from existing wells. Over the next three decades the problem worsened, with no political solution in view, but circumstances altered dramatically in 1976, with an Arizona Supreme Court decision. When the Anamax copper mining company proposed to pump water from one site to another, the FICO farming corporation objected, saying it would be harmed because pumping would reduce the amount of water available to it. The City of Tucson then sought to protect its water interests in the area, claiming that both FICO and Anamax were polluting the basin. In response, the mine objected to the city's transporting of groundwater. After reviewing all of the claims, the court's shocking ruling went against both the city and the mining company, threatening the water use by large numbers of people and major economic interests, but it had failed to explain how the groundwater areas should be defined.

The grave implications of this decision quickly made it a political issue. Barr and Gutierrez, who was now the Senate majority leader, looked to resolve this problem by bringing together representatives of agriculture, mines, and cities. But more than this, both men "believed that the state needed comprehensive groundwater management, and that the time was ripe." Interest in the topic was certainly great, but the longstanding political stalemate over resolving it rested in the parties' different interests, and those had not changed. In this particular slice of the larger conflict, mining companies needed to transport water, but they did not need increased amounts. Cities needed the added water they had been transporting and more, while farmers wanted to continue controlling 90 percent of the water supply. Despite differences and mutual suspicions, however, the parties reached a solution to the court's decision. Much of the success was due to the activities and strategies of Barr and Gutierrez. They hammered out compromises, threatening the parties with "disastrous consequences in the legislature if they did not negotiate." They then took the negotiated settlement to the legislature and forced it to vote the proposal up or down, without allowing amendment. It passed handily.[37]

In essence, the measure solved the issue of transporting groundwater, at least temporarily, by allowing mines to convey it in return for paying damages, when justified, to the affected farmers, and permitting cities to transfer water within their service areas. Barr defended the measure as a temporary solution, saying frankly, "It allows the state to operate until we can figure out how to manage our water resources on a long-term basis."[38] That larger purpose was Barr's goal, and he had incorporated it into the legislation. The measure established a 25-person commission to resolve not only the transportation question, but also the problem of water management, which was far more troublesome. Solving that became more difficult after February 1977, when President Jimmy Carter canceled federal funds for the CAP. When Carter subsequently removed the CAP from his hit list, he made groundwater management a requirement for receiving federal funds. Giving the water commission even more power, the 1977 law required a report from the commission and provided that if the legislature did not pass groundwater legislation by September 7, 1981, the commission's proposal would become law.

The Groundwater Study Commission was established in November 1977, and for the next 14 months its members studied the subject. That first phase was relatively harmonious, but the next one was not. The Commission failed to resolve the major differences and produce a single report. In the summer of 1979, a Draft Report was written and supported largely by representatives of the cities and mines, who constituted a majority, and this prompted agricultural representatives to draft a Minority Report. In November, after further efforts at compromise had collapsed, Governor Babbitt was asked to mediate the negotiations. He organized a rump group of commissioners, including the study commission's co-chairs, Barr and Stan Turley, who met in private for hundreds of hours over the next six months. Exercising great skill, Babbitt pushed the parties toward mutually acceptable compromises, and his knowledge and willingness to work through the details were essential for creating the specific proposal. Others also played important roles, and Jim Bush, who represented the mines, noted, "Barr and Turley were the two heavy hitters that were players" and "they were there all the time."[39] While Turley represented farming interests, Barr was neither a lawyer who knew water law nor a representative of any side. And so, his value came not through arguing the details of particular questions, but from achieving a comprehensive and acceptable solution.

The completed proposal, drafted by the rump group and brought forward by the full commission, represented a sharp change in use of groundwater and focused on conservation and management. It created a Department of Water Resources to administer the act, and it established four Active Management Areas (AMA) in the parts of central Arizona then suffering from serious overdrafting of groundwater. Each AMA had to file a management plan emphasizing conservation and reduced use of groundwater. The greatest differences involved farming, and these included a prohibition on irrigating any new agricultural land, and a limit on drilling new, large wells. Farmers would pay a pump tax to finance the system and use water–measuring devices, and their wells had to be registered and monitored. A mine or other industry could use new groundwater by filing a permit. Cities could increase their water supply by extending their service area, but no new subdivisions could be built without guaranteeing they had a 100-year assured supply of water. Barr and Turley brought the bill to the legislature with a plea from the commission members, who said, "Don't change a comma; don't change anything." Since the measure had won support from all the key players, few legislators were inclined to raise serious objections, though a number voiced some criticisms. But Barr and Turley succeeded in gaining overwhelming approval in both houses. Turley joked, "I never got so few kind words and so many votes in all my years in the Legislature." Barr was effusive, grandly claiming, "This bill says that there will be an Arizona forever," but there was no mistaking the measure's importance. It established a well-designed system for managing and conserving groundwater, although the effectiveness would depend on the future administration of it. As a result, Secretary of the Interior Cecil Andrus approved this plan and permitted the CAP to be completed, and this supplied the additional water that cities needed. Barr had not designed any specifics of the new water system, but his determination to achieve a solution forced the parties together and led to a settlement; one member commented that Barr "harbors an awesome impatience with dawdling." Barr's political skills—his sense of timing, his effectiveness in negotiation, and his ability to convince his colleagues to look at the bigger picture—were crucial in this process.[40]

Air Pollution and Environmental Planning

Like the rest of the country, Arizona grappled with a range of environmental problems starting in the 1960s. Although Arizona had its own particular mix of environmental concerns, like all states, it struggled to build policies that responded to laws, rules, and restrictions emanating from Washington. Barr's approach to this situation was largely pragmatic. He recognized the dangers of air pollution and the economic consequences of regulation, he believed in rational planning and conservation, and he wanted to preserve the maximum opportunity for state authority in this area. Barr was never an aesthetic environmentalist or a preservationist, believing instead in regulated use of resources, and he always remained attentive to the economic impact of regulation, but by the 1980s his understanding of environmental conditions had evolved, and he considered clean air and water as essential to the state.

Arizona's efforts to deal with air pollution began in 1962, when the Department of Health Services was instructed to conduct air pollution studies. Five years later an anti-smog bill set air quality standards and created a Division of Air Pollution Control in the state Board of Health. Pollution received more attention as national apprehension rose, and when Congress passed the Clean Air Act, Arizona also passed a major air pollution measure in 1970, prohibiting "any further degradation of the air quality" by "any industrial polluters." The state health department was tasked with regulating pollution from smelters or coal-fired electricity generating plants. It was also instructed to develop emissions standards for cars, to require emissions control devices on cars when they were available, and to organize a system of vehicle inspection.[41] Mines and utility companies had been seen rightly as major polluters, and a 1971 law allowed prosecution of industrial offenders. Barr had pushed the earlier laws, but he also recognized the increasing impact of vehicle emissions. In 1972 he pushed a legislative committee to confirm industry compliance to the law, after which he then won adoption of a measure to build a vehicle emissions lab and a testing station.

The discussion changed significantly in 1973, after the federal Environmental Protection Agency proposed regulatory measures to reduce air pollution in Arizona. Amidst a swirl of largely negative reaction, Barr worked in stages to craft a position that satisfied policy and political demands. In July he threatened to battle the regulations with legal action and public hearings. In September he placed a story in a Republican Party publication that explained, "At first glance it might appear that Arizona is protesting suggested pollution control. That is not the case. Rather it is, as Barr sees it, 'a direct conflict of constitutional authority.'" Barr argued that certain EPA demands would force the state to exceed its legal authority. He also contended that attempting to legislate a sudden, dramatic change in lifestyle would be politically disastrous. Instead, he argued, "If clean air is the goal, and it should be, we must get the cooperation of the public and progress slowly."[42]

He balanced cautious talk about moving slowly with working vigorously to offer voluntary alternatives. "[H]e singlehandedly cajoled a dozen of Arizona's major industries into a serious effort at developing a broad-based program of voluntary carpooling," and he pursued ways to facilitate this, including a Staggered Hours Committee to reduce rush hour traffic, special parking breaks, and added support for bus systems. More importantly, in 1974 he proposed a mandatory program for vehicle emissions testing, and he defended this to the legislature and the public by claiming, "We fought EPA's plan and told them Arizona is capable of coming up with a plan to get the job done. The failure to instigate a program would mean that our credibility is gone."[43]

While Barr managed to get mandatory emissions testing adopted and to halt implementation of the EPA regulations, conservatives still opposed the program. In 1976, after car owners complained about long waits for testing, Tony West and Jim Skelly sponsored a bill, which many previous supporters cosponsored, to repeal the program. Gutierrez predicted that this would "probably turn out to be the major issue of the session," and he was right.[44] After being defeated several times, the repeal measure passed the House in April, but the Senate voted to make the program voluntary. A conference committee finally produced an alternative that saved the program, easing some of the conditions and referring it to voters, who approved it. In 1980 the program was continued, with additional restrictions, and that approach was repeated in 1986. This abbreviated description of the lengthy process reveals some of Barr's crucial strengths as a political leader: his articulation of messages that appealed to different audiences; his ability to navigate among various participants, in this case, the federal government, Arizona conservatives, and the public; his clever use of legislative strategy, working first in the House, then cooperating with Gutierrez in the Senate, and then through the conference committee; his patient persistence; and his flexibility in adjusting his strategy.

Land-use planning constituted another facet of Barr's approach to environmental concerns, and he articulated the need for rational development. In 1971 he suggested that the legislature might need to acquire title to state trust lands around Tucson and Phoenix in order to prevent urban sprawl, arguing that orderly growth could be obstructed if the trust land "just goes for subdivision land." Instead, he suggested, the legislature could hold the land using some of it for green belts and as "a blocking method for undesirable growth." Two years later, after serving on the Interim Committee on Environmental Future, Barr supported a law that required cities to adopt a general plan for development, enabled them to create a planning agency, and substantially expanded their ability to manage land. He also pushed a state land-use planning law to prevent Arizona from "becoming a huge mass of concrete with the attendant problems." Critics rightly objected that the state measure only provided for an inventory of land, but it was an incremental step toward planning. He envisioned that planning could best be done in a natural resources department, but he recognized the hurdles to forming this unit, and such a department never was created.[45]

By 1975 other land use problems began appearing. Urban growth in the western Salt River Valley was nearing Luke Air Force Base, drawing criticism from the base's new neighbors. Barr's military background heightened his interest in the situation. He was sensitive to concerns about noise, but he pointed out that Luke had been built long before any land development in the area. This, he suggested, argued for protecting the base and demonstrated the importance of land-use planning. Two years later the legislature passed a moratorium on building around military air fields, and in 1978 it instructed counties on planning and zoning around them. In the same year, the legislature approved legislation allowing land transfers. A different kind of problem emerged from 1979 to 1981, as massive flooding in the Salt River Valley prompted support for control projects and reinforced earlier laws restricting building in floodplains.

When Bruce Babbitt became governor, Barr found someone whose interest in planning matched his own, although Babbitt's environmental interests were much broader than just planning. In 1979 the legislature voted for three state land reform measures the governor had requested: "higher rents for urban lands, an end to speculative use of state lands, and authority to work with local governments on urban land-lease negotiations."[46] Over the next two years, Babbitt negotiated with the wide range of interested parties, a strategy that Barr supported, to fashion a plan for orderly development of state trust lands around Phoenix and Tucson. A conflict between the two men killed the measure in the regular legislative session in 1981, but the landmark measure was accepted later that year in a special session. And they cooperated on passing Barr's hazardous waste management plan (1983) and on measures to improve water quality standards (1986). In 1984 Barr again articulated his views on a balanced approach: "Growth is here because we have the very best place to come to. But we have to plan for it and see to it that we use what we have to maintain our environment and surroundings."[47] Barr's response to environmental issues was framed by his concern for economic consequences and a belief in the value of rational planning, but his political sensitivity enabled him to appreciate Babbitt's different perspective.

Education and Mental Health

As the son of an educator who preached the need to educate all children, Barr grew up appreciating the value of education, and he demonstrated this in how he raised his children and what he did in the legislature. Eddie Basha, who worked to improve Arizona schools and served on the Arizona Board of Regents for the state universities, called Barr "a great friend for education" and praised Barr's understanding that "prosperity and growth was predicated on the development of an educated citizenry."[48] This awareness showed in his consistently strong support for educational funding. He led the periodic efforts to increase, stabilize, and equalize funding for K–12 education, and he backed proposals for state-paid kindergarten. But Barr also favored private and parochial schools, and in 1972 he proposed a voucher system that provided a state tax credit of $100 per student. In typical Barr style, he linked his support for both school systems, saying that he favored competition in education; as he remarked, "monopolies of any kind are bad." Claiming that economic pressures might cause private and parochial schools to collapse, which would dump their students on overburdened public schools, he argued for maintaining private and parochial schools through vouchers and for giving more funding to public schools.[49] It was an interesting argument, but it did not convince a majority of his colleagues.

As the graduate of a vocational school, he often thought practically about education, and this led him to support diverse initiatives. He began arguing for bilingual education in 1967, continued during the 1970s, and in 1982 he won the adoption of the Bilingual Education Act. On the other hand, he could sometimes argue, "Education at the primary and secondary level should get back to basics," and blamed parents for encouraging frills. Eddie Basha noted Barr's strong support for vocational education, and Alfredo Gutierrez explained that he intended "to set up five or six of what at that time were called vocational technical schools." But Barr reported that he "had a hard time in Arizona selling vocational education," and only after some struggle was a board for vocational education finally created.[50]

Barr also supported the expansion of higher education in Arizona. He helped create a funding formula to aid community colleges, and he worked even more assiduously to support the growth of the state's three universities, saying, "I fought all my life for the universities' capital construction."[51] And his efforts were needed. Arizona's growth and the rise of college attendance nationally meant that Arizona's college enrollments grew by leaps and bounds. The resulting capital needs meant that every several years the legislature considered additional university funding requests. Usually, these were pared in the early stages of legislative budget decisions, and in leaner years universities got little of what they sought. Overall, however, universities received significant funding that enabled them to expand. Barr remained a consistently strong supporter of university requests and of the institutions' larger purposes. According to Alfredo Gutierrez, Barr decided that Arizona State University (ASU), which only became a university in 1958, needed to be further transformed into a research university. To do this, they adopted a ten-year plan, but this also included additional funding for the University of Arizona (UA) and Northern Arizona University (NAU).

Barr supported the growth of universities without trying to dictate their educational policies, but on several occasions he attempted to intervene directly into their affairs. In 1972 he insisted on seeing student files to determine why the UA turned down so many in-state students. The following year he proposed a law requiring ASU to allow its football stadium to be used for a professional football charity game, and in 1974 Barr and Speaker Stan Akers threatened action if the university refused to allow use of the stadium by a professional football team that some boosters were seeking to attract to the Valley.[52] In 1979 he threatened legislative action after the firing of ASU's popular football coach, Frank Kush. He saw universities, then, as being part of state government, particularly in terms of funding and facilities, and he was willing to follow the urges of colleagues, as when Jim Skelly wanted use of the ASU stadium, or of constituents, who were angry about the Kush firing.

Personal and policy interests also drove Barr's backing for mental health treatment and facilities. Louise Barr noted that his commitment came partly because he was familiar with the family situations of friends and colleagues, and because he had been influenced by his father's beliefs. Forming the Department of Mental Retardation in 1970 from various agencies was part of the general reform of government, and in 1973 the state provided a hospital. Barr and Gutierrez cosponsored a major program change in 1978, including the establishment of group homes. Providing adequate funding levels and provisions for education contributed substantially to their success, but they survived only because the law included a politically controversial provision barring cities from passing restrictive zoning codes against them.

Barr also took pride in his work on another aspect of mental health policy. For two years he labored steadily to win adoption of a program for the chronically mentally ill, and in 1986 he succeeded. This included the opening of five pilot programs in various counties and forming the Division of Behavioral Health. Bob Fannin described Barr's successful strategy of recruiting an expert on the chronically mentally ill from Tucson, and then bringing in legislators, several at a time, and telling them, "Ask this doctor everything you can and learn about this subject and learn about this bill."[53] It was a good example, Fannin said, of how Barr sought legislative approval on complex proposals by offering information, rather than trying to pressure people for their support.

Barr also pursued other social policy questions. In 1974 he questioned why college students and people earning up to $13,000 were eligible for food stamps. The following year he proposed a state homeowner's loan agency to work with lending institutions to promote home-building and allowing cities and towns to loan money for low- and moderate-income housing. It was a classic Barr proposal, combining items that appealed to different groups to increase the likelihood of acceptance. Barr also supported a controversial measure for a Martin Luther King Jr. holiday. First introduced into the House in 1975, it was then introduced in every session from 1981 to 1985 but never made it out of committee. Finally, in 1986 the measure made it to the House floor, but it failed by one vote. As John Kolbe reported, Barr "took a notably high profile on an issue that had almost no support in his own Republican caucus."[54] Serving as Art Hamilton's "most crucial ally" on the measure, Barr was disappointed that so few colleagues could see the rationale for this holiday.

Laws and Order, Crime and Punishment

As a legislator, Barr necessarily dealt with issues of law and punishment. Because he was not a lawyer, he ignored the legal details, but he fully understood the policy and political importance of these matters, and the notion of rationalizing codes was intuitively sensible. Early in his career, Jim Bush approached him about Arizona's failure to adopt the Uniform Commercial Code and asked him to assist the effort. This fit his belief that the state should encourage economic activity, so he got modest legislative funding to study the matter, introduced a bill, and helped get it passed.

New codes were also proposed in other areas of law, and Barr supported revisions of the probate code and the juvenile code. He was more directly and significantly involved in the more politically sensitive revisions of the criminal code. In 1973 a legislative committee began investigating the subject, but the process moved slowly after that, particularly because of policy differences with Democrats, who had gained control of the Senate. Art Hamilton felt that Barr's involvement in resolving this conflict offers "one of the most insightful looks into the personality and style of Burton Barr." It demonstrated his ability to take an issue that was not his own, "but because it was important—it had to pass"; he could focus on it, master the material, and then move to the next issue.[55] Recognizing that passing a bill required agreement from the Democratic Senate, he negotiated a settlement directly with Alfredo Gutierrez, and he brought it back to the House. While the Judiciary Committee Chair, Peter Kay, was furious, his more conservative, combative approach would likely have failed, or at least taken much more time.

While Barr did not campaign on law and order issues or stress them in the legislature, he did support a series of laws in 1968 and 1976 that imposed strict penalties on crime, and he favored restoring the state's death penalty in 1973. With increased penalties for crimes and a larger criminal population, Arizona needed more prisons, and Barr advocated the necessary funding. To deal with prison overcrowding, he argued for work-release programs, and to house more prisoners in the new prisons, he pushed for double-bunking. Here, as on other topics, Barr emphasized research, and when the legislature held a special session in 1983–1984, he directed his staff to learn "everything there is to know" about the prison system.[56] Armed with this independent information, Barr challenged the administration's arguments and produced a compromise, agreeing to allow more convicts work experience outside of prison in exchange for getting more prison beds.

Conclusion: Burton Barr as a Policymaker

During his legislative career Barr worked on a great many other policy matters as well, from raising unemployment benefits to improving state retirement systems, from defining the position of adjutant general to enabling interstate banking. In essence, his interests encompassed the range of Arizona policy-making during this period, but he saw his actions within a sharp lens. For him, the legislative reapportionment in 1966 was *the* dividing point in Arizona history. Power shifted then "from a rural legislature and a rural government to urban government, and everything that exists out there today . . . took place because of the change to urban from rural."[57]

While he was involved to varying degrees on many different issues, Barr was always a central player on the major ones. The transformation of state government, the creation of a new tax system and its implications for education, the creation of AHCCCS, and the passing of the Groundwater Management Act were the defining measures of the era and crucial parts of Arizona's modernizing moment. It is no exaggeration to say that relating the story of Barr's primary political achievements is telling the history of Arizona policy-making and governance during this era.

Barr's role in these developments shifted according to the issue, the players, and the time. Though less involved in crafting particulars of the water law itself, for example, he was instrumental in arranging the initial discussions, in ensuring the participation of the main parties, in devising the strategy necessary to win legislative adoption, and then in achieving this. That was essentially a three-year process; his commitment to reforming the health-care system, especially with Medicaid and AHCCCS, spanned his entire career. Although he drew on Alain Enthoven's managed-competition approach and worked closely with Gutierrez and Babbitt, Barr had consistently introduced new and innovative ideas since before 1970, and his energy and creativity had driven the process.

Barr was a planner and a problem-solver. From experience he knew that these solutions would not last forever. Economic changes would force new tax policy, growth would require additional spending, and new ideas could offer improved programs. Flexibility was, therefore, an essential part of his approach to policy-making. When he lost on Medicaid in 1976, he adjusted to the existing political realities, but he awaited an opportunity to revisit the issue. That realistic approach characterized all of his efforts.

Barr's legislative record included an enormous number of victories that earned accolades from legislators and reporters. But he did not win every vote, nor did he succeed in every attempt to create new programs or government bodies. He lost, for example, in trying to enact no-fault auto insurance, and he failed to create a department of natural resources. What is most striking, however, and what contributed substantially to his overall success and prominence, was his persistence and his willingness to revise proposals and come back with innovative ideas. At the end of every legislative session, some potentially good bills were sidelined and others failed primarily because time ran out before they could be acted on. Sometimes, for example, if the primary sponsor retired, these measures might simply have died. Barr identified those proposals, adjusted them, and added them to a list of new measures that he would introduce in a later session. His record of advancing some proposals—and defeating others—also demonstrated his attention to every stage of the legislative process, from presession planning to conference committees and working with the governor.

Barr's primary arena of activity was in the legislature—on the House floor, the hallways, members' offices, and committee rooms. These were the best places for him to use his extraordinary talents of personal persuasion, to employ his humor, and to negotiate multiple things simultaneously. But he also operated in other modes and places. He helped devise and direct statewide campaigns on tax and education proposals, for example, raising funds, shaping winning arguments, and persuading important people to support the effort. And although not a frequent participant at Republican Party events, he did some public speaking in different parts of the state. Given his success and prominence, the respect he had earned from so many people, his role in making policy, and his contacts throughout the state, it is understandable that people pushed him to run for higher office. But while he was the perfect man at the right time for the legislature, he did not fit so ideally into other political roles.

CHAPTER SIX

Leaving the Legislature and Running for Governor

"By '86, we were packaging people like soap boxes and he didn't package well."

—ALFREDO GUTIERREZ[1]

"Some Republicans were not as supportive of him because they thought he was a compromiser."

—JIM BUSH[2]

"He paid a very high price for having been seen as Mr. All Powerful, All Knowing, Omnipotent, Omnipotence, Omnipresent, Burton Barr."

—ART HAMILTON[3]

"Barr lost 'because of a vicious smear campaign orchestrated from the beginning as an attempt at character assassination. . . . Burt is still tops, while Ev has become an ethical pygmy.'"

—STAN TURLEY[4]

On February 28, 1986, Burton Barr ended the suspense and formally announced his candidacy for governor of Arizona. For several years, knowledgeable political observers considered him the most obvious and strongest Republican candidate, and the previous June, *Arizona Republic* columnist Pat Murphy believed Barr's candidacy was so likely that he should choose his successor as majority leader of the House. A multitude of political and personal factors led to Barr's decision and made it seem almost inevitable. And most observers thought so highly of his skills and record that they were convinced that Barr would win the primary and general elections. Initially, the contest developed as observers had expected, although behind the scenes, there were disturbing problems with the management and direction of his campaign. On July 1 the complexion of the race changed with the late entry of another Republican candidate, archconservative and longtime office-seeker Evan Mecham. His personal attacks on Barr's character, combined with Barr's refusal to confront Mecham on this, were important factors in Mecham's shocking upset victory over Barr in the September Republican primary. The story of the campaign highlights Barr's strengths and weaknesses, as well indicating how Arizona politics were beginning to shift.

Thinking about Running

It was not new in 1985 for people to suggest that Barr run for higher office or for him to think about it. Almost as soon as he rose to prominence as a legislative leader, speculation about this possibility had swirled, mainly because moving up or thinking about it were normal elements of politics. Although Barr loved the legislature and his majority leader position, as an astute politician, he recognized that being considered and especially being courted for a position brought power. What people said and what support they offered constituted valuable political currency. But actually pursuing another office was also a possibility for Barr. His optimism, his enjoyment of a challenge, his sense of civic obligation, and his solution-oriented approach to problems would all enable him to seek and fill another office. If he seemed ideally suited to legislative leadership, his talents were also more than sufficient for him to thrive in another position. Finally, Barr was like most people in that praise and promises of power could turn his head, but his hardheaded approach to politics typically overruled those sorts of distractions.

When Barr's name was mentioned in 1972 as a possible candidate for another post, he said that he was not "being coy," and although focused on passing his legislative program, he was "obviously not going to rule out the possibility of running for any other office."[5] Given Barr's position, this could mean the U.S. House or Senate, the governorship, or another statewide office, but there were reasons against any of these options, especially in the early 1970s. None of the state offices, even governor, had much power, and a congressional seat would require a major campaign every two years, moving his very young children to Washington, and disrupting his wife's career. The U.S. Senate offered more prestige and influence, but it too would mean moving. Moreover, one of the seats was securely held by Barry Goldwater and the other drew several eager Republican candidates. In 1974 John Kolbe noted, "His name pops up in most any conversation about the 1974 governor's race," but he also noted, tellingly, "Barr so relishes the battles he's already in and so loathes the necessary banalities of a statewide political campaign, that it's doubtful he could ever work up the driving ambition to jump into that fray as well."[6]

Three years later, Barr was again roundly suggested for the governorship, but this time he responded more positively to the notion. Though he still worried about limiting his time with his children and about raising the $250,000 needed to run, his real interest in the possibility showed in the *Arizona Republic* headline, "Burton Barr Wrestling with Decision on GOP Gubernatorial Nomination."[7] One incentive was that the race seemed fairly open in the fall of 1977. No strong Republican had stepped forward, although Barr had encouraged Sandra Day O'Connor to run; Democrats expected a contest for the nomination to include at least Wesley Bolin, who in October had ascended to the governor's post after Raul Castro resigned, and Bill Schulz, an apartment magnate with strong political interests. Barr had enough interest in the possibility to commission a poll on his chances, but conditions changed dramatically in March 1978, when Bolin died. With Bruce Babbitt now governor and the likely nominee, Barr saw a strong candidate and someone he liked, so he dropped his interest.

In 1980 political observer Bernie Wynn noted that Barr "constantly is being urged to run for governor, Congress, [or] the U.S. Senate," but he found it relatively easy not to pursue any national office.[8] Republicans urged him to run against Babbitt in 1982, but he respected the governor and worked productively with him, so he demurred again to this "ongoing thought," saying, "I'm not interested in running for any other office."[9] In 1984 he reiterated his basic reaction to the option. "I'm not afraid to try for governor, but I just don't want the office. I think people make big mistakes when they let their egos carry them beyond what they're supposed to be. I love the camaraderie of the [legislature]. I love the system."[10] But by 1984 the opportunities for a gubernatorial bid were different than at any previous time, and while Barr approached the decision cautiously and recognized the various drawbacks, he moved steadily toward a commitment.

The most important difference was his family. Throughout his legislative career he had genuinely put his family first. As John Kolbe reported, "One remembers the frantic last day of the legislative session a few years ago when all activity suddenly ground to a halt. Why? Barr had gone home to coach a soccer game."[11] But with his oldest child entering high school, Barr knew that in a few years his children would require less of his time. His wife also expressed her support for his candidacy. "Louise Barr wants her husband to run," reported a major profile piece on Barr in 1984. She noted, "He's a master of the game. Why sit around and tell Bruce what to do, when he could do it better himself?"[12]

The political situation at this point also influenced Barr's decision. Bruce Babbitt would not be seeking reelection this time, and would instead be pursuing a presidential nomination, just what Barr had over the years frequently chided him for considering. But while the race had no incumbent, it did have a very viable Democratic candidate. Bill Schulz had switched from Republican to Democrat in the 1970s and sought the 1978 gubernatorial nomination until Babbitt stepped in. Two years later he ran a very strong race against Barry Goldwater for the Senate, losing by only one percent of the vote. By 1983 Schulz was focusing on the next gubernatorial race, traveling the country to research different state governments. He also investigated Arizona government, pestering Barr "with his incessant inquiries about the legislative business," but Barr also confessed, "he admires the thoroughness with which the Democratic aspirant is preparing himself for the governorship."[13] Able, personable, articulate, informed, organized, with name recognition and the personal wealth to finance a strong campaign, Schulz was not only a formidable candidate, but Barr also respected and liked him.

Arizona Republicans, who had been highly frustrated by Babbitt's successes, now worried about beating Schulz, and, as they had for over a decade, tried to persuade Barr to run. They had one advantage this time: Congressman John McCain was friends with Barr, he was running for Goldwater's Senate seat, and he "envisioned an unbeatable McCain-Barr top-of-the-ticket."[14] Equally important, this fit into the plan of national Republican leaders, who were looking for ways to become the majority party. Determined to expand the party's control of only one-third of the nation's governorships, they believed Arizona was one of the states that Republicans should control. They also considered the office crucial to achieve redistricting of congressional districts after the next U.S. Census was taken. Keven Ann Willey reported, "High-level discussion among Reagan's political adviser, Edward Rollins; Republican National Committee Chairman Frank Fahrenkopf, Jr., and incoming chairman of the Republican Governors Association, Gov. John Sununu of New Hampshire, have focused on ways to get Barr to run."[15] These leaders thought to persuade Barr by emphasizing party loyalty, and who better to make this case, they thought, than party leader President Ronald Reagan.

In June 1985 Barr took his family on vacation to Washington, and after seeing many of the sights and getting a tour of the Supreme Court from Justice Sandra Day O'Connor, he received a phone call from McCain to set up a trip to the White House to meet the president. Although it was allegedly just for "a quick greeting," Barr sensed a larger purpose, but even had he wanted to, he could not decline the invitation or the opportunity for his family. After meeting and charming the family, President Reagan met privately with Barr and did ask him to run. The family and many observers believed that the president's request played a major role in shaping Barr's decision. To reporters after his meeting and to others later he maintained a "no-but-maybe" position, but he later explained, "If you are in the aura of the Oval Office, and the President of this nation turns to you and says, 'I want you to run for governor,' you haven't got really a lot to say."[16]

Barr remained publicly noncommittal into the fall, but he now talked about running as a possibility, "between 25 and 30 percent," rather than simply saying no. The failed effort by some Republicans to convince businessman Ralph Watkins to run further increased the pressure on Barr, although he said he would not make any decision until after the October referenda on funding Maricopa County highways. A potential race got much easier in September, when Bill Schulz ended his candidacy because his daughter's serious health problem required his time. Barr commented, "I'm edging more and more closely to a final decision. A lot of the negatives have been mitigated."[17]

A final consideration was the changing attractiveness of the legislature. Barr had always loved its camaraderie and solving problems, but after 20

Figure 15. The Barr family and President Ronald Reagan. Burton S. Barr Collection.

years as majority leader, the longest stretch for any current state leader, stepping down began to seem not unreasonable. Staying in power got both easier and harder. It was easier because his reputation grew: "Nothing moves through the House, they say, unless Burton Barr gives the word," or as Jim Skelly put it, "Barr always gets his way." But that reputation and past success also made it harder. The determination of senators in 1983 to beat him delayed finding a compromise solution, grievances accumulated among some longer-serving House members, and some of Barr's stories and techniques became familiar and thus less effective. Some members "seemed immune to his charms, you know, who would just get angry at his humor."[18]

The character of the legislature was also shifting, to some extent. Conservatives were less pragmatic and more hardline on social and moral issues, while freshmen were more willing to challenge the chamber leadership. Thus, in 1982 Barr reported that the job "isn't as much fun as it used to be," particularly because in previous years "we had a camaraderie that was greater than we have today." This meant that "the team concept isn't as easy to achieve," and as a consequence, "it takes more time and more effort to achieve goals." Looking back at this time, Alfredo Gutierrez concluded, "I think he overstayed his welcome. I think he was facing open rebellion because of it." While rebellion may be too strong a term, particularly since Barr remained generally successful in winning his issues, legislative sessions in the early 1980s were more contentious. Tellingly, in later reflecting on this period, his close leadership colleagues, Joe Lane and James Sossaman, both described him as being "tired of his legislative role" and "burned out." If Barr was thinking, then, of ending his legislative career, "What better way to go out," asked Lane, "than to go out as Governor?"[19]

Starting to Run

In October Barr said he would not decide until January, but this only postponed an announcement of what he had decided. And for a good reason: according to state law, if Barr formally announced his candidacy before the last year of his term began, he would have to resign his office. In October, a Committee for Good Government organized with the goal of raising $1 million for a Barr campaign, while also gathering signatures of people willing to support Barr. Although officially separate from Barr, this independence was primarily for legal reasons, and the committee was clearly operating with his agreement. Probably the strongest evidence that Barr had decided was that "most of Barr's colleagues predict Barr will opt to run for governor" and win. On January 22, 1986, Barr ended "the worst kept political secret in Arizona" and openly declared his intention to run for governor.[20]

Barr knew from the outset, of course, that this campaign would differ greatly from any he had experienced or run before. Although he had participated, sometimes heavily, in several statewide referenda campaigns, his own experience as a candidate was limited. In his first several campaigns he energetically walked the neighborhoods, but thereafter he essentially relied on his record and his safe district to guarantee reelection. He attended some events and sent out campaign literature in conjunction with his two district running mates, but one of them, Tony West, claimed that Barr had coasted in his campaigns. Because of his experience in raising and dispensing campaign funds, Barr understood about the increasing costs and knew of some small campaigning devices, like balloons at county fairs, but he had not experienced a statewide contest nor did he understand how greatly they had changed over the years. By the 1980s, campaigns in many states, including Arizona, had become complex operations, requiring money, press management, events and speeches, use of volunteers, direct mail, television, polls, and skilled management.

Barr's first significant campaign decision involved McCain's proposal that they link their campaigns, using McCain's manager, Jay Smith, who had run several Arizona races, to direct the effort. Barr was excited about the idea and asked Smith to meet with Bob Fannin. The son of Paul Fannin, the former governor and senator, Bob was the major organizer of Barr's unofficial organizing and finance committee, a close political confidante, and the chairman of Barr's campaign committee. Fannin turned down the idea of a joint effort, drawing on his father's experience with that approach in 1970, but he also ignored Smith's suggestion to produce media for both campaigns. He also dismissed Smith's report of a survey done by the Republican governors showing that Barr "had a potential problem with likely Republican primary voters." Smith concluded from their conversation that Fannin was "ignorant of modern campaign techniques."[21]

The alternative to using Smith was hiring another consulting firm, so Fannin and Barr interviewed consultants from Arizona, Washington, Texas, and California. On the recommendation of Stuart Spencer, a well-known Republican guru who had run Ronald Reagan's California campaigns, they hired the Dolphin Group, headed by Bill Roberts, Spencer's former partner. McCain advised Barr that this was not a top firm, but Fannin countered that they were experienced and that Roberts, who was older and had a military background, would work well with Barr. Roberts began working in October, and in December he came to Phoenix for several days. Unfortunately, Roberts was seriously ill, and after removing himself from active involvement, he sent another campaign coordinator.

The campaign staff expanded in March, adding Mike Boyd as press coordinator, and by summer, it included a state organizational chairman, an events organizer, a speech writer, plus various finance people, media assistants, and others. Campaign financing was very well structured, holding 15 to 20 fund-raisers, plus several sit-down dinners, as well as raising money by direct mail. In only two months of preliminary activity in 1985 they raised $112,000, and although Barr estimated that he needed $1.5 million to $2 million for the campaign, there was never any question of his ability to raise the money.

The campaign officially opened on February 28 with a morning event in Phoenix, an afternoon presentation in Tucson, an evening dinner back in Phoenix, and then weekend speeches in Yuma and Flagstaff. The Phoenix event was elaborately staged and more like a victory rally than an announcement. In a room decorated with blue and gold balloons, a Dixieland band entertained a crowd of 600 cheering well-wishers at an early-morning breakfast. In attendance to offer support were three former governors, former state chairman Harry Rosenzweig, plus other dignitaries, while Senate President and longtime friend Stan Turley chaired the event. Besides giving the campaign a rousing start, this power event aimed to discourage any potential Republican opposition, since party leaders, and Barr, wanted to avoid any divisive primary battle that could hurt the GOP's chances in the general election. As further evidence of Barr's strength, the campaign staff released a petition endorsing Barr's candidacy signed by 16 of 18 Republican senators and 37 of 38 Republican representatives.

One candidate was already in the race, Calder Chapman, a city councilman from Williams, but he had no experience, visibility, or money, and no one considered him a serious candidate. The focus of attention was Attorney General Bob Corbin, who was just completing his second term and who had previously crossed swords with Barr over AHCCCS. GOP leaders feared that Corbin might run, as much to thwart Barr as to serve himself. On the day of Barr's announcement, Corbin declared there was "a good chance" he would run, touting a poll of Pima and Maricopa voters showing that he led Barr by 21 to 17 percent. It was a short campaign. The next day Corbin said he would not run and pledged to support Barr. While he claimed the decision reflected his lack of interest in being governor and desire to remain attorney general, the Barr event clearly showed the overwhelming preference of GOP leaders and indicated that any other candidacy would be difficult.

The Race is On

Having launched the campaign with a splash and eliminated a serious primary opponent, Barr's team had achieved two major goals. Now, they needed to implement a successful strategy for the rest of the campaign. Without primary opposition, they could focus on the general election, looking to attract Democrats and independents, while still appealing to GOP voters. Barr's strengths were his accomplishments as a legislative leader, his encyclopedic knowledge of state policies and problems, his personal friendships with current and former lawmakers across the state, his personal qualities of integrity and humor, and, as the *Arizona Republic* would later say in its endorsement of Barr, "an uncanny knack for getting complex problems resolved."[22] Building on those considerable strengths was one part of the strategy; the second part was addressing his weaknesses, which were political.

Barr's political limitations were highlighted by the 1985 Republican governors' poll, which showed that 56 percent of Republican voters recognized his name, but only 26 percent felt favorably, while 14 percent had a negative view. Low name recognition was likely because he represented a Phoenix district. The unfavorable views partly reflected a belief outside of Phoenix that he had channeled benefits to the Phoenix area, while slighting the rest of the state. Responding to this would be a bit complicated, for as well as overcoming the traditional anti-Phoenix feelings of some Tucsonans, in the rest of the state he would have to finesse his urban focus and his belief that Arizona's future required building its cities. The unfavorable rating was also because conservatives perceived him as liberal, and because, as James Sossaman explained, "He had been so close with Babbitt those years and, in some people's minds, did Babbitt's bidding."[23] Moreover, Barr had a limited history with the GOP rank and file.

Barr's campaign strategy had to be built around his decision to remain in the legislature as majority leader for the spring 1986 term. He assured people, "I'm not going to be any different than I've ever been." John Kolbe reported Barr's belief that running for governor "would not alter his frenetic legislative pace, or dim his interest in the wide variety of issues facing lawmakers in 1986."[24] To accomplish this, Barr pledged to campaign in the evenings and on weekends until the legislative session ended.

In the previous November, when his candidacy seemed likely, Barr had begun his pre-campaign travel by going to Tucson. Congressman Jim Kolbe observed, "Burt will run well in southern Arizona, but he's got a selling job to do," noting that southern Arizona voters were sometimes "a little paranoid" about lawmakers from Maricopa County.[25] In January Barr started a general tour of the state, first traveling south to Sierra Vista, Benson, and Douglas, then going to Prescott, Flagstaff, Lake Havasu City, and back south to Nogales. Barr's message to rural communities claimed familiarity and awareness, and promised future access. Speaking in Holbrook at a Lincoln Day dinner, Barr explained that he already knew Navajo County and its people, and that as governor he would be their "friend in the state capitol," for "I truly believe that all 15 counties are part of the same family."[26] At another event in Show Low he claimed to have fished and camped everywhere in the state; in Williams he noted that he had a cabin in nearby Flagstaff and had "known Williams for 30 years." In every rural community from Sedona to Safford, he offered an economic plan focused on tourism, he emphasized the need to improve education, and he reiterated the value of his experience and his commitment to hard work. Despite these efforts, in mid-June he announced, "My first problem is to establish myself in a statewide campaign," and he began a tour with John McCain to increase his name recognition.[27]

Barr stressed these same themes in speaking to metropolitan audiences, adding the goal of improving transportation. Although he several times mentioned as a hopeful omen the rise in Republican voter registration numbers, he did not make party ties the focus of his presentations. He spoke critically about some of Governor Babbitt's actions, explaining what he would have done differently, but he did not make a strong partisan argument. Instead, from its inception, his campaign was relatively neutral on questions of party. In his statement of candidacy, he wrote specifically about working with people as individuals, "which has meant looking beyond their political affiliation." He justified bipartisanship as being positive and productive, for his gaining the respect of legislators "on both sides of the political aisle," meant that "Arizona folks have been able to reap the rewards of such cooperation."[28] This accurate description of Barr's approach to policy-making and his view of party offered some advantages in a general election against a Democratic candidate, but it did not help him appease critical Republican voters.

Arizona Democrats witnessed a sharply contested primary for governor, with three candidates active starting in the fall and making formal declarations in February. Phoenix businessman Dave Moss was the first to declare and the least likely to win, and he dropped out of the race shortly before the September primary. Tony Mason was the second to announce. A lawyer who had served in the Attorney General's and the Maricopa County Attorney's offices and who lost a close congressional race in 1976,

Mason had gone from a private legal practice to an investment firm. Although criticized for being too close to developers, he won endorsements from Governor Babbitt and Phoenix Mayor Terry Goddard, and he focused on dealing with pollution and on strengthening education and the economy.

The front-running Democratic candidate was Carolyn Warner, who had been state superintendent of schools since 1974. Warner denounced the "old politics" of faction and partisan conflict, promised leadership and negotiation, and highlighted the goals of better transportation; pollution control, with jail terms for polluters; support for agriculture and mining; and a vigorous anti-drug policy. Having held office for 12 years, Warner had statewide visibility and a record to run on but also to defend, since many criticized her for the state's educational failings. More troubling criticisms were that she lacked "much substance," with some Democrats complaining that she had "a show-business type of personality," that as superintendent she had done "nothing but make speeches and blame the legislature," and that if elected, she "would be the quintessence of a ceremonial governor." After Dave Moss eventually withdrew from the race, he described her as being "shallow on the issues" and dealing too much in clichés, and the *Arizona Republic*, in endorsing Mason claimed that Warner had a "lackluster" record and had failed to be "a leader and policymaker in public education."[29]

But Warner also had numerous supporters, and in the early March poll she had a substantial 60–14 lead over Mason. Even more significant was her wide 48–30 lead over Barr. Like Barr, she focused on the general election, but more than that, she launched a highly aggressive campaign that concentrated on Barr and ignored her Democratic competitors. Speaking in Yuma in March, she accused him of "leaning heavily on special interests and partisan politics," and she asserted that the legislature had "done nothing" about toxic waste, blaming that on Barr. She criticized Barr's success at compromise by saying, "It is basically a choice between leadership and dealership," and she equated Barr with "the old politics of piecemeal solutions."[30] In April she attributed a statement to Barr about air pollution that "stunned" her (although Barr denied having made the statement), and she purported to be worried about Barr's campaign funds, because "he has so many special interest groups backing him." Accelerating her claims, she argued that Barr "should be fired" for having the legislature refer issues to voters; in May she accused him of "allowing" the King holiday bill to fail while voting for it "just covered his political posterior."[31]

A Troubled Campaign

Despite Barr's advantages in having widespread Republican leadership support and substantial financial resources, his campaign struggled through the initial spring months and into the summer. His difficulties included his vulnerability as the current majority leader, the campaign strategy, and campaign management. Continuing to serve as majority leader while running for governor created serious problems, as two *Phoenix Gazette* columnists predicted. Richard de Uriarte warned Barr that as a compromising legislator, "You're going to have to take hundreds of stands that are going to alienate somebody." John Kolbe warned that Barr seemed to be tempering his views and that his colleagues were helping him avoid controversy.[32]

In fact, both warnings proved accurate. The piecemeal nature and the timing of legislative actions hurt Barr in March, as he defended Phelps Dodge from pollution charges and suggested that the state needed to wait for air pollution data before proposing legislation. In April some state legislators were reported as saying that the session was in "chaos" and "running in circles," and Senator Tom Gabaldon, (D-Flagstaff) claimed that it was because of "Barr's race for the governor's seat," for "he basically is setting the agenda because of his position."[33] In reality, legislative schedules are always somewhat confused, and while Barr was splitting his time and less efficient than in the past, the charges also represent partisan and election year politics.

Other events and statements fueled a perception that Barr was dodging issues. In April, when the Senate produced a compromise on a bill restricting the use of groundwater in artificial lakes, Senate President Stan Turley said it was done to avoid putting Barr in a difficult position. House Whip Joe Lane said baldly, "Everything we do, we're concerned about Burt," and to that end, "We look at every bill and every issue."[34] While Barr said that he had not requested that action on the bill, this sort of situation fueled criticism like the claim in a *Phoenix New Times* article that "Barr's supporters know that he is dropping out of sight on the hot items this session." This was evident, the article argued, in Barr's failure to vote on a mandatory seat belt law, and it offered an apparently telling admission about Barr backing away from the limelight from Speaker James Sossaman: "I think we have to be careful about how we say this, but I think that perception is probably correct."[35]

But while the author presented Sossaman's statement as a weak defense of Barr's not voting, it is more directly a comment on the visibility of Barr's leadership on issues. Other critics offered a different explanation for Barr's nonvoting, claiming it was because he was distracted by working on his campaign. Finally, while the article alleged that Barr "essentially voted both ways" on excluding Planned Parenthood from getting family-planning money, in reality he voted for the amendment, which failed, and then for the larger appropriation measure.

If journalists failed to portray the complexities of legislative operations and decision-making carefully, politicians were even more prone to mistakes and misrepresentation. Warner's criticisms of Barr and the King holiday are particularly noteworthy. In dismissing Barr's vote for the holiday, Warner sneered that Barr had "allowed his right-wing colleagues to have their way." John Kolbe observed, Barr "doesn't allow or disallow his colleagues to do anything. They are all independently elected officials." Whether Warner's statement reflected her "stunning political naiveté," as Kolbe suggested, or was a more cynical attack on Barr, it highlights the problems arising from Barr's continuation in office.[36] Making laws may not be like making sausage (to cite an old adage), but the process is highly complex, subject to fits and starts, requires cajoling and negotiation, and often ends in failure. When this session concluded, some important legislation had passed, other measures failed, and the *Arizona Republic* termed it a productive session. This type of assessment was crucial for Barr, given his emphasis on his success as a legislative leader, but the expectations for success were unclear. To a fair extent, Barr's gubernatorial hopes depended on what the public believed and understood about this.

These problems of perception and leadership were heightened by the campaign's strategy of presenting Barr as a leader and touting his expertise. This was evident in campaign materials like the "Dear Neighbor" letter that cited his personal history and six legislative achievements, but offered no program information. Similar to this was the one-page leaflet that, along with his biography and achievements, listed challenges facing the state without explaining what Barr proposed to do about them. His five-page "Statement of Candidacy" referred to his experience and some legislative accomplishments, cited his belief in hard work, projected the state's future growth, hoped that youth would participate in government, mentioned his love for Arizona, and included two paragraphs on issues—one on tourism and another on education—and neither offered any policy ideas.

Newspaper reports of Barr's speeches in rural areas mirror these campaign materials. A newspaper report of a candidate forum in April noted that he "offered no specific proposals," and instead of defending his role in the criticized program for highways, he joked about it, saying, "Bulldozers will be everywhere. You'll never be able to get on Grand Avenue again in our lifetime." Apart from this bit of levity, however, Barr at this occasion and so many others behaved like a stodgy statesman, rather than the interesting, informed purveyor of ideas he had been in the legislature and, at times in previous years, in public speeches. Barr's makeover was completed by one more step. Keven Ann Willey noted that in the past Barr's pants were always "fraying at the hems," and "his shirt was generally rumpled, his tie stained and his hair disheveled." But the campaign changed that. Bruce Merrill saw Barr at a Phoenix Suns basketball game and noted, "He had a razor haircut, and he was wearing a $500 suit. It was Burt, but it didn't look anything like him. They were packaging him for California, not Arizona."[37]

Poor organization and management also plagued the campaign. In November Bob Fannin had tried to hire Rick Collins as campaign manager, but Collins declined, and the position was never filled. The Dolphin Group's consultant, Bob Wolfe, was young, relatively inexperienced, and unfamiliar with Arizona. Most important, as Alfredo Gutierrez observed, Barr "was such a dominant character" that a successful manager had "to be equally dominating," something Wolfe could not be. The problem extended to other campaign staff, and press secretary Mike Boyd felt that "Burt just resented that there were a bunch of 30-year-old, runny-nosed kids so highly involved in his campaign."[38]

It was more than their youth that troubled Barr about his staff. His rapid-fire style of discussion and constant motion made him intolerant of sitting in meetings, especially about how he should perform. Mike Boyd observed mildly, "He wasn't particularly good at taking advice," adding, "Burt really didn't seem to listen very closely, didn't seem to really give a whole lot of credence to the so-called experts."[39] As a legislator, Barr had problems with time management, and he did not improve as a candidate; for example, he showed up a half hour late to his campaign opening. He compounded the problem by refusing help, such as insisting on driving himself to events in the Phoenix area, but sometimes getting lost and needing to call for directions.

The problems were not all Barr's, however. The Southern Arizona headquarters was not opened until April 11, a striking failing, given Barr's need to attract Tucson voters. Even more damaging was the Dolphin Group's failure to organize volunteers or to use Arizona leaders. This closed-shop mentality was inexplicable to party leaders like GOP state chairman Burt Kruglick, who recognized Barr's need to connect better with party activists. Jane Hull observed "very little grass roots in that organization" and "very little use of a lot of people." A conspicuous example of this involved an offer from former Senate President Marty Humphrey and former

Governor Jack Williams to spend the month of May campaigning with Barr in rural communities. The Dolphin Group rejected the idea, saying, "The consultant should have total control of the campaign." While Fannin later explained this as "miscommunication," it was a major lost opportunity, and Barr was understandably unhappy.[40]

By June it was apparent that the situation could not be allowed to continue and Bob Wolfe had to go. This left Barr essentially in control of his campaign and solely dependent "on Bob Fannin for any type of information or advice."[41] But Fannin, forced to be the liaison with the Dolphin Group, had neither the expertise to run the campaign nor the stature to force Barr's cooperation. Nevertheless, Barr felt invigorated, determined to restart the campaign, and began a rural tour with John McCain. He also had grounds for happiness, since despite the battering by Warner and the missteps of his campaign, the polls showed he had gained five points on Warner and led her 35 to 33 percent.

But despite the new beginning, management problems persisted, since Barr essentially took over his own campaign. Not until early August, when the Dolphin Group sent Lee Stitzenberger, did the campaign have a manager. More problematic were Barr's speeches. Mike Boyd described Ron St. John, the campaign's speechwriter, as experienced and very able, but added, "Ron would write speeches, and Ron would write issue papers for Burt, and Burt just plain and simply ignored them." The problem dated from the campaign's beginning, because newspaper reports about the opening event noted that his record of achievement was cited "in a printed statement which bore no relation to Barr's 12-minute speech." Barr had spent 20 years talking to reporters and making speeches, and as Peter Burns said, "He could give a whole speech without any notes," or he could just talk with a reporter "and use his analogies and his metaphors and his visuals . . . and he'd just give all of these wonderful quotes."[42] The success of Barr's political career had rested on his ability to remember and organize material, to talk to people, and to persuade them.

But the campaign trail, speaking to many and larger audiences, differed greatly from the legislature and required another approach. John Kolbe felt that Barr's campaign speeches demonstrated an "utter inability to control his rhetoric. I mean he would just babble on and on and on, and it was so full of insider stuff." Joe Lane hosted Barr in rural Arizona, where "Burt made a 45-minute speech, and to that hall in Douglas, that's 30 minutes too damn long. And I kept signaling him, standing in the back of the room, I kept doing everything I could, and Burt was going a hundred miles an hour. And I could see those guys starting to look at their watches."

Lane tried to offer him advice, saying, "Burt, go there and [be] short, sweet, concise, bang. Smile a lot, don't wiggle your eyebrows, don't act like a clown, because they will think you're an idiot."[43]

Alfredo Gutierrez, who later founded a marketing and consulting company, explained that for campaigns, "We do a lot of research, and we come down to three or four message themes to be repeated eight thousand times. The candidates know not to vary from those." But Barr "wouldn't stay with a message." Speaking one day in Williams, for example, he declared drugs to be the state's number one issue; the next day in Kingman he put economic development in the top spot. Gutierrez also noted that Barr "was one of the wittiest [guys], and his sarcasm . . . was devastatingly funny, but it was devastating." Barr's humor, so useful in dealing with legislators, was a hindrance in communicating with voters. Sue Sossaman described an event in Sun Lakes with several hundred people: "And every time somebody would ask a question, I mean, Burt was just on a roll. Everything was a joke and there was nothing serious about anything."[44]

If Barr's joking lost him votes in Sun Lakes, one particular joke proved far more costly. Speaking to the Phoenix Chamber of Commerce, Barr was asked about a sensitive tax issues. To solve a budget crisis in 1983, the legislature had passed a temporary half-cent increase in the sales tax, but in 1984 it became apparent that those revenues were essential, so the tax was made permanent.[45] Barr had exercised the most influence on these decisions, and he was asked why a tax initially passed as a temporary measure was made permanent. Barr could have responded that the state's economic condition had not improved as expected, or that cutting the tax would mean devastating spending cuts, or that this should be seen in the context of a decade of tax cuts—arguments he had used to gain legislative support. Instead, he leaned into the microphone, wiggled his eyebrows and said, "I lied. Next question." The room broke into laughter, and, as John Kolbe said, "I don't think there were five people there who thought it was meant in any serious kind of way, and yet you put that on paper. . . ."[46] It not only read differently than it sounded, but the meaning of a sarcastic joke could be twisted into evidence of something else.

The Plot Thickens: Evan Mecham Enters the Contest

Evan Mecham had a long history of running for office. A devout Mormon and a car dealer from Glendale, he had pursued his political aspirations with religious conviction and like a second career. Early on he had attempted to parlay a state senate seat (1960–1962) into a seat in the U.S. Senate, but he was defeated by incumbent Carl Hayden. He had then lost the Republican nomination for governor three times (1964, 1974, and 1982), and in 1978 he won the nomination but lost the election to Bruce Babbitt. After his fourth loss in 1982, Mecham vowed never to run again, but the lure of office was too strong. His entry into the 1986 race came after an ostensible draft effort that Max Hawkins started in May. In June Hawkins gave a press conference to support his petition drive for Mecham and, in a six-page statement, to denounce Barr as undeserving to hold public office. The petition drive was successful—it needed less than 3,400 signatures—Mecham submitted the forms in late June, and on July 1, Mecham announced he would seek the nomination.

But while Mecham was running for the fourth consecutive time, this campaign was quite different. His previous races had featured archconservative proposals to make drastic cuts to the state budget, let all existing federal programs expire, support a constitutional amendment to stop federal involvement in any welfare program, end state authority over land-use planning, and end the one-person, one-vote rule. In this campaign Mecham's published program had none of the radical proposals he had previously touted, and it appeared relatively innocuous, calling for things like efficiency in state government, improved education, and establishing a state weights and measures department. But the focus of his campaign was quite different.

When Mecham entered the race, the first issue he mentioned was his opposition to the one-cent sales tax increase and his determination to repeal it. Throughout the following weeks of the campaign, he hammered away at this and at Barr, denouncing it as a "liar's tax," claiming that Barr's joke had been a serious admission of his dishonest intent. When asked by Stan Turley how he would make up for the substantial lost revenue from repealing the tax, he said blithely that this could be done through increased governmental efficiencies. Mecham's early explanations of his candidacy also revealed a personal grievance, for he claimed that Barr "promised" to support him fully in his 1978 gubernatorial race, but that instead Barr had told contributors not to support Mecham and instead to contribute to legislative races.[47]

Mecham's campaign theme was a "New Beginning," and he focused on attacking the Arizona power structure, whose existence he said he had discovered while serving in the state senate in the early 1960s. He identified the public manifestation of this as the Phoenix 40, a group of prominent persons who met and discussed public concerns, but whom Mecham described as manipulating the activities of state and local government. "With me in the race," said Mecham, "we're not just going to talk about water and air and nice little things like that." Instead, he proposed to talk about taxpayers and "who's getting the goodies packages from state government." His campaign, he said, was asking voters to "wipe out the control of special-interest government and replace it with an administration that will govern with favor for none and equal consideration for all." He identified Barr as an important representative of this power elite and special interest government, their "bag man," and said that when voters learned "the truth, . . . they will find [Barr] unacceptable for governor."[48]

Over the succeeding weeks, Mecham made a series of charges against Barr, dredging up old allegations about Barr's intervention on behalf of grocers in 1974, and repeating accusations about Barr's landholdings made in a recent *New Times* article. Mecham called for investigations by the House Ethics Committee, the attorney general, and the Maricopa county attorney, but those authorities responded that there was no evidence or no actionable issues. Then, within a few weeks of the September 9 primary, Mecham issued two 12-page tabloid publications that he mailed successively to 380,000 registered Republican voters. Having accused the state's major papers of bias against him, and with the experience of running an alternative newspaper from 1963 to 1973, Mecham decided that direct mailing would be his most effective means of campaigning.

Providing only slight information about Mecham, the publications focused mostly on Barr. By reprinting articles and copying every critical allegation ever made against Barr, Mecham assembled a massive number of charges, even though many had been previously refuted, and others were transparently flimsy.[49] The most serious were recent charges that Barr profited by inside information and bought land where the highways he promoted would be built. But Barr's defense demolished the charges. He noted that he had no advance knowledge of the routes, that many of his parcels had been purchased years previously, that many were not close to the routes, and that his "ownership" typically consisted of a very small share, less than three percent, of a limited partnership.

Mecham's approach relied on a distrust of politicians and government that had grown since the 1960s, on the post-Watergate prominence of investigative journalism, and the increased frequency of and familiarity with negative political campaigns. Mecham's negative campaign began by using the earlier publications and repeating Warner's accusations, but the use of innuendo, exaggeration, and gross distortions put this in a different category. Mecham's assault on Barr was startling in the extent of the charges and because it constituted most of Mecham's campaign. Tony West, who was ideologically much closer to Mecham than Barr, said, "That was the first time that we'd ever seen that vicious of an attack on a statewide candidate that was so personal and, particularly, on somebody who had earned his spurs and worked hard in the vineyard and toiled and produced a better Arizona."[50] Barr's supporters found the attacks even more offensive because many believed Barr to be precisely the opposite of Mecham's distorted view: an honorable, honest, and decent person.

Barr's supporters and friends were especially confused and upset, then, by Barr's mode of response to Mecham. Earlier in the campaign, when assaulted by Warner's charges, he said that he would "not get down in the gutter with her. I'm going to run a positive campaign." On another occasion he told the press that he had "no intention of criticizing his opponents. 'I don't have time,' he said. 'I'm so enthused about tomorrow.'" When asked directly by reporters about particular issues, he corrected the false statements and gave facts to counter the charges, but his speeches did not discuss other candidates, let alone attack them. After Hawkins made his allegations, Barr said he would not "get into a shouting match" with him, and after Mecham's initial attack, he stated that he was "not going to criticize or attack."[51]

Nearly all of his political friends strongly urged him to respond directly to these attacks, imagining television, radio, or newspaper ads, but Barr refused, considering the charges ludicrous, distasteful, and something that should not be dignified with a prominent response. Mike Boyd and Lee Stitzenberger also argued for combating this, but said that Barr worried about alienating some of Mecham's supporters. Somewhat lost in subsequent discussions was exactly how Barr should have responded to Mecham's charges and with what effect. Refuting them would be shifting the debate to Mecham's terms; responding to only some of the massive number of charges would turn attention to those that were ignored. The more effective response would have to discredit Mecham, including a direct attack on him, pointing out his more extreme views, casting doubt on his claims to have been drafted, emphasizing his personal hostility to Barr, and suggesting that his proposal to repeal the sales tax would force drastic cuts in vital programs. But this, too, would have changed the focus of Barr's campaign; it would have, arguably, alienated some of Mecham's supporters; and it would have violated Barr's deeply held objection to personal attacks. Ultimately, Barr decided that people would realize that Mecham was not a serious candidate and the charges were bogus, allowing Barr to continue presenting a positive vision and focused on the general election. The campaign had accumulated substantial funds and was planning a major television effort after the primary.

Polls were crucial in shaping the campaign's strategy. A poll released July 19 showed a major gain for Mecham, with Barr's June lead of 42 to 5 percent having shrunk to a much narrower 38–17 advantage. In the August 9 poll Barr reversed the trend and increased his lead, rising to 44 percent versus 18 percent for Mecham. In September the margin narrowed significantly, but it was still 35–20 for Barr, and the campaign remained confident that this would hold in the election. But private polls showed something else. A pollster working in mid-August for GOP candidates discovered surprisingly high negative and no opinion responses in Barr's House district and disturbingly high levels in a nearby district. This information was brought to the campaign, but Barr would not change his mind. Alfredo Gutierrez reported that tracking polls by Democrats revealed slippage in Barr's number, but Barr's campaign people would not listen. Even worse, they were so confident of the outcome that they stopped taking their own tracking poll 10 to 12 days before the primary.

The Failed Campaign and the Lost Election

It was past midnight when Burton Barr and his family walked to the podium in his campaign headquarters at the Phoenix Hilton Hotel. The crowd of supporters, so exuberant and hopeful at the beginning of the evening, was now somber and silent, in stunned disbelief about what had apparently occurred. With tears evident on faces in the audience and on the dais, Barr made a statement, not a concession speech. Harkening back to his World War II experiences, as he often did, he spoke of fighting battles through life and of the difficulties they bring. "The battle is not over yet," he claimed, but the consistent and painful pattern of the long night's tally of election results contradicted that claim.[52]

He lamented the negative character of the campaign he had faced and spoke with satisfaction about his positive approach, saying, "The last thing I wanted to do was hurt anybody." He declared it sad that political figures could be flagrantly attacked, thinking of the innumerable times he had implored people to participate in public life. This could not be allowed to continue, he argued, "if our society is to survive." Poignantly, he added, "I just hope we can come to a conclusion that winning isn't everything and that there is concern for decency." Listening at his own headquarters to these televised remarks Evan Mecham claimed surprise and innocence. "I seem to be hearing him saying he was attacked. Let me make this clear. I never attacked Burton Barr personally." The problem, he asserted, was that Barr "never came out on the issues."[53]

The basic election results were simple and dramatic: Barr had taken only 45.9 percent of the vote, while Mecham, who had won only 38 percent in the primary four years earlier, had garnered 54.1 percent of this vote. Barr had won only four counties, including three of the smallest. Most strikingly, he had lost both of the populous counties: Pima (44.0 percent), and worse, since it was his home county, Maricopa (47.3 percent). The Barr campaign's strategy of traveling in rural Arizona, when over 80 percent of the Republican turnout came from the two urban counties, had been disastrous.

The first explanation for this shocking upset offered by most commentators and observers was the impact of Mecham's attacks. Bob Evans, a Barr supporter, said, "I'm disappointed to discover that mudslinging has been so very effective." He explained, "During the campaign, I was pleased that Barr did not choose to respond, but it is abundantly clear that response was necessary." GOP State Chairman Burt Kruglick, who had taken the unusual step of breaking with neutrality and endorsing Barr, blamed Barr's defeat directly on Mecham's allegations. Barr lost, said Kruglick with surprising candor, because "he miscalculated the intelligence of the voting public by not answering Ev Mecham's charges almost immediately. The public responded by saying, 'Hey, there must be something to what he (Mecham) is saying.'"[54]

The defeat involved more than this, of course. It had been possible in part because Barr and most political folks underestimated Mecham. Having seen him for decades, watched his continuous pursuit of office, and heard his extremely conservative, somewhat conspiratorial views, they were not inclined to take him seriously. But this time Mecham ran a different campaign. His attacks on Barr masked that effort, to some extent, but he also stayed largely on his single message. Some of those who voted for him would be surprised a year later when he unveiled his proposals, or by his candid statements, like describing the United States as a Christian nation, or referring to "pickanninies." Since roughly half of the state's registered voters had not lived in Arizona in 1980, they did not know his history.

The campaign was clearly flawed in strategy and organization, and Barr bore major responsibility for those. Failing to hire experienced advisers, he then failed to listen to those he had. Like a lawyer defending himself, his effort to direct his own campaign was foolish. He was also far too self-assured, confusing his knowledge of policy and small groups with an understanding of statewide political campaigns. But while responsible for these and other shortcomings, other people and parts of the campaign also shared the blame.

The campaign's misuse of polling was a serious error. There is no reason to think the polling methods were faulty or the data was wrong, but the interpretation of the data was certainly flawed, as pollster Earl de Berge suggested. Certainly the trend toward Mecham from August to September should have caused concern—and might have led to a different decision on responding to the attacks—but more disturbing was the very high number of undecided voters. The best explanation for the upset is that decided voters held their preference, while previously undecided voters went well over 3–1 for Mecham. Failing to read the polls, to keep taking polls, and to react to them was disastrous.

The decision to concentrate on the general election made sense in January and March, but not after May, when Mecham began hinting about entering the race. Barr later suggested that it was hard for the campaign to shift gears, but the difficulty seems more emotional than logistical, since there were three months before the primary. But while the arrangement of tours and speaking events consumed Barr's time, other parts of the campaign were also not redirected to confront Mecham. Barr had a major advantage over Mecham in money; he could and should have used it on advertising. Many observers also felt that the campaign erred by not linking Barr more directly with McCain and Reagan, and legislators said that their offers to send testimonials about Barr to their constituents were rejected. Failing to connect with party leaders was a particularly big mistake because, as Jon Kyl explained, Barr "was not seen as the party candidate," and he needed to assuage the feelings of the faithful.[55]

One possibility for success remained, despite all of the deficiencies, and that was to mount a vigorous drive to mobilize Barr's supporters. Bob Fannin remembered that at some point in the campaign the advisers thought this would be valuable, agreeing "maybe it's important to have a good 'get out the vote' in Pima County and Maricopa County, and get Burt's voters out," but in the end, "this did not happen—there was not a good organization for that purpose." Burt Kruglick confirmed that "Barr did not 'get out the vote' among his supporters." The very low turnout figure for this election may reveal that voters felt cross-pressured or confused, and thus did not vote, but it is apparent that Barr's campaign did not mount an effort and that his supporters did not vote.[56]

Clearly the Barr campaign had deficiencies in basic management of advertising, polling, and mobilizing supporters, but flawed campaigns can win. The ultimate and most serious weakness is evident in Lee Stitzenberger's post-election confession, "If we'd known that Burt was in trouble, we would've corrected it. We did not know."[57]

Power, Campaigns, and History

Barr's loss stemmed from weaknesses in his campaign, including his own failings, but other factors over which he had limited control also played a role. Art Hamilton explained, "Burton Barr paid a tremendous price for all the power he had amassed." As the reality and impression of that power grew, giving him credit "for every good thing that has happened in the state," he also became vulnerable, because people "also blamed him for every bad thing that had happened since Barry Goldwater was in short pants."[58]

The grievances were not only abstract, however; some were personal. "You cannot do the job he did for as long as he did it," Hamilton noted, "without stepping on a lot of toes." Some of this was simply an inherent part of the legislative and political process, involving choices and decisions, but Barr had been strikingly successful. Reflecting after his loss on his weaknesses, Barr said that in his drive to solve problems, "I don't always consider the ramifications of my actions," and that people might feel he "didn't care enough for them." There had certainly been occasions when his solutions had bypassed people or even run over them. More than that, while Jim Skelly might not have resented Barr because, as he had noted, "Burt always wins," others did.[59]

Some people had feelings stronger than resentment. In her preelection analysis, Keven Ann Willey noted that his work "has earned him enemies," people who "have seized upon his first statewide race as an opportunity to air their gripes." Some years later, Alfredo Gutierrez expanded on this, saying that "there were people out there who really didn't like Burt" and who "thought for the most part that he was bad." This included powerful business interests, like Keith Turley, the head of the Arizona Public Service utility company, who "was the hate part" of Barr's love-hate relationship with business. Some farmers and cattlemen, Gutierrez suggested, "felt he had run over everything" and were upset by how "the economics of water changed, the economics of farming changed." Barr's supporters saw his ability, humor, and decency, and they saw the positive side to his efforts, that he tried to be inclusive in his negotiations and compromises. But as Gutierrez put it, Barr "wasn't Santa Claus. . . . He was one tough guy."[60]

In July 1985, when Barr was still struggling with whether to run for governor, he mused to reporter Joel Nilsson, "Do I want to develop a new style, spend a year campaigning"?[61] But while he recognized intellectually that a new style would be needed, adjusting to it was more difficult. The ideal campaign, given Barr's experience, would have been essentially an extension of what he had done for 20 years: talking about policy and the state's future. But the reality of campaigning was not just the obvious difficulty of staying on message; it was also adjusting and reacting to what an opponent was saying. During the first half of the primary, with no real Republican opponent, Barr continued to present his own, somewhat bland message, even though Carolyn Warner challenged him. Mecham's entry into the race demanded that he adopt another campaign style, with a defense and an offense, and that he address the issues behind Mecham's campaign, but he did not want to do that.

In reality, Barr was the best candidate for Mecham to face, for Mecham's conservative populism resonated best against someone with Barr's experience. And as Art Hamilton observed, "Mecham did a masterful job of being the populist, anti-government guy, Mr. Outsider, who wasn't going to be controlled by all those downtown Phoenix boys," and he played to an instinctive sympathy for the underdog.[62] In this context, Barr became a symbol of government for people upset with it for whatever reason. But Barr was even more of a target as Mr. Magic, for his ability to conjure up solutions to problems delighted many but infuriated others. To those concerned with ideological purity, Barr was anathema. This was true for Mecham and his supporters, but also for some like liberal Representative John Kromko (D-Tucson), who preferred Mecham to Barr because of his commitment to ideology.

Barr's essential task in the election was to explain the value of negotiation and compromise in a political setting. This is always challenging, for as Garry Wills noted, "Praise of the political leader *as a compromiser* is so rare that, when we find an example of it, it sounds more like satire than sincere praise."[63] The task was essential because this election largely revolved around competing notions of leadership. Posing a distinction between "dealership and leadership," Warner had castigated Barr, claiming that he made private deals while she would reach agreements through open, public meetings. Although her campaign rhetoric probably simplified her position, and she essentially ignored that Barr's primary political role involved public debates and decision-making, the central thrust of her argument was that private negotiations were wrong. While public discussions and decision-making are essential in democracy, ignoring the problems of public posturing and the need for private and personal engagements to assist in public policy decisions was either naïve or political posturing. Barr saw discussions with interested parties as a key part of successful leadership, and he demonstrated his effectiveness in this time after time.

Mecham offered a different notion of leadership, a crusading style, a belief that a leader's task is to articulate and fight for principles. This style is appealing, particularly in times of public frustration, and it fits well with a populist approach to politics, either Mecham's conservative slant or John Kromko's approach from the other end of the ideological spectrum. With this kind of approach to leadership, engagement is combat and victory is total, but the most common result is stalemate. Evan Mecham, as his behavior as governor would show, viewed disagreement as basic, often permanent, and the result of wrong beliefs.

Barr followed a basic set of beliefs, but he did not see leadership as primarily battling for ideology or for partisan gain; instead, he believed that leaders should identify and solve problems. He took a collegial approach to decision-making because he felt that everyone had some contribution to make, and he saw persons on the other side of an issue as potential allies on the next one. He considered planning, flexibility, public debate, and private negotiation as parts of leadership. It was an approach that had served him well for 22 years in the legislature, but in the 1986 campaign criticism from the left and the right seemed to tarnish its value.

Barr's task in 1986 was far more difficult than it initially appeared. Supported by the leaders of his party, well-funded, with tremendous knowledge and political skills, and without a highly popular opponent, he seemed very likely to win the election. Instead, his candidacy called up a deeper current of frustration with Arizona's transition from rural to urban, as well as offering an opportunity for various individuals and political groups to express dissatisfaction for past defeats at his hands. Most disturbing to him was Mecham's campaign assault on his integrity. Barr's obvious goal was explaining his vision for Arizona and how to achieve it, and while not as informative as one of his one hour monologues to a reporter, his campaign accomplished that for those who were looking and listening. But the larger and far more difficult task he faced, once Mecham entered the race, was explaining why the crusading and "lay it on the table" styles of leadership were flawed, why his approach was better, and that he was a master not just of obtaining settlements but of including competing interests. During the campaign he did mention his basic commitment to this approach, but he did not give it the importance and central place in his campaign that it needed. His loss reshaped Arizona's future.

CHAPTER SEVEN

An Itch to Serve

Life after the Legislature

"I think Burt was genuinely hurt after his defeat, and quite frankly, he wanted to wash his hands of politics as much as he could, but of course he could never do that."

—CHRIS HERSTAM[1]

"My game has always been to work toward a solution. Some people called it wheeling and dealing. But in politics you have to learn to accommodate."

—BURTON BARR[2]

"We should recognize the people that help build a community. We also should hold him up as a model."

—YVONNE GARRETT[3]

"I'm struck by the Japanese tradition of declaring people to be living treasures; and certainly in my experience in Arizona politics, if we had a living treasure, it was Burt."

—TERRY GODDARD[4]

Life changed quickly for Barr after his loss in the primary election. The campaign was over, the reporters were gone, his legislative career was ended, and at the age of 69 he had to decide what to do next. His campaign wounds were deep, but the message he had delivered for two decades, calling people to participate in public life, reflected his core belief in the value of service. He could neither resist the invitations that quickly arrived, nor could he avoid seeing things that needed to be done. During the next decade he continued to serve his community. When he died, family and friends grieved his passing, but political commentators began assessing his impact on Arizona and Arizona politics, and the significance of his leadership.

Living with Loss

The morning after the primary defeat, Louise Barr awoke "devastated because I couldn't believe that it had happened," and intended to stay in her room when she heard Burt in the kitchen telling the children that this defeat was nothing compared to his experience at Anzio. While comparisons with that horrific battle might have felt appropriate then, hearing his pep talk helped her and reassured the children. Burt knew, of course, he had things to do that day. He went with Louise to his campaign headquarters later that morning and thanked his campaign workers. Afterward, one worker said, "The boss was exuberant. He's not going to fade away. He's in good spirits." He also issued a formal concession to Mecham, although he did not mention him by name.[5]

Two days later Barr spoke at length to reporter John Kolbe about his feelings and plans. Dismissing the claim by Mecham campaign chairman Max Hawkins that the charges against Barr were not personal, Barr retorted, "I don't think anyone could get more personal" than to question "my integrity on everything." He felt that making such attacks was not "decent." In reality, he charged, the attacks had a distinctly personal basis, for "these are people who want to get even."[6] Political rumors in the state were swirling, with moderate Republicans and Democrats upset at the Mecham and Warner victories and their negative campaigns, and Eddie Basha suggesting that he might run as independent candidate if Bill Schulz did not, but Barr refused to discuss his political plans. While skimming over most policy topics, Barr did suggest that Mecham's narrow focus on repealing the sales tax ignored the state's many needs, including the AHCCCS program. As for himself, he already had work, serving as the honorary chair of the Phoenix all-Indian rodeo, aiding Basha in pushing a constitutional amendment to raise the spending limit on education, and assisting Phoenix Mayor Terry Goddard.

A month later, Barr was finishing his legislative duties, working with his staff on a bill to extend the AHCCCS program. He had still not endorsed Mecham. Louise had offered her services to Schulz, who was now on the ballot as an independent candidate for governor. Barr deliberately left his intentions vague, dangling different pieces of information. He explained that he would not have sought the nomination if Schulz had run as initially planned, but he declined to endorse Schulz. He mentioned the tug of his long Republican loyalties, yet he also noted pressures on him to "be a good boy. Wrong." Mecham's attacks, he said, were not "going to be forgotten."[7]

Barr's bitterness about the attacks added to his sadness at losing the election, missing the opportunity to serve, and disappointing his family and friends. It was galling to have lost to Mecham, a sense that grew after his defeat, when the Mecham and Warner victories prompted Bill Schulz to run as an independent, which eventually allowed Mecham to squeak into office. These feelings mixed with the recognition that he bore some responsibility for the loss. Charlie Stevens, Alfredo Gutierrez, Joe Lane, and many others had sought to advise him about aspects of the campaign, but he had not listened well. While he mostly tried to hide his feelings from his family, his son Mike saw that he was "incredibly shocked" and depressed by the loss, which he took personally. Others also saw the pain he felt. Don Isaacson said the effect "was tremendous, I mean just visibly, you could see the impact on him." Charlie Stevens thought he "was probably more hurt than most people would be" because he felt his extensive efforts for Arizona and for so many people had been unappreciated. Mike felt that he finally recovered after four or five months, and he was "again dabbling in politics."[8]

Although severely tested, Barr's optimistic outlook returned, and he resumed his normal busy lifestyle, one more demanding than most 69-years-olds would enjoy. But while the campaign wounds healed, they left a scar. A year after the election Barr confessed, "Of all the things that happened to me in this world, that was the worst, it was the hardest to take. I've never carried a grudge in my life, but I will never forgive what they did to me."[9]

Working with the Legislature Still, Very Still

Barr's departure from the legislature took him from a life he had loved and a role he had filled so ably. It also removed the institution's greatest source of information about state policy and legislative operations, and the loss was magnified by the retirement of other leading lawmakers like former Speakers Frank Kelley and Stan Turley, and the shift of Speaker James Sossaman to the Senate. But Barr still had many friends in the House in 1987, and given those friendships and his expertise, many legislators contacted him, asking his advice about particular issues or legislative procedures and using him as a sounding board. He, in turn, reached out to them. This interaction prompted conversations that Barr enjoyed, and it gave him welcome contact with friends and his former life, but it was also risky. Barr had no desire to antagonize the governor, or to be the basis for anti-Mecham organizing, but he was also determined to maintain a role in public life, including contact with other political figures. This forced Barr to evaluate exactly what kind of public role he did want, especially in relationship to the governor and the legislature, but as the governor's troubles mounted, this became increasingly difficult.

Rick Collins, who had become the chief of staff for new House Speaker Joe Lane, consulted Barr frequently, almost daily in the beginning of the legislative term, asking, "How do we run this place?" Don Isaacson, another staffer and friend, also communicated with Barr. Some legislators who had worked closely with Barr, like Art Hamilton, continued their collaboration, with Hamilton calling him "with incredible regularity to find out what he was thinking, what people were saying, what advice he would give." Others, like Jack Jewitt, who chaired the House Transportation Committee, admitted publicly that he "periodically" asked Barr's opinions on some matters. As the session developed, however, relations between the legislature and Mecham deteriorated. This made some legislators seek Barr's advice more often, while others communicated less.[10]

Immediately after taking office, Mecham had generated added controversy by cancelling the state's Martin Luther King Jr. Day, an act he compounded in subsequent months by criticizing King and making racist comments. He caused more insult and antagonism because of other insensitive and foolish remarks, like the claim that working women caused the high divorce rate, and he developed an increasingly adversarial relationship with the press. While these actions worsened his public standing, he furthered damaged his chances of achieving his policy goals by his confrontational approach with the legislature. He began by proposing to drop the sales tax by one cent, which would have removed essential state revenues, and with no plan for how to compensate for this, the legislature rejected the proposal. Other Mecham proposals created further concern and opposition. Chris Herstam, one of the Republican moderates, explained, "When the agony started for me in 1987, I regularly talked to Burt Barr," and solicited his advice on various specific issues. But Herstam recognized the nature of Barr's situation and his concerns, and he asserted, "In no way did he try to sabotage Ev Mecham. He didn't want to have anything to do with Mecham or any influence on Mecham's success."[11]

Private conversations with legislators were one thing, but Barr also had to decide about speaking in public. Before January he had agreed to speak in April at a monthly economic-forecasting event. This had not seemed a particularly sensitive political topic, but when April rolled around, the legislature was confronting a Mecham budget plan aimed at freezing state salaries and cutting education spending. Barr cared about government and education, so he used the forecasting forum to address them. Arizona's economic growth, he explained, depended on seeming "predictable," but the current confrontational atmosphere in state government was reducing business confidence in the state and the willingness to move to Arizona. He rejected claims that universities were "elitist," arguing that they were crucial avenues for success and needed higher levels of funding.[12] In these remarks and the relatively few other occasions when he spoke in public after his defeat, Barr addressed matters that he cared about and tried to avoid talking about Mecham except as he directly affected those issues—a distinction that the governor and some in the public found difficult to see.

The legislature's increasingly strained relationship with the governor prompted speculation about Barr's role. In May an *Arizona Republic* story entitled "Ghost in the Machine: Invisible Barr Still Haunting the Legislature" made this a public issue. Mecham officials refused to comment publicly, but speaking anonymously, a close Mecham aide claimed that Barr "is trying to ruin Ev by any means that he can. He's trying to embarrass him, trying to cause problems publicly with the perception that [Mecham] is not getting along with the legislature." Of the numerous legislators who were interviewed, some mentioned consulting with Barr on occasion and that "he has not faded away," but they scoffed at the notion that Barr was actively manipulating the legislature. One legislator remarked that Barr cared about his friends, about Republicans maintaining a legislative majority, and about Arizona's challenges. "To see that as a conspiracy is absurd," he claimed. Senate Minority Leader Alan Stephens dismissed the notion that Barr had stirred up opposition to the governor, pointing to the spontaneous and widespread "opposition that people are showing against Mecham."[13]

And that opposition was becoming more serious and prevalent. In May, the Mecham Watchdog Committee, founded in January 1987, transformed itself into the Mecham Recall Committee and began gathering signatures to force an election. In July, 13 legislators issued a statement criticizing the governor's behavior. During the next four months, prompted by the governor's increasingly problematic comments and actions, politicians, eventually including Barry Goldwater, began calling for Mecham to resign. Barr was carefully and deliberately not a party to any of this. "I don't talk recall," he said, noting that people would call to invite his participation. He also stated, "I'm not plotting against him, even though he still brings up my name."[14] (Mecham commonly remarked that Barr, Babbitt, and Gutierrez had cared only for themselves and "little about the results to the state as a whole."[15])

Mecham's troubles worsened in October, as evidence of an unreported campaign contribution surfaced, and then evidence that he had misappropriated campaign funds to aid his business. In November the recall leaders submitted enough signatures to force a recall election, set for May, but other events were moving more quickly. A grand jury indicted Mecham in January, but the legislature also began action. Starting on January 15, the House heard the case against the governor, and on February 8 it voted to impeach him. Three weeks later the Senate began meeting as an impeachment court, and on April 4, 1988, it voted to convict him and removed him from office. Throughout this furor, Barr made no public comments, and Speaker Joe Lane reported subsequently that, "Burt never called me or said one word to me ever about the impeachment of Mecham, ever."[16]

For two years Barr had been tied to Mecham—first by the accusations, then by hurt, then by concern that any public statement or contact with legislators might seem an effort to spite Mecham, and finally by the suspicion that he was somehow orchestrating Mecham's downfall. In reality, after he recuperated and recovered in late 1986, Barr began creating a new role for himself in 1987, one that allowed him to talk privately with legislator friends, to respond to requests for advice, and to participate in major public causes on his own terms. Although he remained hurt and upset by the accusations and their unjust consequences, he did not pine for the office or scheme about revenge against Mecham. Here, as in other times of difficulty, his optimistic and pragmatic outlook on life guided his behavior, and he focused on moving ahead and finding new ways to contribute.

New Challenges

Barr had no time to wait for new challenges; they found him. The day after Barr's shocking defeat, Phoenix Mayor Terry Goddard asked him to serve as an adviser and work on a variety of projects for the city, and Barr agreed. Having seen Barr work on the 1981 gas tax dispute and Peoria's annexation attempt in 1985, Goddard had firsthand evidence of Barr's skills. Barr's arrangement with the city was simple: he took no salary and had no office, just using any available space, but he did insist on getting a parking place.

Valued for bringing people together and solving complex problems, he offered Goddard advice as requested. Serving as essentially a "minister without portfolio," he dealt with "[w]hatever Phoenix had trouble with or what we needed legislative help with," said Goddard. He worked to reshape the city's relationship with the legislature, but his involvement there had limits, for he would not address matters involving differences with certain legislators. Barr was also valuable because of his contacts and his ability to raise money, and he combined those in support of several causes. In 1988, when the city sought voter approval for a $1 billion bond campaign to fund a wide range of city buildings, programs, and initiatives, Barr raised funds to finance the support campaign. One of the buildings funded by this measure was an impressive city library, but money was needed to furnish the building. Barr volunteered to help and brought all of his persuasive powers to bear. Asked by a potential donor what could be named after him for a $5,000 gift, Barr said "a restroom," and talked the person into contributing hundreds of thousands of dollars.[17] In recognition of these efforts, the library was named for Barr after his death.

Many of the problems he dealt with were thorny. In 1982 the federal Indian Bureau announced plans to close the Phoenix Indian School, a valuable, three-acre site in north-central Phoenix, opening the question of how the land might be used. Barr worked extensively in the initial negotiations, which involved a potential swap of land with Baron Collier, a developer—always a controversial issue in Phoenix. Goddard explained, "He did almost all of our fieldwork on Collier and the land swap for the Indian School." Barr provided an analysis of the Colliers, "an intelligent way of dealing with them, which was respectful for what they needed and what the city needed out of the park," and then handled complex negotiations with the Colliers and monitored this through congressional hearings. While the matter was not finally resolved until 1996, the end result was city ownership of the land.[18]

Barr was also the city's point man in trying to attract major league sports franchises. For some years the city had been attempting to attract a football team, seeking unsuccessfully to entice the owners of the then Baltimore Colts and the Philadelphia Eagles to relocate to a city hungry for professional football. Barr helped conclude a deal with Bill Bidwell, who, in January 1988, agreed to move his St. Louis Cardinals to Phoenix. Phoenicians were overjoyed, but a year later they were furious because the team suddenly jacked up ticket prices to the highest in the league. In a meeting of community leaders with Cardinals officials, Barr started by asking, "Exactly when did you hire the Ayatollah to do your public relations?"[19]

Invoking the Iranian leader, whose name had become a popular American symbol of harsh and extreme behavior, conveyed the seriousness of the team's problem, which Barr then helped resolve. Although Phoenix was not as well positioned to obtain a major league baseball franchise, Barr was part of the presentation team in 1988 that attempted to persuade league owners to award an expansion franchise to Phoenix, laying the groundwork for a later, successful effort.

While he was willing to help on problems like these, Barr cared more deeply about three major projects connected to his vision for development of the Phoenix area. The first of these was the Rio Salado Project, a plan for developing the dry bed of the Salt River, which had originated in the 1960s and taken form through the 1970s. In 1980 the legislature had voted to create a Rio Salado Development District, and the management group soon finalized a mixed-use plan for a 17-mile stretch of the river bottom. In 1986 the legislature, with Barr's support, voted to allow Maricopa County voters to decide whether to levy a property tax to fund the project. Barr strongly supported the plan and served as finance chair of the committee to campaign for it. This matched Barr's desire for urban land-use planning and economic development, and he saw it as a plan of "courage and foresight" that would be a "centerpiece" of beauty and development in the Valley. "It's the single greatest opportunity we are ever going to have, the one real chance to provide in the urban area a mixed-use plan . . . that exists nowhere else (in the country)."[20] A majority of voters felt differently and rejected the plan in November 1987, although Tempe and Phoenix would later develop their own plans for parts of the river bed.

At the same time, Barr worked to raise campaign funds for another valley-wide initiative. The ValTrans proposal called for a Valley transportation system to include 103 miles of elevated rail lines, 1,200 buses, and additional highways, to be paid for by a half-cent sales tax. This also represented a longtime interest of Barr's; he had been pushing transportation planning for 15 years, and most recently he had been a major advocate of the highway system adopted and funded by Maricopa County voters in 1985. This new proposal, however, proved to be a train too far. Although the initial polls were favorable, the measure went down in defeat in March 1988 by a 3–2 margin. Here, too, Phoenix, Tempe, and Mesa would later create a different version of the defeated project and develop a light-rail mass transit system.

The third major campaign in which Barr was involved was a statewide effort that his friend Eddie Basha helped to lead. Arizona Citizens for Education (ACE) in 1990 sought to raise $5.8 billion in various taxes over 10 years to improve the state's education system, which at the time was near the middle of the state rankings. While the educational arguments were strong, bad economic conditions also doomed this initiative to defeat.

During these same years of his public campaign efforts, Barr worked for certain private groups. He served on the board of Brophy College Preparatory School, the high school his son Mike attended, and also on the board of directors of the University of Phoenix, a for-profit institution that he had supported because he felt it provided expanded educational opportunities. He was active in Episcopalian Services, his church's social service organization; he served on the board of the Housing Opportunity Center, an organization that Terry Goddard set up in 1991; and with Alfredo Gutierrez, he co-chaired the fund-raising efforts for Friendly House, a longtime Phoenix institution that provided services to immigrants.

Mecham's removal from office ended Barr's formal exile from the governor's office, but his desire to avoid association with the impeachment or its consequences kept him at some distance. Still, his expertise was too valuable to waste, and in September 1988, he accepted an appointment from new Governor Ross Mofford to chair a state task force on welfare reform. In 1993 he agreed to help Governor Fife Symington negotiate gaming compacts with Indian tribal leaders. Barr also resumed a political role, being involved in two gubernatorial races, though on personal rather than partisan grounds. In 1990 he backed Goddard, serving on his campaign committee and attending meetings of the steering committee. In 1994 Symington sought his support, and although he had a relationship with the governor, he instead supported his good friend Eddie Basha, the Democratic candidate.

At the same time that he was pursuing all of these activities, he was in partnership with Alfredo Gutierrez. Captain Chaos had also retired from legislative service in 1986, but as a man of 41 he looked for gainful employment. Partnering with Bill Jamieson, a former Babbitt administrator, he organized Jamieson and Gutierrez, a public policy and issues management company that grew quickly to handle a range of business, public affairs, and political clients. In 1986, when Barr left the legislature, he had also sold his company. Although he retained a position and an office, his interest in that business had declined and he no longer fit there. Gutierrez's firm gave him a new base. "We had offices . . . and a conference room and all the newfangled things that were coming about then—the fax machines and cellular phones—and so Burt would come in every day."[21]

After a while Gutierrez began asking him to take a formal role with the firm, but Barr refused. He did not need the money, he did not want to burden the firm, he was only around for a limited time each day, and he wanted to remain a free agent. But Gutierrez persisted, in part because he was involved in the "strategic approach to almost everything we did." Finally, after two or three years, he formally joined, and for a salary, "just to satisfy Louise." His continuing, daily presence in the office later prompted staff and even partners to ask Gutierrez, "Didn't Barr have a hobby?" "No," he would say, "We are his hobby; we are *the* hobby."[22] And so, operating from the Jamieson and Gutierrez office, he worked, satisfying that itch to serve, working only on projects he believed in, helping raise funds for the library and other causes, and trying to establish an ASU campus in downtown Phoenix.

Final Days

After 1990 the pattern of Barr's life changed. With Goddard's departure from the mayor's office, he no longer served the city nor worked out of a city office. The ACE campaign was the last sustained campaign in which he played a major role. He remained active, but at 73 he had shifted from "perpetual motion" to "usually in motion," and he could take overseas trips with Louise. But things changed further because his kidneys began to fail, influenced perhaps by the hepatitis and other injuries he suffered in World War II. It took him little time to decide not to pursue a transplant, knowing what that would involve and because he believed that a kidney should go to a younger person. This meant daily medication and dialysis multiple times a day. He and Louise told the children that his condition was serious but not immediately threatening, but he informed almost no one else, wanting no sympathy or special attention. He was determined that, as much as possible, he would not let this stop him from doing things. When he first began treatments, his son Mike thought he "went out of his way to make it appear that he was healthier than he was, healthier than ever."[23] For a while this did seem true, and he was helped in 1993, when he got a machine allowing him to do dialysis overnight, instead of during the day.

He continued his connections with close friends by phone or sharing lunch. Eddie Basha spoke with him regularly and lunched with him at the China Doll restaurant. Basha was amused because Barr "couldn't ever remember people's names, but he had this Burt Barr way. He'd say 'Hi there!'" to all the people he recognized. Barr was also a creature of habit: "He always had the chow mein. I said 'God, Burt, don't you . . .' 'Nope, I'll have chow mein.'" Terry Goddard also "kept in pretty close touch," mainly by phone, but every three or four months Barr would take him to lunch at the University Club. Barr never mentioned his health problems, although during one lunch he fell asleep three times. Instead, he asked about

Goddard: he "wanted to know about me. How things were going." But the meetings always included a discussion of family, and increasingly they "had an unusual amount to do with his children." His breakfasts with Chris Herstam followed a related pattern. "We would always start with the kids," reflecting the strongest lesson he learned from Barr: "nothing was more important than family." After that, they talked about contemporary politics, his second love, and then "military history was there again, which played such a role in his life." Meeting in Barr's last year, Herstam observed his physical deterioration and the unsteadiness, but he also saw "the sparkle in his eye was there."[24]

Burton Barr died on January 13, 1997, the result of a general physical deterioration caused by kidney failure. The man who had joked about retiring while taking his children to Cub Scouts and Brownies was surrounded by his grown children, each having graduated from college and with developing careers. Alfredo Gutierrez would later say that Burt had made a deal with the Lord to have one last day, for drawing on his last reserves of energy he rallied to talk with family and friends in his hospital room and share their company while watching part of a football game on television. The next day he died.

A January 16 memorial service at All Saints Episcopal Church drew a packed audience that heard tributes from Eddie Basha, Alfredo Gutierrez, Charlie Stevens, former Governor Bruce Babbitt, and Senator John McCain. Six days later, Barr was buried in Arlington National Cemetery, a soldier's funeral befitting his years of valorous service on the nation's behalf. The ceremony began in the Fort Meyer Chapel, adjacent to the Cemetery, with family, the Arizona congressional delegation, Senators Kyl and McCain, Supreme Court Justice O'Connor, Charley Stevens, Alfredo Gutierrez, Burt's wartime friend Mike Daley, and employees of Jamieson and Gutierrez. First, Daley eulogized Barr, who had saved his life and recommended him for the Congressional Medal of Honor. Then, because some others felt too emotional to deliver remarks, Charlie Stevens offered a second eulogy. The mourners left the chapel on this rainy, gloomy day, and over a hundred soldiers marched alongside the caisson for the mile to the grave site. And there, with some final words, Burton Barr was laid to rest.

Final Words and Larger Meanings

At the time of his death, Barr was appreciated as a marvelously engaging character, praised for his accomplishments in passing noteworthy legislation, and lauded for his pragmatic, civil, bipartisan approach to policy-making and public engagement. While the passage of time dims some memories, and new voters, either those from other places or those newly come of age, may have no memories of Barr at all, a core of Arizonans have continued to look back on Barr's era and successes and regret their passing. Such feelings for the past are not unique; one reason that people study history is to learn and understand its lessons. That is, of course, no simple task. But if interpreting the past is difficult, then applying its findings can be even more troublesome.

Burton Barr was undeniably a person of great abilities and talents. He was engaging, humorous, compassionate, interested in others, hardworking, and vastly energetic—all highly desirable characteristics for a political leader. His capacity for understanding people and complex issues, plus his determination to solve problems, enabled him to negotiate and forge coalitions, making him an outstanding transactional leader. While his lengthy tenure as majority leader reinforced his opportunities for success in the legislature, his influence did not depend on friendships or on punitive measures or threats; he did not withhold campaign funds or deny committee chairmanships to the uncooperative. Rather, his power rested, first and foremost, on his powers of persuasion, which is also evident in his business and post-legislative successes.

Barr demonstrated an impressive ability to bore incisively into an issue, to find the essential value or strength, and to identify areas of weakness or unanswered questions. Terry Goddard remembered with admiration how Barr came to a meeting, "took control, had a clear agenda, and . . . knew the questions to ask to get that agenda to completion. And I've never seen anybody who was better at it." Bob Fannin described his efforts to explain a particular proposal, and Barr said, "Quit talking that way. Just tell me, is this something that is going to help, who's this going to help, and who is going to be against it." While his connection with a proposal would move far beyond this level, he started with a clear, simple assessment.[25]

Barr practiced inclusiveness because it was a cherished value of his and because he knew it was generally important for achieving solutions. Whether it was discussions over groundwater or deliberations regarding indigent health care, he ensured that all of the necessary parties were at the table. Within the legislature, he took a pragmatic approach to seeking success. As a Republican leader, he worked for and funded the success of the party's legislative nominees, regardless of their ideological perspective. He looked beyond ideology and personality, telling Fannin, for example, "Not everybody is going to like everybody here. We can't choose our cellmate.

We have to deal with who's here."[26] And so he did, whether they were conservative or liberal, Republican or Democrat, congenial or grumpy.

Added to these general leadership traits, the personal relationships that Barr developed over his years in office also aided his efforts. In his tribute to Barr in 1997, John Kolbe quoted a lawmaker who often battled with Barr: "Of course, if he runs [for office] I'll do anything for him. I love the man." Barr's character and generosity built strong friendships that inspired deep affection and support. His good friend Eddie Basha recounted Barr's request for a contribution to support ValTrans. Basha, who opposed the program, turned him down. Barr repeated his request, and Basha realized, "Out of sheer respect for Burt, and because of the friendship, and because of everything that he did for this state, I couldn't turn him down."[27]

Barr also made enemies and attracted critics, people who crossed swords with him and mostly lost—like the leaders of the state's traditional economic interests, and some conservatives and liberals who disliked his willingness to find compromises and his ability to win. He preferred persuasion and compromise, but on occasion he could use the power of his position. Although typically self-controlled, his confrontations with Governor Babbitt sometimes spilled over into anger and grudges, reflecting his frustration at the unusual position of suffering political defeat. The quality of his political skills in most circumstances is put in stark relief by his failings as a gubernatorial candidate. Although recognizing the challenges before entering the race, once he became a candidate and was operating outside of his familiar environment, he plunged ahead without seeking or accepting advice, insisting on doing things his way. His shocking election loss served as a painful education.

While Barr's leadership skills were impressive and especially well-suited for legislative situations, his accomplishments were also possible because of the particular historical era in which he functioned. Barr came to the legislature at a special and propitious time. Across the nation, citizens were pushing for reform and modernization of state government to meet new challenges, and a flood of ideas were arising about how to renew the role of states as vital participants in a federal system. In Arizona, the state's urban and economic growth had created opportunities and possibilities, the old partisan divisions bore limited relationship to the current issues and needs, and both the necessity and direction for change were visible, comprehensible, and attainable.

Barr understood some of this. He talked emphatically about the urban character of society, about the need to create urban institutions, a transportation system and infrastructure, and social policies that responded to new requirements for education, physical health, and mental well-being. Growth demanded radical revisions in tax policy, environmental and planning controls, and the introduction of water management. A governmental system forged in the early twentieth century for a lightly populated state had become grossly inefficient and inequitable for Arizona in the 1960s and after. By transforming state government into an effective instrument, and by using that instrument to create important state policies, Barr shared in a movement that changed not only state government, but also the larger federal system.

The central significance of reapportionment was also clear to Barr, and he described the years after 1966 as "a completely different era." He also understood how the shift had affected the parties. Democrats were "in disarray," shocked at being out of power and struggling to understand and respond to the problems of Arizona's new urban society.[28] This gave Republicans an unbridled opportunity to lead from 1966 until roughly 1974, when Democrats began electing supporters of modernizing efforts, while conservatives became somewhat more influential in Republican ranks. Thereafter, the abilities and flexibility of Republican legislative leaders Stan Akers, Frank Kelley, and Stan Turley, plus the skillful efforts of Democrats Alfredo Gutierrez and Art Hamilton, allowed Barr to pursue support for legislative initiatives where he could find it. In the process, Barr became not just the most powerful man in the state, but he had used his power to be the most effective and productive leader.

Barr's departure from the center political stage in 1986 has rightly seemed to later observers of Arizona politics as a watershed, but was his departure a cause or a consequence of this change? Why did he decide to leave the legislature to run for governor in 1986, and what if he had not done so? Running for governor might or might not have been the wise choice, and retirement from political office was another option, but for a few years before his decision Barr had been feeling that legislative activities were less "fun" than before, and colleagues suggested he was "tired" or that he had "overstayed his welcome." His wife, Louise, later observed, "It was a reasonable time for him to go." Barr concluded in May 1986, "I have reached the end of the legislative level. I don't have any other hills to climb."[29] If this reflected a lack of positive challenges, Barr may also have felt uninterested in confronting the changing attitudes of legislators. Some seemed "immune to his charms," viewing his humor as a failure to take issues seriously. Legislative norms were altering, as freshmen were less likely to remain silent and more apt to challenge the leadership. A restiveness with long-term, older leadership was stirring in the House, and younger, ambitious politicians were looking for their chances.

Barr had surmounted earlier rumblings and challenges, but these had a somewhat different tenor, and there was reason to think that an era was ending. The most obvious change was the people. Babbitt was retiring as governor, as were Barr's key legislative partners: Gutierrez, Kelley, and Turley. A second, though less obvious, shift was in the focus of government. The central challenge that Barr and his allies confronted in 1966 was to modernize state government and its policies, and that had been largely accomplished. Important challenges remained, of course, and policies on taxes, education, and other issues would perennially need revision, but the capacity of state government had been fundamentally altered, and policies addressing Arizona's urban needs had been put in place—an accomplishment that also mirrored larger national patterns.

Partisan politics had also changed by 1986. Rural, Pinto Democrats no longer dominated that party; its vote and focus were largely urban. Republicans had picked up some of the rural support, but their major gains were in suburban areas. More significant, especially for Barr, was the role of conservatism in the Arizona GOP. Conservatives of various stripes had always been among the party's leaders and represented in the legislature, but dealing with Arizona's modernizing moment required actions that did not fit a simple conservative agenda. By 1986, with many of those needs addressed and the original imperative less clear, conservatives, particularly those of a certain type, were more insistent that their demands be met.

Evan Mecham was not simply the embodiment of that sentiment, for his history and flaws were his own, but his presence and success in 1986 indicate something of the rising conservative trend in the party and the state. Labels can be misleading, but they can also provide a shorthand guide to larger differences. In this case, contemporaries used the terms "archconservative" and "ultraconservative" to designate persons holding more extreme conservative views, particularly those focused on moral issues and (morally, it seemed) opposed to taxes. Mecham fits into that category, but a larger movement, which Mecham did not direct, was active. For example, in 1986 the number of new legislative candidates jumped to 186, up from only 25 in 1984, while a record number of 16 Republican incumbents faced primary challenges. Moderate Republicans and Democrats charged that "ultraconservative candidates are putting together 'hit lists.'"[30]

Elections must be viewed in context, and Arizona's 1986 election fits within a national trend of rising conservatism within the Republican Party and the state. But that election should not be viewed as simply an undifferentiated part of a broad pattern. Its components, actors, and consequences were distinctive and particular to the state. Mecham's negative attacks on Barr and Barr's refusal to respond actively gave the party nomination to a highly polarizing candidate; the unique, independent candidacy of Bill Schulz enabled Mecham to win the election. In office, Mecham did make a difference because he changed the focus of state policy debates to the King holiday and the consequences of repealing it, to cutting taxes, and to slashing educational funding. His confrontational style and personal gaffes promoted divisions; the evidence of his misdeeds fueled the recall and forced investigations. Whatever the justice of his impeachment and conviction, they invigorated hostility and division within the Republican Party, prompting primary challenges and fueling the fires of anger that burned for years.

Had Barr been elected, his policies and style would have been radically different than Mecham's, of course, and the travails of the Mecham era would have been avoided. Whether Barr could have succeeded as governor in bridging an already growing divide over policies is unclear, but it is absolutely certain that Mecham's election and its consequences helped develop a politics of hostility and ideological narrowing. More important than this sort of counterfactual speculation, however, is the attraction of Barr's model of political and legislative leadership. Running through the post-Barr years of political discussions in Arizona, and periodically popping up in newspaper columns or magazine stories, is the memory of Barr's bipartisan, solution-oriented approach. With a current political system riven by partisanship, harsh rhetoric, and negative campaigns, and with major concerns over failure to resolve key issues, the desire to look to the past for answers is understandable, but is that memory, that image, correct?

This book argues that Barr was a highly effective leader, that he made and helped make major policy changes, and that he practiced an open, inclusive politics. This was not some sort of "golden era," for there were clearly shortcomings, failures, and conflict, but it was a time in which much was accomplished. What has changed? Term limits, for one thing. In 1992, Arizona, like many states, adopted term limits for state legislators, restricting members to eight years in one house. This reduced the opportunities for legislators to build long-term relationships with each other and to develop the kind of expertise that Barr established. Intense partisanship and the use of "wedge politics"—focusing on issues that divide—make it more difficult to be productive. Stan Barnes, who served in the legislature for six years after Barr left, argued that politics shifted and "disagreements started becoming personal." Art Hamilton said that the legislature had shifted from spending most of its time "on how to get the place to work" to spending most of its time on "hand-to-hand combat."[31]

Structure is important, but so, too, are culture and relationships, and Barr was masterful in cultivating them. As a very small example, in 1973 Barr proudly announced to the House that his new daughter, Suzanne, a Republican, "has been assigned to two committees: Yelling and Screaming and Eating and Changing." The Democratic leader, Craig Daniels, responded in kind, saying that he had intended to protest this early partisan decision, but that after he had heard the committee assignments he decided "that sure sounded like Republicans."[32] Leadership is a relative relationship; it depends not only on the abilities and characteristics of the leader, but also on the interests and receptivity of followers. And it rests on how the larger body politic understands leadership. If leadership means crusades and a search for purity, then politics can only be a battle. But if politics is the art of the possible, and leadership involves the effective practice of politics, then the results can be very different. Responding with frustration to criticism of Barr shortly after his defeat, a journalist wrote, astutely, "The *real* danger in politics is not that you might get a dealmaker, but that you might not."[33] Barr was not only the quintessential dealmaker, he helped at least some people understand why that was important.

Notes

These notes are intended primarily to provide the sources for quotations. The Essay on Sources (p. 238) offers a general assessment of both primary and secondary sources used in writing this volume.

Abbreviations

ADS	*Arizona Daily Star*
ALAR	Arizona State Library, Archives, and Public Records
AR	*Arizona Republic*
BBC	Burton S. Barr Collection, Arizona Collection, Arizona State University Libraries
HMB	H. M. Barr Subject Files, 1927–1937, Portland Public School Archives
PG	*Phoenix Gazette*

Introduction

1. *On Heroes, Hero-Worship and the Heroic in History* (New York: Fredrick A. Stokes & Brother, 1888), 2.

2. Garry Wills, *Certain Trumpets: The Call of Leaders* (New York: Simon & Schuster, 1994), 23–24.

3. Shawn Hubler, "Meet the Most Powerful Man in Arizona," *Tucson Citizen Magazine*, April 7, 1984, 2.

4. Govenor Bruce Babbitt, letter to the Arizona Legislature, January 10, 1983; Govenor Babbitt, *Opening Message to the Arizona Legislature, 1983* (Phoenix: Governor of Arizona, 1983), 1, 2.

5. Keven Ann Willey, "Consistent Betting on a Full House," *AR*, May 8, 1983, B1, B4.

6. Ibid.

7. Joe Lane, interview by Jack Pfister, transcript, February 1, 1999, 5.

8. Willey, "Consistent Betting on a Full House."

9. Catie Robin, "The Teddy Bear Who Runs the House," *Arizona: The Arizona Republic*, January 3, 1982, 4; Steven Tragash, "Adaptability Helps House's Majority Leader Remain in Charge," *AR*, April 4, 1976, B-2; Bernie Wynn, "The Riddle of Barr: Does He Try Harder?" *AR*, March 30, 1973, 31; John Kolbe, "Rip, Chew, Talk, Fight or Juggle: Burt Barr Keeps Action Going," *PC*, October 1, 1973; Hubler, "Meet the Most Powerful Man in Arizona"; John Kolbe, "'Barr Factor' Haunts Prolonged Special Session," *PG*, February 14, 1980; Art Hamilton, interview by Jack Pfister, July 1, 1998, transcript, 14.

10. Ralph Waldo Emerson, *Complete Works of Ralph Waldo Emerson*, vol. 2, *Essays First Series*, "History," http://www.rwe.org/complete-works/ii-essays-i/i-history.html.

11. Tracey Arklay, "Political Biography: Its Contribution to Political Science," in *Australian Political Lives: Chronicling Political Careers and Administrative Histories*, ed. Tracey Arklay, John Nethercote, and John Wanna (ANU E Press, Canberra, 2006), 19.

12. Wills, *Certain Trumpets*, 20.

13. Ibid., 13.

14. Robin, "The Teddy Bear Who Runs the House," 4.

15. Such was the contention, for example, by some critics of President George H. Bush's shift in 1990 on raising taxes.

16. Willey, "Consistent Betting on a Full House," B4

17. Tragash, "Adaptability Helps House's Majority Leader Remain in Charge," B-2.

18. Thomas P. O'Neill Jr., *Man of the House: The Life and Political Memoirs of Speaker Tip O'Neill*, with William Novak (New York: St. Martins' Press, 1987), 381.

19. Joel H. Silbey, *Martin Van Buren and the Emergence of American Popular Politics* (New York: Rowman & Littlefield, 2002); American Political Science Association, *Toward a More Responsible Two-party System* (New York: Rinehart, 1950); Austin Raney, *Curing the Mischiefs of Faction: Party Reform in America* (Berkley: University of California Press, 1975); John H. Aldrich, *Why Parties? The Origin and Transformation of Political Parties in America* (Chicago: University of Chicago Press, 1995); Arthur Paulson, *Realignment and Party Revival: Understanding American Electoral Politics at the Turn of the Twenty-First Century* (Westport, CT: Praeger, 2000); David W. Rohde, *Parties and Leaders in the Postreform House* (Chicago: University of Chicago Press, 1991); Anthony King, ed., *The New American Political System*, 2nd ed. (Washington, DC: AEI Press, 1990).

20. David M. Wrobel, "The Politics of Western Memory," in *The Political Culture of the New West*, ed. Jeff Roche (Lawrence: University Press of Kansas, 2008), 332–63.

21. William Deverell,"Politics and the Twentieth-Century American West," in *A Companion to the American West*, ed. William Deverell (Malden, MA: Blackwell, 2004), 450.

22. Jeff Roche, introduction to *The Political Culture of the New West*, ed. Jeff Roche (Lawrence: University Press of Kansas, 2008), 5.

23. Samuel Lubell, *The Future of American Politics*, 3rd ed. (New York: Harper & Row, 1965), 30, 31.

24. *The American West: A Twentieth-Century History* (Lincoln: University of Nebraska Press, 1989), 283. See also Lisa McGirr, *Suburban Warriors: The Origins of the New American Right* (Princeton, NJ: Princeton University Press, 2001).

25. Paul Kleppner, "Politics without Parties: The Western States, 1900–1984," in *The Twentieth-Century West*, ed. Gerald Nash and Richard Etulain (Albuquerque: University of New Mexico Press, 1989), 295–338.

26. Ibid., 328.

27. Jon Kyl, interview by Jack Pfister, August 18, 1997, transcript, 9; John Kolbe, interview by Jack Pfister, January 12, 1999, transcript, 7.

28. See, for example, Jon C. Teaford, *The Rise of the States: Evolution of American State Government* (Baltimore: Johns Hopkins University Press, 2002).

29. Roche, introduction to *The Political Culture of the New West*, 7.

Chapter 1

1. Quoted from *The Dehumanization of Art and Other Essays on Art, Culture, and Literature* (Princeton, NJ: Princeton University Press,1968), cited by http://www.successories.com/iquote/author/1959/jose-ortega-y-gasset-quotes/1.

2. Stephanie Strasser, interview by Jack Pfister, July 10, 2005, transcript, 11.

3. Ibid., 6.

4. Thomas Kessner, *The Golden Door: Italian and Jewish Immigrant Mobility in New York City, 1880–1915* (New York: Oxford University Press, 1977), 37, 129–31.

5. David Samuel Barr, interview by Philip R. VanderMeer, October 30, 2013, notes in the author's possession. Barr, a grandson of Hy's brother Samuel Max, explained that his grandfather would not talk about his family's past.

6. Robert D. Johnston, *The Radical Middle Class: Populist Democracy and the Question of Capitalism in Progressive Era Portland, Oregon* (Princeton, NJ: Princeton University Press, 2003), 53.

7. William Toll, *The Making of an Ethnic Middle Class: Portland Jewry over Four Generations* (Albany: State University of New York Press, 1982), 194.

8. He died in 1976.

9. E. Kimbark MacColl, *The Growth of a City: Power and Politics in Portland, Oregon, 1914–1950* (Portland, OR: Georgian Press, 1979), 284.

10. *Oregonian*, November 6, 1976, C9.

11. H. M. Barr, "Fitting the School to the Needs of the Individual Child," ms., p. 3; HMB, copies in BBC.

12. Ibid., 5.

13. H. M. Barr, "A New Year for Oregon Schools," ms., pp. 7–8; HMB, copies in BBC.

14. H. M. Barr, "Have You X-Rayed Your Prejudices?," ms., part 2, p. 4; HMB, copies in BBC.

15. H. M. Barr, "Are We Sincere About Our International Affairs?," ms., pp. 1, 8, 9; HMB, copies in BBC.

16. See Johnston, *The Radical Middle Class*, 191–232.

17. *AR*, January 10, 1967, and February 2, 1982.

18. Merle Miller, *Ike the Soldier: As They Knew Him* (New York: G. P. Putnam's Sons, 1987), 310.

19. Miller, *Ike the Soldier,* 310.

20. Story from Barr interview by Pfister; Burton Barr to Brigadier General John S. D. Eisenhower, September 27, 1990, private letter in BBC; and Miller, *Ike the Soldier,* 316–17.

21. Two similar versions of this story are in Catie Robin, "The Teddy Bear Who Runs the House," *Arizona: The Arizona Republic,* January 3, 1982, 4, based on reminiscences by Harry P. Smith, mimeographed sheet [n.p., 3rd Division?, n.d.]; and *AR,* January 12, 1986.

22. *AR,* April 10, 1981; Lloyd Clark, *Sun City Daily News,* February 11, 1997, AA1; Lloyd Clark, interview by Jack Pfister, December 22, 1999, transcript, 6.

23. Military records for medals in Military Records, BBC.

24. Mike Barr, interview by Jack Pfister, December 4, 2000, transcript, 11–12.

25. Louise Barr, interview by Jack Pfister, September 2, 1997, transcript, 6.

26. Mike Daley, interview by Jack Pfister, January 11, 2001, transcript, 3.

27. *AR,* January 12, 1986, C2.

Chapter 2

1. Eddie Basha, interview by Jack Pfister, November 16, 2000, transcript, 4.

2. Lloyd Clark, interview by Jack Pfister, December 22, 1999, transcript, 9.

3. Peter Burns, interview by Jack Pfister and Brent Brown, October 21, 2003, transcript, 13.

4. Major General W. S. Paul to H. M. Barr, December 20, 1945, Barr Military File, BBC.

5. Larry Shelp, interview by Jack Pfister, October 3, 2003, transcript, 15.

6. Quotations from ibid., 13–14.

7. Basha, interview, 3–4.

8. Richard Kaplan, interview by Jack Pfister, October 17, 2003, transcript, 7–9.

9. Colonel Leon L. Kotzebue to Burton S. Barr, December 14, 1951, Barr Military File, BBC.

10. "Operation FRAN Set Feb. 26," *Javelina Journal,* Phoenix, Arizona, vol. 2, no. 1, February 1956, 1.

11. Clark, interview, 9.

12. *AR,* May 23, 1964.

13. Shelp, interview, 14.

14. Basha, interview, 4.

15. Shelp, interview, 8.

16. Kaplan, interview, 3.

17. Ibid., 7.

18. Shelp, interview, 18.

19. Michael Barr, interview by Jack Pfister, December 24, 2000, transcript, 3.

20. Louise Barr, interview by Jack Pfister, September 2, 1997, transcript, 5.

21. Michael Barr, interview, 9.

22. Stephanie Straser, interview by Jack Pfister, July 10, 2005, transcript, 3, 4, 14.

23. Michael Barr, interview, 3.

24. Nikki Corral, interview by Jack Pfister, August 23, 2004, transcript, 8.

25. Steven Tragash, "Adaptability Helps House's Majority Leader Remain in Charge," *AR*, April 4, 1976.

26. Robin, "The Teddy Bear Who Runs the House," 4.

27. Michael Barr, interview, 3; Suzanne Barr, interview by Jack Pfister, June 13, 2005, transcript, 6.

Chapter 3

1. Burton Barr, interview by Jack Pfister, April 12, 1994, transcript, 5.

2. Alfredo Gutierrez, interview by Philip VanderMeer, July 6, 2012, transcript, 5.

3. J. Morris Richards, *History of the Arizona State Legislature, 1912–1967,* 18 vols. (Phoenix: Arizona Legislative Council, 1979), vol. 16, part 2, p. 58.

4. Barr, interview, 7.

5. David Berman, *Arizona Politics and Government: The Quest for Autonomy, Democracy, and Development* (Lincoln: University of Nebraska Press, 1998), 18.

6. Daniel J. Elazar, *American Federalism: A View from the States* (New York: Thomas Y. Crowell, 1966), 93.

7. Heidi J. Osselaer, *Winning Their Place: Arizona Women in Politics, 1883–1950* (Tucson: University of Arizona Press, 2009), 163.

8. Malcolm E. Jewell and Samuel C. Patterson, *The Legislative Process in the United States* (New York: Random House, 1966), v.

9. Jon C. Teaford, *The Rise of the States: Evolution of American State Government* (Baltimore: Johns Hopkins University Press, 2002), 20.

10. *Tucson Daily Citizen*, January 25, 1972, 27; James Elton McMillan Jr., *Ernest W. McFarland: A Biography* (Prescott, AZ: Sharlot Hall Museum Press, 2004), 293.

11. Barr, interview, 5; Richards, *Arizona State Legislature*, vol. 10, part 1, p. 20; vol. 13, part 2, p. 1; and Inskeep quoted in vol. 16, part 2, p. 78.

12. Richards, *Arizona State Legislature*, vol. 15, part 1, pp. 24–25, and vol. 10, part 5, p. 30. Dean E. Mann, "The Legislative Committee System in Arizona," *Western Political Quarterly* 14 (December 1961): 938; and Alan Rosenthal, *Legislative Performance in the States: Explorations of Committee Behavior* (New York: Free Press, 1974), 29.

13. Harry Bandouveris, "The Code," *Arizona Days and Ways Magazine*, November 21, 1965, 6; Richards, *Arizona State Legislature*, vol. 16, part 2, p. 202.

14. Jack A. Brown, interview by Brent Brown, December 17, 1996, transcript, 1.

15. Bandouveris, "The Code," 5; Jack DeBolske, interview by Jack Pfister, June 9, 1997, transcript, 2.

16. Richards, *Arizona State Legislature*, vol. 16, part 1, p. 45; vol. 16, part 2, p. 17.

17. Ibid., vol. 13, p. 105; vol. 16, part 1, p. 28, vol. 16, part 2, p. 58; Alfredo Gutierrez, interview by Jack Pfister, March 4, 1997, transcript, 8.

18. DeBolske, interview, 2; Barr, interview, 4; Bruce B. Mason and Leonard E. Goodall, "Arizona," in *Impact of Reapportionment on the Thirteen Western States*, ed. Eleanore Bushnell, (Salt Lake City: University of Utah Press, 1970), 58; Gutierrez, interview, 8; *AR*, April 17, 1973, 6; *AR*, April 20, 1973, 8.

19. Richards, *Arizona State Legislature,* vol. 16, part 2, p. 79; Gutierrez, Pfister interview, 8; Barr, interview, 5. Giss's parliamentary knowledge was substantial, but many in the legislature had only a cursory understanding. Even Stan Turley, who served as House Speaker (1967–1969) and Senate president (1983–1987) confessed to some confusion. Stan Turley, interview by Jack Pfister and Melanie Sturgeon, April 15, 1994, transcript, 5.

20. Turley, interview, 3–4.

21. Barr, interview, 4–5.

22. As another example of this practice, Phoenix adopted a new city charter in 1948.

23. Griffenhagen & Associates, *Report on General State Organization* (Chicago: [n.p.], 1949), vol. 1, 9.

24. Berman, *Arizona Politics and Government,* 50.

25. Gutierrez, VanderMeer interview, 2.

26. Ibid.

27. *AR,* July 16, 1967, 18-A.

28. Barr, interview, 4; Stan Turley, *The Kid from Sundown* (Mesa, AZ: Cox Printing, 2002), 177.

29. Barr, interview, 5.

30. Turley, *The Kid from Sundown,* 177.

31. Pritzlaff retired from the House in 1969 and later served in the Arizona Senate, 1974–1982; he died in 2005. His son-in-law, Fife Symington III, was governor of Arizona from 1991 to 1997.

32. *AR,* January 10, 1967.

Chapter 4

1. Jon Kyl, interview by Jack Pfister and Brent Brown, August 18, 1997, transcript, 8.

2. John Kolbe, "Academy Awards for Legislators Almost Canceled, But Here Goes," *PG,* June 19, 1975.

3. Michael Clancy and Dolores Tropiano, "All Loved Ex-speaker, Barr None," *AR,* January 19, 1997.

4. John Kolbe, "Rip, Chew, Talk, Fight or Juggle: Burt Barr Keeps Action Going," *PG,* October 1, 1973.

5. Bernie Wynn, "The Riddle of Barr: Does He Try Harder?" *AR,* March 30, 1973, 31.

6. John Kolbe, "Burton Barr Always Gets His Way," *PG,* February 26, 1982.

7. I am using this term as did James MacGregor Burns (*Leadership* [New York: Harper and Row, 1978]), which effectively combines the categories that some other analysts use, where "traits" include innate personality, "skills" are learned, and "style" involves relationships. See Peter G. Northouse, *Leadership: Theory and Practice* (Thousand Oaks, CA: Sage Publications, 2010).

8. Malcolm Edwin Jewell and Marcia Lynn Whicker, *Legislative Leadership in the American States* (Ann Arbor: University of Michigan Press, 1994), 4. See also Alan Rosenthal, *Heavy Lifting: The Job of the American Legislature* (Washington, DC: CQ Press, 2004).

9. For a published use of the adage, see Ralph Wright, *All Politics Is Personal* (Boston: Marshall Jones Company, 1996); Louise Barr, interview by Philip VanderMeer, June 4, 2013, tape; Louise Barr, interview by Jack Pfister and Brent Brown, September 2, 1997, transcript, 9; Keven Ann Willey, interview by Jack Pfister, October 22, 2003, tape.

10. Catie Robin, "The Teddy Bear Who Runs the House," *Arizona: The Arizona Republic*, January 3, 1982, 4; Tony West, interview by Jack Pfister and Brent Brown, October 12, 2000, transcript, 10; Nicki Cornell, interview by Jack Pfister, August 23, 2004, transcript, 8; Alfredo Gutierrez, interview by Philip VanderMeer, July 6, 2012, transcript, 12; Peter Burns, interview by Jack Pfister, October 21, 2003, transcript, 8, 12, 14; James, Skelly, interview by Jack Pfister and Brent Brown, October 25, 2000, transcript, 6.

11. Burton Barr, interview by Jack Pfister, April 12, 1994, transcript, 17; Wynn, "The Riddle of Barr."

12. Terry Goddard, interview by Jack Pfister, May 19, 2000, transcript, 7; Jim Bush, interview by Jack Pfister, 7; Skelly, interview, 5; Charles Stevens, interview by Brent Brown, September 11, 1997, transcript, 7; John Kolbe, interview by Jack Pfister, January 12, 1999, transcript, 5.

13. Willey, interview; Kolbe, interview, 5; Louise Barr, Pfister interview, 12; Don Isaacson, interview by Jack Pfister and Brent Brown, September 21, 2000, transcript, 4.

14. Cornell, interview, 8.

15. Jack DeBolske, interview by Jack Pfister, June 9, 1997, transcript, 7–8; Shawn Hubler, "Meet the Most Powerful Man in Arizona," *Tucson Citizen Magazine*, April 7, 1984, 2. When Keven Ann Willey slightly criticized a family member in a story, Barr stopped talking to her for four days until she explained the inadvertence of the offense. When another *Arizona Republic* columnist, Tom Fitzpatrick, wrote stories accusing Louise Barr of improper activities, Barr refused to speak to him for a year.

16. Hubler, "Meet the Most Powerful Man in Arizona."

17. Stevens, interview, 7; West, interview, 7.

18. Art Hamilton, interview by Jack Pfister, July 1, 1998, transcript, 12.

19. Cornell, interview, 4; Collins, interview, 3; Susan Schultz, "The Good, the Bad, and the Powerful," *Phoenix*, August 1979, 138; and Alfredo Gutierrez e-mail to Jack August, January 5, 2009 (forwarded to Jack Pfister, January 9, 2009).

20. Stevens, interview, 6–7; Burns, interview, 8; Kyl, interview, 10; "Burt Barr Dies; Last Man to Run the Whole Show," *Arizona Capitol Times*, January 17, 1997, 2; Louise Barr, Pfister interview, 12.

21. Alfred Gutierrez, interview by Jack Pfister, March 7, 20, 1997, transcript, 14; Willey, interview; Keven Ann Willey column, *AR*, January 19, 1997.

22. Burns, interview, 7; Joe Lane, interview by Jack Pfister, February 1, 1999, transcript, 4; Schultz, "The Good, the Bad, and the Powerful," 140; Kolbe, "Burton Barr Always Gets His Way."

23. Gutierrez, Pfister interview, 11.

24. Lane, interview, 4.

25. Hamilton, interview, 5,7.

26. Ibid., 14.

27. Lane, interview, 4; James Sossaman, interview by Jack Pfister and Brent Brown, November 16, 2000, transcript, 12.

28. Willey, *AR*, March 24, 96; Chris Herstam, interview by Jack Pfister and Brent Brown, August 19, 1997, transcript, 13.

29. Al Kluender, "Observations by Al Kluender, member of the 27th and 28th Arizona Legislatures," ms. in possession of the author; Skelly, interview,14, 5–6; Jack A. Brown, interview by Brent Brown, December 17, 1996, transcript, 2.

30. Alan Rosenthal, *Heavy Lifting: The Job of the American Legislature* (Washington, DC: CQ Press, 2004), chap. 6.

31. Burns, interview, 14; Gutierrez, VanderMeer interview, 13.

32. Rick Collins, interview by Jack Pfister, December 29, 1998, transcript, 7–8; Burns, interview, 10.

33. Hamilton, interview, 11–12.

34. Lane, interview, 4.

35. Steven Tragash, "Adaptability Helps House's Majority Leader Remain in Charge," *AR*, April 4, 1976.

36. Burns, interview 7; Collins, interview, 3; Hamilton, interview, 11; Brown, interview, 2; Tragash, "Adaptability Helps House's Majority Leader."

37. Jane Hull, interview by Jack Pfister, December 29, 1998, transcript, 8; Gutierrez, Pfister interview 12; Sossaman, interview, 11.

38. Hull, interview, 8; Barr, interview, 17.

39. Hamilton, interview, 12: Gutierrez, e-mail to August; Goddard, interview, 7.

40. Hubler, "Meet the Most Powerful Man in Arizona."

41. John Kolbe, "Candid Lessons in Leadership—About Barr and Gutierrez," December 13, 1979; Tragash, "Adaptability Helps House Majority Leader"; Hubler, "Meet the Most Powerful Man in Arizona"; Kyl, interview, 8; Kluender, "Observations."

42. Stevens, interview, 7; John Kolbe, "Tax Rebates on Homes a Sham, but Lawmakers Won't Admit It," *PG*, May 29, 1975.

43. Rosenthal, *Heavy Lifting*, 211.

44. Willey, interview.

45. Gutierrez, VanderMeer interview, 7; Gutierrez, Pfister interview, 13; Skelly, interview, 4–5.

46. Lane, interview, 4.

47. Hubler, "Meet the Most Powerful Man in Arizona"; West, interview, 8; *AR*, January 19, 1986; Skelly, interview, 3.

48. Kolbe, interview, 6; *AR*, January 19, 1986; Herstam, interview, 14–15; Kyl, interview, 9. Since West took Barr's money, one wonders whether he included himself as one of Barr's 15 pocket votes.

49. Burns, interview, 12; Herstam, interview, 13; Collins, interview, 3; Hamilton, interview, 11.

50. Gutierrez, VanderMeer interview, 13.

51. Cornell, interview, 3; Burns, interview, 14.

52. Herstam, interview, 12; Collins, interview, 8; Steven Tragash, "Adaptability Helps House's Majority Leader"; Eddie Basha, interview by Jack Pfister and Brent Brown, November 16, 2000, 9.

53. Stevens, interview, 6; Schultz, "The Good, the Bad, and the Powerful," 142.

54. Burns, interview, 7.

55. Skelly, interview, 4. But, as Skelly reported, the measure was passed that year by initiative.

56. Skelly, interview, 7.

57. John McCain, interview by Brent Brown, June 10, 1997, transcript, 2; Isaacson, interview, 5; Wynn, "The Riddle of Barr"; Arizona, *Journal of the House of*

Representatives, 27th Legislature, 1965–1966, 664; Stevens, interview, 8. See also Isaacson, interview, 4.

58. Basha, interview, 9.

59. Tragash, "Adaptability Helps House's Majority Leader"; Schultz, "The Good, the Bad, and the Powerful," 138; *AR*, January 3, 1986.

60. Hamilton, interview, 12; Collins, interview, 8; Isaacson, interview, 7.

61. Sossaman, interview, 13–14.

62. Keven Ann Willey, "GOP Senators Gunning for House Leader," *AR*, January 30, 1983; Hamilton, interview, 15.

63. Burns, interview, 15; Robin, "The Teddy Bear Who Runs the House"; Wynn, "The Riddle of Barr."

64. Hull, interview, 4; West, interview, 11; Kyl, interview, 10; Lane, interview, 13; Herstam, interview, 12.

65. West, interview, 10; *AR*, January 19, 1986; Tragash, "Adaptability Helps House's Majority Leader."

66. Tragash, "Adaptability Helps House's Majority Leader"; Stevens, interview, 7; Tragash, "Adaptability Helps House's Majority Leader."

67. Herstam, interview, 13; Basha, interview, 8; Stevens, interview, 6; Kyl, interview, 9; Asa Bushnell, "More Hot Air Than Logic," *Tucson Citizen*, February 19, 1976.

68. Stevens, interview, 10; West, interview, 11.

69. Gutierrez, Pfister interview, 15.

70. Tragash, "Adaptability Helps House's Majority Leader"; Kolbe, interview, 5; West, interview, 14; Wynn, "The Riddle of Barr."

71. Tragash, "Adaptability Helps House's Majority Leader."

72. Les Schlangen, "Action against Markets Spurs Change in Weights-Agency Plan," *AR*, March 24, 1974.

73. Tom Fitzpatrick, "Many Worship at Altar of Political Kingfish," *AR*, March 20, 1983, and *AR*, March 21, 1983; Hubler, "Meet the Most Powerful Man in Arizona"; Gutierrez, Pfister interview, 18. These charges were repeated by Evan Mecham in the 1986 gubernatorial campaign and discussed by Keven Ann Willey, "Barr Keeping Chin Up in Try for Governor," *AR*, September 6, 1986.

74. Keven Ann Willey, "GOP Caucus Argues over Ethics Plan," *AR*, April 26, 1983.

75. Bernard M. Bass, with Ruth R. Bass, *The Bass Handbook of Leadership: Theory, Research, and Managerial Applications*, 4th ed. (New York: Free Press, 2008), 103.

76. Jewell and Whicker summarize the key components of the institutional context as the legislature's institution power, its representative character, partisan polarization, rules, and professionalization. Jewell and Whicker, *Legislative Leadership in the American States*, 32–33.

77. On legislative studies, see especially John Burns, *Sometime Governments: A Critical Study of the 50 American Legislatures* (New York: Bantam Books, 1971); Duane Lockard, "The State Legislator," in *State Legislatures in American Politics*, ed. Alexander Heard (Englewood Cliffs, NJ: Prentice Hall, 1966), 98–125; and Alan Rosenthal, "The State of State Legislatures: An Overview," *Hofstra Law Review* 11 (1982–1983): 1185–1204.

78. Turley, interview, 13, 2; Pat Conner, interviewed with Paul Bergelin, audio file, June 13, 2012, ALAR, http://azmemory.azlibrary.gov/cdm/singleitem/collection

/legoral/id/78/rec/111; Louis Gonzalez, interview by Paul Bergelin, April 26, 2012, audio file, ALAR, http://azmemory.azlibrary.gov/cdm/singleitem/collection/legoral/id/75/rec/106; Keven Ann Willey, "Novice Legislators Discover a Chase after Paper Data," *AR*, February 13, 1983; Turley, *Kid from Sundown*, 180.

79. Jim Fickess, "Symington: Man of Contradictions," *Arizona Business Gazette*, January 16, 1997; Connor, Bergelin interview; Turley, interview, 5.

80. Schultz, "The Good, the Bad, and the Powerful," 140; Willey, "Novice Legislators"; Joe Lane, interview by Patricia Roeser, March 31, 2008, audio file, ALAR, http://azmemory.azlibrary.gov/cdm/singleitem/collection/legoral/id/100/rec/65.

81. Leo Corbet, interview by Dana Bennett, January 15, 2007, audio file, ALAR, http://azmemory.azlibrary.gov/cdm/singleitem/collection/legoral/id/9/rec/35; Gonzalez, interview.

82. Schulz, "The Good, the Bad, and the Powerful"; Lane, interview, 11; Hamilton, interview, 6.

83. Bernie Wynn, "Barr Woos Freshman; Woman Focuses on Leadership," *AR*, June 22, 1979.

84. Polly Rosenbaum, interview by Zona D. Lorig, tape, Phoenix, July 8, 1996, to September 6, 1996, AHS, Tempe, quoted in Carol S. Palmer, "Challenging Tradition: Arizona Women Fight for the Equal Rights Amendment" (master's thesis, Arizona State University, 2007), 46; Heidi J. Osselaer, *Winning Their Place: Arizona Women in Politics, 1883–1950* (Tucson: University of Arizona Press, 2009); Hull, interview, 3; Barr interview, 14.

85. Turley, ALAR interview; John Kolbe, "Senate GOP Leaders Lay Groundwork for Classic Trap," *PG*, July 5, 1984; Gonzalez, ALAR interview.

86. John Kolbe, "Keeping GOP in Strong Voice Will be Task of Akers, Barr," *PG*, November 2, 1974; John Kolbe, "Agony Will Have Bearing on Battle of Chamber Leaders," *PG*, May 3, 1976; Bernie Wynn "Rep. Kelly Chosen as House Speaker," *AR*, November 6, 1976.

87. Cornell, interview, 7.

88. "Frank Kelley, Who Once Led Arizona's House, Dies at 65," *AR*, November 17, 1988.

89. Art Hamilton, interview 2 with Jack Pfister, June 6, 2005, transcript, 5; Skelly, interview, 14.

90. Herstam, interview, 3; John Kromko, interview by Paul Bergelin, May 23, 2012, audio file, ALAR, http://azmemory.azlibrary.gov/cdm/singleitem/collection/legoral/id/82/rec/71.

91. Barr, interview, 7–8; Bernie Wynn, "You Can Call Burton Barr a Lot of Things, but You Can't Call Him Boring," *AR*, November 30, 1980.

92. Gutierrez, VanderMeer interview, 7–8; Alfredo Gutierrez, interview by Carol Palmer, October 3, 2006, audio file, ALAR, http://azmemory.azlibrary.gov/cdm/singleitem/collection/legoral/id/1/rec/1.

93. Kyl, interview, 9.

94. Although the report does not discuss directly the existing conditions in Arizona, the rankings and recommendations are very useful. The Citizens Conference on State Legislatures, *State Legislatures: An Evaluation of their Effectiveness* (New York: Praeger Publishers, 1971), 107–12.

95. Quotation from Gutierrez, VanderMeer interview, 3, 6. In 1975 this organization became the National Council of State Legislatures. See Richard H. Leach, "A Quiet Revolution, 1933–1976," *The Book of the States, 1976–1977* (Lexington, KY: Council of State Governments, 1976), 21–17; and Eugene W. Hickok Jr., *The Reform of State Legislatures and the Changing Character of Representation* (Lanham, MD: University Press of America, 1992), esp. 48–51.

96. John DeWitt, "Senators Can't Match Barr's 'Shovel Diplomacy,'" *ADS*, February 3, 1980; Kyle, interview, 8.

97. DeBolske, interview, 10, 3; Stevens, interview, 5.

98. Skelly, interview, 5; Hull, interview, 3.

99. Hull, interview, 4; West, interview, 4–5.

100. Berman, *Arizona Politics and Government*, 63, 62; *Arizona Legislative Review*, May 19, 1965, 1. Jason Crabtree LaBau offers an extended analysis of this in "Phoenix Rising: Arizona and the Origins of Modern Conservative Politics" (Ph.D. diss., University of Southern California, 2010).

101. Barr, interview, 13.

102. Kolbe, "Keeping GOP in Strong Voice."

103. Brown, interview, 2.

104. Hamilton, interview 2, 5; Cornell, interview, 6.

105. Gutierrez, Pfister interview, 11, 9.

106. Kyle, interview, 8; Lane, interview, 4–5.

107. *PG*, January 13, 1970; John Kolbe, "'Barr Factor' Haunts Prolonged Special Session," *PG*, February 14, 1980.

108. Willey, "GOP Senators Gunning for House Leader"; *Tucson Citizen*, February 10, 1983; Kolbe, "Senate GOP Leaders Lay Groundwork"; Hamilton, interview, 2, 4.

109. Raul Castro, with Jack L. August, *Adversity is My Angel: The Life and Career of Raul Castro* (Fort Worth, TX: TCU Press, 2009), 91.

110. See Berman, *Arizona Politics and Government*, 112–16; *AR*, March 22, 1968.

111. Barr, interview, 13; *Tucson Daily Citizen*, January 25, 1972.

112. Gutierrez, interview, 25.

113. Burns, interview, 9.

114. John Kolbe, "Barr-Babbitt Brawl a Contrast in Style and Loyalties," *PG*, May 4, 1981.

115. John DeWitt, "Veto Left Rift between One-Time Pals Babbitt, Barr," *ADS*, May 3, 1981.

116. Hubler, "Meet the Most Powerful Man in Arizona," 2.

117. Jewell and Whicker, *Legislative Leadership in the American States*, 31–55.

118. Ibid., 20.

Chapter 5

1. John Kolbe, interview with Jack Pfister, January 12, 1999, transcript, 7.

2. Alfredo Gutierrez, interview with Jack Pfister, March 4, 1997, transcript, 16.

3. Michael Murphy, "Burton Barr Dies, Legislative Legend," *AR*, January 14, 1997.

4. Governor Samuel Goddard, "Farewell Address," *Arizona Legislative Review*, May 27, 1966, 6.

5. Jon Kyl, interview by Jack Pfister, August 18, 1997, transcript, 9.

6. Alfredo Gutierrez, interview by Philip VanderMeer, July 6, 2012, transcript, 16.

7. John Kolbe, "Rip, Chew, Talk, Fight or Juggle: Burt Barr Keeps Action Going," *PG*, October 1, 1973.

8. *AR*, May 23, 1964.

9. *AR*, November 15, 1970.

10. *AR*, March 11, 1967.

11. Voters rejected proposals to change the State Mining Inspector and the Arizona Corporation Commission into appointive posts, while the legislature never passed other measures (e.g., the department of natural resources). For comparative analysis of others states, see Jon C. Teaford, *The Rise of the States: Evolution of American State Government* (Baltimore: Johns Hopkins University Press, 2002), 202–8.

12. *AR*, November 12, 1972; Craig Daniels, "Where They Failed," *AR*, May 13, 1973.

13. Quotation from George C. McLeod, "Barr Bound to Arizona," *Tucson Daily Citizen*, January 25, 1972. On state governments and federalism, see Teaford, *Rise of the States*, 195–230; Carl W. Stenberg, "Federalism in Transition: 1959–79," *Intergovernmental Perspective* 6 (Winter 1980): 4–13; Thomas R. Dye, *American Federalism: Competition Among Governments* (Lexington, MA: Lexington Books, 1990), 5–25; Richard P. Nathan, "Federalism—the Great 'Composition,'" in *The New American Political System*, ed. Anthony King, 2nd ed. (Washington, DC: AEI Press, 1990), 231–62.

14. Peter Burns, interview by Jack Pfister, October 21, 2003, transcript, 2.

15. Arizona Academy, *Arizona's Tax Structure: Revenue Needs and Revenue Sources* (Phoenix, 1962), 19, as reported in Dan Cotbran, "The Arizona Budget in an Age of Taxpayer Revolt," in Zachary A. Smith, *Politics and Public Policy in Arizona*, 2nd ed. (Westport, CT: Praeger, 1996).

16. *AR*, December 23, 1967, editorial, 6.

17. Burton Barr, interview by Jack Pfister, April 12, 1994, 11–12.

18. *Tucson Citizen*, December 25, 1967.

19. Even adjusting for inflation in the value of housing, this was roughly a one-quarter decrease in residential property taxes.

20. *PG*, March 28, 1973.

21. *Prescott Courier*, November 10, 1977.

22. *PG*, November 27, 1978.

23. Art Hamilton, interview by Jack Pfister, July 1, 1998, transcript, 11.

24. Don Harris, "1% Increase in State Sales Tax Probably Will Continue," *AR*, November 4, 1983.

25. Shawn Hubler, "Meet the Most Powerful Man in Arizona," *Tucson Citizen Magazine*, April 7, 1984, 2.

26. Terry Goddard, interview by Jack Pfister, May 19, 2000, transcript, 6.

27. Jack DeBolske, interview by Jack Pfister, June 9, 1997, transcript, 11–12.

28. Dennis Farrell, "Barr Says Arizona's Health Care Is a 'Mess,'" *PG*, December 31, 1970; Grant Smith, "Everybody Has Tonic for Sick Health Care," *AR*, April 25, 1971.

29. Grant Smith, "Barr Leads Drive to Fund Total Health Plan for Arizonans," *AR*, April 26, 1971; Farrell, "Barr Says Arizona's Health Care Is a 'Mess.'"

30. *PG*, June 2, 1972; *Tucson Daily Citizen*, April 26, 1974; Smith, "Barr Leads Drive to Fund Total Health Plan for Arizonans."

31. *AR*, April 27, 1973.

32. Gutierrez, VanderMeer interview, 18, 19; Athia Hardt, "State Is Expected to Change Health Care of the Indigent," *AR*, November 11, 1972; "Barr Gives Medicaid Assurance," *PG*, February 8, 1973.

33. Burns, interview, 6.

34. Steven Tragash, "Adaptability Helps House's Majority Leader Remain in Charge," *AR*, April 4, 1976, B-2.

35. Isaacson, interview, 2; McCain, interview, 3.

36. *AR*, September 30, 1984.

37. Desmond D. Connall Jr. "A History of the Arizona Groundwater Management Act," *Arizona State Law Journal* 2 (1982): 319.

38. Ibid.; *Prescott Courier*, July 15, 1977.

39. Jim Bush, interview by Jack Pfister and Brent Brown, October 5, 2000, transcript, 7.

40. Ibid.; Richard DeUriarte, "Babbitt Signs Water Reform Measure, *AR*, June 12, 1980; John Kolbe, "Groundwater Laws: Decision Time," *PG*, December 7, 1979.

41. *AR*, May 3, 1970.

42. "Arizona Majority Leader Blasts EPA Measures," *The Republican Voice of Arizona* (September 1973), 1; *AR*, April 10, 1974.

43. Kolbe, "Rip, Chew, Talk"; *AR*, April 10, 1974.

44. *Scottsdale Daily Progress*, March 1, 1976.

45. Don Warne, "Barr Suggests Legislature Block Sprawl," *PG*, October 4, 1971; *PG*, May 10, 1973.

46. *AR*, April 22, 1979.

47. Rod Platt, "Involved, Supportive Public Key to Good Government, Barr Says," *PG*, August 1, 1984.

48. Eddie Basha, interview by Jack Pfister and Brent Brown, November 16, 2000, transcript, 6, 7.

49. *PG*, October 14, 1972.

50. *Prescott Courier*, November 10, 1977; Basha, interview, 4; Gutierrez, VanderMeer interview, 8–9; Barr, interview, 9.

51. Barr, interview, 9.

52. The university said it was following the policy of the Western Athletic Conference, protecting stadium improvements financed by student fees, and feared competition for Valley sports dollars. *AR*, February 7, 1974.

53. Bob Fannin, interview by Jack Pfister and Brent Brown, February 26, 1999, transcript, 4.

54. John Kolbe, "Small Attack on Barr Reveals Warner Weakness," *PG*, May 22, 1986.

55. Hamilton, interview, 11.

56. *AR*, January 19, 1986.

57. Barr, interview, 6.

Chapter 6

1. Alfredo Gutierrez, interview by Jack Pfister and Brent Brown, March 20, 1997, transcript, 17.

2. Jim Bush, interview by Jack Pfister and Brent Brown, October 5, 2000, transcript, 8.

3. Art Hamilton, interview by Jack Pfister, July 1, 1998, transcript, 13.

4. Stan Turley, "News Release," September 29, 1986, reprinted in *The Kid from Sundown*, 168.

5. George C. McLeod, "Barr Bound to Arizona," *Tucson Daily Citizen*, January 25, 1972.

6. John Kolbe, "Rip, Chew, Talk, Fight or Juggle: Burt Barr Keeps Action Going," *Tucson Citizen Magazine*, April 7, 1984, 2.

7. *AR*, October 27, 1977.

8. Bernie Wynn, "You Can Call Burton Barr a Lot of Things, but You Can't Call Him Boring," *AR*, November 30, 1980.

9. Don Harris, "Two Possible GOP Opponents for Babbitt Withdraw," *AR*, June 10, 1981.

10. Shawn Hubler, "Meet the Most Powerful Man in Arizona," *Tucson Citizen Magazine*, April 7, 1984, 2.

11. John Kolbe, "Barr None: Presidential Lobbying Won't Pay Off," *PG*, June 24, 1985.

12. Ibid.

13. Bob Schuster, "Burton Barr Won't Stray from His House," *The Arizona Spirit*, July 10, 1985.

14. Joel Nillson, "Blind March to Judgment," *AR*, March 14, 1986.

15. Anne Hoy and Keven Ann Willey, "Barr Hears President's Battle Call," *AR*, June 2, 1985.

16. Ibid.; Burton Barr, interview by Jack Pfister, April 12, 1994, transcript, 16; Stephanie Strasser, interview by Jack Pfister, July 10, 2005, transcript, 8.

17. Joel Nilsson, "Barr's Gubernatorial Dilemma: A 'Hint' of Things to Come?" *AR*, July 22, 1985; Rosemary Schabert, "Barr May Be Eyeing Race for Governor," *Mesa Tribune*, September 14, 1985.

18. "Barr's Flub Didn't Faze General Bradley," *PG*, April 18, 1981; Kolbe, "Burton Barr Always Gets His Way"; Alfredo Gutierrez, interview by Phil VanderMeer, July 6, 2012, transcript, 21.

19. Catie Robin, "The Teddy Bear Who Runs the House," *Arizona: The Arizona Republic*, January 3, 1982, 3; Gutierrez, VanderMeer interview, 21; James Sossaman, interview by Jack Pfister and Brent Brown, November 16, 2000, transcript, 5; Joe Lane, interview by Jack Pfister, February 1, 1999, transcript, 11.

20. Keven Willey, "Barr Candidacy Pushed by Group Aiming to Raise $1 Million by Year's End," *AR*, October 27, 1985; John Kolbe, "'I'm Ready to Go' in Race for Governor, Barr Says," *PG*, January 22, 1986.

21. Jay Smith to Jack Pfister, March 30, 2006; Nilsson, "Blind March to Judgment."

22. *AR*, August 27, 1986.

23. Sossaman, interview, 10.

24. Kolbe, "'I'm Ready to Go' in Race for Governor, Barr Says."

25. "Barr to Polish Image in Tucson Area," *ADS*, November 8, 1985.

26. *Tribune News* (Holbrook, AZ) and *Herald* (Snowflake, AZ), February 2, 1986.

27. Karen Kirk, "Barr Begins State Travels to Raise Name Recognition," *PG*, June 14, 1986.

28. Burton Barr, "Statement of Candidacy," ms. copy, BBC.

29. John Kolbe, "Warner's Candidacy is Official," *PG*, February 25, 1986; Don Harris, "Too Late to Change Now: Carolyn Warner's Style, Drive 'Are What You See,'" *AR*, April 20, 1986; *AR*, September 3, 1986; *AR*, August 27, 1986.

30. Tony Carroll, "Bring Governor to the People," *Yuma Daily Sun*, March 6, 1986; Bob Schuster, "Warner Focuses Best on Platform Issue," *Chandler Arizonan*, March 11, 1986.

31. Emil Venere, "Warner 'Stunned' at Barr's Air Position," *Tempe Daily News*, April 8, 1986; Karen Kirk, "Pollution Offensive Promised," *PG*, April 14, 1986; John Kolbe, "Warner, Barr Spar over Commitment to King Holiday," *PG*, May 20, 1986.

32. Richard de Uriarte, "Burton Barr, Beware!," *PG*, March 17, 1986; John Kolbe, "Barr's Unique Problem: For a Candidate He's Too Visible," *PG*, March 17, 1986.

33. *Mohave Daily Miner*, April 9, 1986.

34. Howard Fischer, "Senate Juggles Lake Bill with Barr in Mind," *ADS*, April 11, 1986.

35. Doug MacEachern, "Politicking Out of the House," *New Times*, April 16, 1986.

36. Kolbe, "Small Attack on Barr Reveals Warner Weakness."

37. John Kolbe, "Gubernatorial Hopefuls Trade Potshots at Forum," *PG*, April 17, 1986; Keven Ann Willey, "Barr Keeping Chin Up in Try for Governor," *AR*, September 6, 1986; Bruce Merrill, interview by Beth Isaak, November 14, 2003, quoted in Beth Isaak, "Mr. Magic and the 1986 Gubernatorial Primary," unpublished seminar paper, 22, in BBC.

38. Gutierrez, Pfister interview, 19; Mike Boyd, interview by Jack Pfister and Brent Brown, 1999, transcript, 4.

39. Boyd, interview, 5.

40. Jane Dee Hull, interview by Jack Pfister, December 29, 1998, transcript, 5; Nillson, "Blind March to Judgment."

41. Boyd, interview, 4.

42. Boyd, interview, 4; John Kolbe, "Barr Formally Launches Campaign for Governor," February 28, 1986; Peter Burns, interview by Jack Pfister, October 21, 2003, transcript, 9.

43. John Kolbe, interview by Jack Pfister, January 12, 1999, transcript, 7; Lane, interview, 10.

44. Gutierrez, Pfister interview, 17; Sossaman, interview, 10.

45. See the discussion of this in chapter 5.

46. Kolbe, interview, 7. Many people remembered and referred to Barr's joke, but with slightly varying particulars. The two most specific descriptions mention either the Chamber of Commerce or the Rotary.

47. Mecham campaign materials, mailing #1, "Integrity #1 Issue," 5, in BBC; Laurie Roberts, "Mecham Bids for Governor a Fifth Time; Republican Criticizes Barr, Democrats," *AR*, July 2, 1986.

48. Roberts, "Mecham Bids for Governor"; Rosemary Schabert Case, "Mecham Announces Candidacy," *Mesa Tribune*, July 2, 1986.

49. The details of the allegations in Mecham's tabloids are far too lengthy for discussion here, but Willey's article, "Barr Keeping Chin Up in Try for Governor," offers a brief explanation.

50. Tony West, interview by Jack Pfister and Brent Brown, October 12, 2000, transcript, 8–9.

51. Kolbe, "Warner, Barr Spar"; Don Harris, "'Enthused' Barr Rallies GOP Officer Corps," *AR*, June 22, 1986; Don Harris, "State GOP Figure Urges Apologies," *AR*, June 11, 1986; Roberts, "Mecham Bids for Governor."

52. Don Harris, "Mecham and Warner Win," *AR*, September 11, 1986.

53. Rosemary Schabert Case, "Barr Finds Comfort in Family, Friends," *Mesa Tribune*, September 11, 1986; Harris, "Mecham and Warner Win"; Rose Schabert Case and Simon Fisher, "Mecham Stuns Barr," *Mesa Tribune*, September 10, 1986.

54. Case and Fisher, "Mecham Stuns Barr"; Harris, "Mecham and Warner Win."

55. Kyl, interview, 9.

56. Bob Fannin, interview by Jack Pfister, February 26, 1999, transcript, 7; Carol Sowers, "Governor Hopefuls Vow to Run on Issues," *AR*, September 11, 1986.

57. Nilsson, "Blind March to Judgment."

58. Art Hamilton, interview by Jack Pfister, July 1, 1998, transcript, 13.

59. Don Harris, "Barr Upbeat Despite Suffering Defeat," *AR*, September 11, 1986.

60. Willey, "Barr Keeping Chin Up in Try for Governor"; Gutierrez, Pfister interview, 27.

61. Nilsson, "Barr's Gubernatorial Dilemma."

62. Hamilton, interview, 13.

63. Garry Wills, *Certain Trumpets: The Call of Leaders* (New York: Simon & Schuster, 1994), 23–24.

Chapter 7

1. Chris Herstam, interview by Jack Pfister and Brent Brown, August 19, 1997, transcript, 9.

2. Burton Barr, quoted in Joe Kullman, "An Active Voice, Burton Barr Shows No Signs of Slowing Down," *Phoenix Business Gazette*, June 8, 1987.

3. Yvonne Garrett, in "Burt Barr Remembered for Fund-Raising Efforts," *AR*, October 10, 1997.

4. Terry Goddard, interview by Jack Pfister, May 19, 2000, transcript, 7.

5. Louise Barr, interview by Jack Pfister, September 2, 1997, transcript, 11; Harris, "Barr Upbeat Despite Suffering Defeat."

6. John Kolbe, "Mecham's Personal Attacks Might Cost Barr's Endorsement," *PG*, September 13, 1986.

7. Laurie Roberts, "Barr Shuns Endorsement of Mecham," *AR*, October 8, 1986.

8. Mike Barr, interview by Jack Pfister, December 4, 2000, transcript, 7; Don Isaacson, interview by Brent Brown and Jack Pfister. September 21, 2000, transcript, 10; Charles Stevens, interview by Brent Brown, September 11, 1997, transcript, 10–11.

9. Anthony Sammer, "Burton Barr: Goddards's Volunteer Chief of Staff," *PG*, October 14, 1987.

10. Isaacson, interview, 10; Art Hamilton, interview by Jack Pfister, July 1, 1998, transcript, 14; Steve Yozwiak, "Ghost in the Machine: Invisible Barr Still Haunting the Legislature," *AR*, May 3, 1987.

11. Herstam, interview, 7, 8.

12. "2 Ex-legislators Criticize Mecham as Confrontational," *AR*, April 16, 1987.

13. Yozwiak, "Ghost in the Machine."

14. Kullman, "An Active Voice."

15. "Governor Lists Credits of His Terms, Avoids Attacking Press during Speech," *AR*, August 13, 1987.

16. Joe Lane, interview by Jack Pfister, February 1, 1999, transcript, 6.

17. Goddard, interview, 11; Garrett, "Burt Barr Remembered for Fund-Raising Efforts."

18. Goddard, interview, 12, 18.

19. Ibid., 17.

20. "Barr Named to Direct Rio Salado Tax Effort," *Mesa Tribune*, February 11, 1987.

21. Alfredo Gutierrez, interview by Jack Pfister, March 4, 1997, transcript 19.

22. Ibid.

23. Mike Barr, interview, 10.

24. Eddie Basha, interview by Jack Pfister and Brent Brown, November 16, 2000, transcript, 7, 9; Goddard, interview, 15, 16; Herstam, interview, 16.

25. Goddard, interview, 15; Bob Fannin, interview by Jack Pfister, February 26, 1999, transcript, 3.

26. Fannin, interview, 5.

27. John Kolbe, "A Master of Modern Legislative Arts," *PG*, January 5, 1997; Basha, interview, 7.

28. Burton Barr, interview by Jack Pfister, April 12, 1994, transcript, 6, 13.

29. Louise Barr, interview by Phil VanderMeer, June 4, 2013, tape, author's possession; Steve Meissner, "House Dynamo Itching to Take Over State's Top Post," *ADS*, May 18, 1986.

30. Laurie Roberts, "Right Wing Preparing 'Hit Lists,' 'Ambushes,' State Moderates Say," *AR*, July 7, 1986.

31. Steve Goldstein, "Raising the Barr," *Phoenix Magazine*, January 2009, 66; Art Hamilton, interview by Jack Pfister 2, June 6, 2005, transcript, 3.

32. "At the Capitol," *AR*, April 13, 1973.

33. Deborah Laake, "Snuffing the Wheeler-Dealers," *New Times*, October 1–7, 1986.

Essay on Sources

One of the real limits to writing histories of state legislatures or legislators is that, unlike congressmen, typically very few state legislators leave collections of personal papers documenting their legislative work, and Arizona has been no exception. Despite his long tenure in office and his leadership position, Barr left none, nor did others. A few lawmakers may write memoirs of one sort of another, but those are insufficient as the basis for a broad-based history. Published sources—newspapers, magazines, government documents, and other reports—are highly informative, of course, but in lieu of personal papers, one can get some inside understanding of legislative life through interviews.

Interviews

Fortunately, interviews were available for undertaking this study. The primary ones were done by Jack Pfister and Brent Brown—sometimes separately, sometimes together—and they are invaluable. They asked their interviewees about themselves (as part of a larger history of Arizona politics they hoped to do), and about their views of and interactions with Burton Barr. I initially received these interviews in transcript form. This allowed me to make effective use of them, but although the transcriptions are generally good, they were not edited to compensate for verbal pauses, to correct misspellings of names, to fill in gaps in the transcription, or to add any explanatory material. I discovered the audio versions of the tapes late in my work on this book, but I used them to check for missing words and when I had questions about a transcript. This uncovered various missed words, and occasionally these resulted in correcting false impressions ("contemptuous" rather than "contentedness"). Even more important, some interview material was not transcribed; a whole page of the Jon Kyl interview was missed. Consequently, in using these transcriptions whenever I encountered a statement that seemed at all questionable, I listened to the audio tapes of the interviews. Another caveat on usage is that by their nature oral interviews do not include punctuation, and while the transcriptionist(s) did an overall excellent job on getting the words, on occasion I thought that the punctuation was wrong, and so I entered my own. The Arizona State University Archives holds the audio recordings and original transcripts in the Burton S. Barr Collection.

The Arizona State Library, Archives and Public Records, also holds interviews conducted for its Legislative Oral History Project. It currently holds interviews with 51 legislators, some of whose service overlapped with Barr. These interviews are most useful here for the general sense of the legislature. Finally, I conducted very helpful additional interviews with Alfredo Gutierrez, Louise Barr, and David Samuel Barr.

Published Sources

Newspapers provided good coverage of the legislature when it was in session—the end of session reports were particularly valuable—and I relied on the dailies of the two major cities—the *Phoenix Gazette* and the *Arizona Republic*, as well as the *Tucson Daily Citizen* and the *Arizona Daily Star.* For additional Phoenix area stories, I consulted the *Mesa Tribune* and the *Scottsdale Daily Progress*, and for "outer state" reactions, I read the *Yuma Daily Sun*, the *Kingman* (Mohave) *Daily Miner* and the *Prescott Courier.* The *Phoenix Business Gazette* periodically had useful stories, as did the *Phoenix New Times* and *Phoenix Magazine.* Newspaper clippings in the Vertical File in the Arizona Room of the Burton S. Barr Library also included material on Barr for when the legislature was not in session.

Detailed coverage of legislative actions is available in the *Arizona Legislative Review* (1959–1982), which was replaced by the *Arizona Capitol Times*, which provides more news stories and also publishes valuable compilations of data on state politics—elections, officeholders, referenda. The records of proceedings in each chamber, *Journal of the House of Representatives* and *Journal of the Senate*, also include lists of committees, committee assignments, bills, sponsorship, and staff. The *Legislative Action on House Bills* and the companion *Legislative Action on Senate Bills* help one track the progress on bills. *Parliamentarily* [sic] *Speaking: A Handbook for Legislators: When to Say It, What To Say, How to Say It* (Phoenix: House of Representatives, Chief Clerk's Office, 1975) shows the effort to assist legislators in learning parliamentary procedure. The Arizona State Library, Archives and Public Records, also has collected basic biographical information on state legislators, accessible at http://www.azlibrary.gov/officials/BrowseLeg.aspx.

The indispensable source of contextual information on state governments in this era is the Council of State Governments' annual publication, *The Book of the States* (Lexington, KY). Also useful are the *Yearbook of the National Conference of State Legislative Leaders* (Milwaukee, WI: National Conference of State Legislative Leaders, 1966–1975) and the National Municipal League's monthly *State Legislatures Progress Reporter* (October 1965–1970).

The Barr Family

U.S. Census records provide basic data on Barr's family, and some additional information came from an interview with David Samuel Barr, the grandson of Hy's brother. A search of Portland records by Connie Lenzen uncovered some basic information about Burt and his brother Wallace in the Benson Polytechnic High School yearbook, information from Oregon vital records, obituaries in the *Portland Oregonian* newspaper, occupation and residence data on family members from R. L. Polk's *Portland City Directory*, 1911–1950. She also transmitted correspondence from D. Evans, the Portland Public Schools records manager, and material in the H. M. Barr Subject Files, 1927–1937, which included a published article by H. M. Barr—"The School as an Agency for Building Citizenship," *Oregon Parent-Teacher* 14 (December 1933): 5, 13—and various speeches and radio talks: "A New Year for Oregon Schools," "Fitting the School to the Needs of the Individual Child," "Education in Other Lands," "Are We Sincere About Our International Affairs?" and "Have You X-Rayed Your Prejudices?," copies of which are in the Burton S. Barr Collection, Arizona State University Library.

New York and Jewish Heritage

The literature on the history of immigration to the United States and of Jewish immigration, especially to New York, is extensive. A good general introduction is Alan M. Kraut, *The Huddled Masses: The Immigrant in American Society, 1880–1921*, 2nd ed. (Wheeling, IL: Harlan Davidson, 2001). For the history of Jews in New York City, I used Moses Rischin, *The Promised City: New York's Jews, 1870–1914* (Cambridge, MA: Harvard University Press, 1962); Irving Howe, *World of Our Fathers: The Journey of the East European Jews to America and the Life They Found and Made*, 2nd ed. (New York: Schocken Books, 1989); and Thomas Kessner, *The Golden Door: Italian and Jewish Immigrant Mobility in New York City, 1880–1915* (New York: Oxford University Press, 1977), while Gotham Center for New York History, "Garment Industry History Initiative" is a useful introduction to the garment industry (http://www.gothamcenter.org/garment/).

Portland and Oregon

The history of Portland and its people are well covered in various works. Two general histories of use are Carl Abbott, *Portland in Three Centuries: The Place and the People* (Corvallis: Oregon State University Press, 2011) and Jewel Beck Lansing, *Portland: People, Politics, and Power, 1851–2001* (Corvallis: Oregon State University Press, 2003). E. Kimbark MacColl, with Harry H. Stein, discuss the city's foundations in *Merchants, Money, and Power: The Portland Establishment, 1843–1913* (Portland, OR: Georgian Press, 1988), and continues the analysis in E. Kimbark MacColl, *The Growth of a City: Power and Politics in Portland, Oregon, 1914–1950* (Portland, OR: Georgian Press, 1979). William Toll discusses the different stages of Jewish migration and community formation in *The Making of an Ethnic Middle Class: Portland Jewry over Four Generations* (Albany: State University of New York Press, 1982). Robert D. Johnston analyzes the city's political culture and the important political battles (notably over education) that occurred during the Barr family's first decades of residence in Portland in *The Radical Middle Class: Populist Democracy and the Question of Capitalism in Progressive Era Portland, Oregon* (Princeton, NJ: Princeton University Press, 2003).

American Military, World War II, and After

The reorganization of the U.S. military that led to the creation of the Reserve Officer Training Corps that Barr participated in is discussed in Stephen Skowronek, *Building a New American State: The Expansion of National Administrative Capacities, 1877–1920* (New York: Cambridge University Press, 1982), and the history of the U.S. Army Reserve is available from Richard B. Crossland, *Twice the Citizen: A History of the United States Army Reserve, 1908–1983* (Washington, DC: Office of the Chief, Army Reserve, 1984) and GlobalSecurity.org, "U.S. Army Reserve—History," http://www.globalsecurity.org/military/agency/army/usar-history.htm.

The main patterns of World War II are conveniently discussed in A. Russell Buchanan, *The United States and World War II*, 2 vols. (New York: Harper & Row, 1964) and *American Military History*, ed. Richard W. Stewart, vol. 2, *United States Army in a Global Era, 1917–2003* (Washington, DC: Center of Military History, United States Army, 2005). For detailed analyses of the various campaigns—like Charles R. Anderson, Algeria-French Morocco November 8, 1942–November 11, 1942 (Washington, DC: Center of Military History, United States Army, 1993)—I consulted the numerous works published by the U.S. Army Center of Military History, including the CMH Series available at http://www.history.army.mil/html/bookshelves/resmat/ww2eamet.html#tab_1, and the *U.S. Army in World War II Series* at http://www.history.army.mil/html/bookshelves/collect/usaww2.html.

The main source of information on Barr's specific military activities comes in a letter from Colonel D. D. Spahr to Mrs. Burton S. Barr, December 31, 1964, which lists Barr's decoration and awards; copies of the "General Orders," which included the descriptions of actions for which Barr received these awards; the "Transcript of Military Record," which he received in April 1977; correspondence from the army in 1946; and correspondence from his commission as lieutenant colonel, copies of which are in the Burton S. Barr Collection, Arizona State University Library. Donald G. Taggart, *History of the Third Infantry Division* (Washington, DC: Infantry Journal Press, 1947) contains information on the engagements of Barr's division, and Merle Miller includes stories about Barr in *Ike the Soldier: As They Knew Him* (New York: G. P. Putnam's Sons, 1987).

Leadership

The literature on leadership is enormous, partly because it takes so many forms. The most useful assessments of this literature and its innumerable categories and terms are Bernard M. Bass, with Ruth R. Bass, *The Bass Handbook of Leadership: Theory, Research, and Managerial Applications*, 4th ed. (New York: Free Press, 2008); Bernard M. Bass and Ronald F. Riggio, *Transformational Leadership*, 2nd ed. (Mahway, NJ: Lawrence Erlbaum Associates, 2006); Peter G. Northouse, *Leadership: Theory and Practice* (Thousand Oaks, CA: Sage Publications, 2010); and Barbara Kellerman, *Followership: How Followers Are Creating Change and Changing Leaders* (Boston: Harvard Business Press, 2008). These studies are invaluable for understanding the array of attributes, characteristics, contexts, and influences. Since my focus was political and historical, I found greater immediate use from Garry Wills, *Certain Trumpets: The Call of Leaders* (New York: Simon & Schuster, 1994); James MacGregor Burns,

Leadership (New York: Harper and Row, 1978); and James MacGregor Burns, *Transforming Leadership: A New Pursuit of Happiness* (New York: Grove Press, 2003).

American Politics

Byron E. Shafer and Anthony J. Badger, eds., *Contesting Democracy: Substance and Structure in American Political History, 1775–2000* (Lawrence: University Press of Kansas, 2001) is an excellent introduction to the literature and concepts of political history; John H. Aldrich, *Why Parties?: The Origin and Transformation of Political Parties in America* (Chicago: University of Chicago Press, 1995) gives a useful history of the rise, decline, and shift of political parties. Some of the various studies of voter behavior in postwar politics are attentive to the timing of change, including Samuel Lubell, *The Future of American Politics*, 3rd ed. (New York: Harper & Row, 1965) and Everett Carll Ladd Jr., with Charles D. Hadley, *Transformations of the American Party System: Political Coalitions from the New Deal to the 1970s*, 2nd ed. (New York: W. W. Norton, 1978).

John A. Andrew provides a concise discussion of the 1960s in *Lyndon Johnson and the Great Society* (Chicago: Ivan R. Dee, 1998), while Michael Schaller and George Rising succinctly survey *The Republican Ascendancy: American Politics, 1968–2001* (Wheeling, IL: Harlan Davidson Inc., 2002). Several essays in Steve Fraser and Gary Gerstle, eds., *The Rise and Fall of the New Deal Order, 1930–1980* (Princeton, NJ: Princeton University Press, 1989) as well as W. H. Brands, *The Strange Death of American Liberalism* (New Haven, CT: Yale University Press, 2001) assess changes in liberalism. Kevin P. Phillips, *Post-Conservative America: People, Politics and Ideology in a Time of Crisis* (New York: Random House, 1982) and Donald T. Critchlow, *The Conservative Ascendancy: How the Republican Right Rose to Power in Modern America*, 2nd ed. (Lawrence: University Press of Kansas, 2011) discuss the rise of conservatism, while Geoffrey Kabaservice tells the story from the other side in *Rule and Ruin: The Downfall of Moderation and the Destruction of the Republican Party, From Eisenhower to the Tea Party* (New York: Oxford University Press, 2012).

State Government and Federalism

Jon C. Teaford, *The Rise of the States: Evolution of American State Government* (Baltimore: Johns Hopkins University Press, 2002) analyzes the changing role of state governments and is especially effective in explaining the profound change in the effectiveness, activity, and efficiency of state governments from the 1960s to the 1980s. Ballard C. Campbell, *The Growth of American Government: Governance from the Cleveland Era to the Present* (Bloomington: Indiana University Press, 1995) scrutinizes the transformation of government, primarily the federal, but also examines how state governments functioned, especially on fiscal matters. Larry Sabato's *Goodbye to Good-Time Charlie: The American Governor Transformed, 1950–1975* (Lexington, MA: Lexington Books, 1978) is a useful study of changes in state government during this crucial era.

Insightful analyses of the changes in state governments and federalism during this era are Carl. W. Stenberg, "Federalism in Transition: 1959–79," *Intergovernmental Perspective* 6 (Winter 1980): 4–13; Thomas R. Dye, *American Federalism: Competition Among Governments* (Lexington, MA: Lexington Books, 1990); and two essays in Marilyn Gittell, ed., *State Politics and the New Federalism: Readings and Commentary* (New York: Longman, 1986): Marilyn Gittell, "Studying the States," 1–8; and Steven D. Gold, "Recent Developments in State Finances," 314–43; while Ann O'M. Bowman and Richard C. Kearney provide a useful overview of *State and Local Government*, 8th ed. (Boston: Wadsworth, 2011). Daniel J. Elazar's classic study of *American Federalism: A View from the States*, 3rd ed. (New York: Harper & Row, 1984) and Larry N. Gerston, *American Federalism: A Concise Introduction* (Armonk, NY: M. E. Sharpe, 2007) are interesting approaches to significant changes in the basic patterns of federal-state power relationships.

Legislatures

Several classic studies of legislatures are useful not only for their general insights but also for their assessments of contemporary conditions: Malcolm E. Jewell and Samuel C. Patterson, *The Legislative Process in the United States* (New York: Random House, 1966); Alexander Heard, ed., *State Legislatures in American Politics* (Englewood Cliffs, NJ: Prentice Hall, 1966); and Malcolm E. Jewell, *The State Legislature: Politics and Practice*, 2nd ed. (New York: Random House, 1969). Alan Rosenthal provides a more recent perspective in *Heavy Lifting: The Job of the American Legislature* (Washington, DC: CQ Press, 2004).

Thomas G. Alexander and David Roy Hall focus on "State Legislatures in the Twentieth Century," in Joel Silbey et al., eds. *Encyclopedia of the American Legislative System*, 3 vols. (New York: Charles Scribners' Sons, 1994) 1:215–32, and other essays in those volumes also address aspects of the state legislative experience in the postwar era. Two notable studies aimed at improving state legislatures: the report sponsored by the American Political Science Association, *American State Legislatures*, ed. Belle Zeller (New York: Thomas Y. Crowell, 1954) was followed 25 years later by The Citizens Conference on State Legislatures, which published *State Legislatures: An Evaluation of Their Effectiveness* (New York: Praeger Publishers, 1971) and John Burns, *The Sometimes Government: A Critical Study of the 50 American Legislatures* (New York: Bantam Books, 1971). The historical transformation of legislatures is covered in Richard H. Leach, "A Quiet Revolution, 1933–1976," in *The Book of the States, 1976–1977* (Lexington, KY: Council of State Governments, 1976), 21–27; Alan Rosenthal, "The State of State Legislatures: An Overview," *Hofstra Law Review* 11 (1982–1983): 1185–1204; and Eugene W. Hickok Jr., *The Reform of State Legislatures and the Changing Character of Representation* (Lanham, MD: University Press of America, 1992), esp. 47–55. Malcolm Edwin Jewell and Marcia Lynn Whicker wrote the seminal study on *Legislative Leadership in the American States* (Ann Arbor: University of Michigan Press, 1994), but practitioners like Thomas P. O'Neill, *All Politics Is Local and Other Rules of the Game* (New York: Times Books, 1994) and Ralph Wright, *All Politics Is Personal* (Boston: Marshall Jones Company, 1996) provide another perspective.

The West and Western Politics

Starting points for assessing the West are Clyde A. Milner, Carol A. O'Connor, and Martha A. Sandweiss, eds., *The Oxford History of the American West* (New York: Oxford University Press, 1994); David M. Wrobel and Michael C. Steiner, eds., *Many Wests: Place, Culture and Regional Identity* (Lawrence: University Press of Kansas, 1997); and William Cronon, George Miles, and Jay Gitlin, eds., *Under an Open Sky: Rethinking America's Western Past* (New York: Norton, 1992), particularly Michael E. McGerr's essay "Is There a Twentieth-Century West?" Michael P. Malone and Ross Peterson, "Politics and Protests," in *The Oxford History of the American West*, 500–33, surveys a century of Western politics; Paul Kleppner's particularly useful analysis of "Politics without Parties: The Western States, 1900–1984" is in *The Twentieth-Century West: Historical Interpretations*, ed. Gerald D. Nash and Richard W. Etulain (Albuquerque: University of New Mexico Press, 1989), 295–338. Jeff Roche, ed., *The Political Culture of the New West* (Lawrence: University Press of Kansas, 2008) includes essays offering a cultural approach to Western politics, while the essays in Richard Lowitt, ed., *Politics in the Postwar American West* (Norman: University of Oklahoma Press, 1995) take a range of approaches. William Deverell surveys themes and literature of "Politics and the Twentieth-Century American West," in *A Companion to the American West*, ed. William Deverell (Malden, MA: Blackwell, 2004), 442–59, and Robert W. Cherny outlines "Research Opportunities in Twentieth-Century Western History: Politics," in *Researching Western History: Topics in the Twentieth Century*, ed. Gerald Nash and Richard Etulain (Albuquerque: University of New Mexico Press, 1997), 83–117.

Arizona Political History and Politicians

Thomas E. Sheridan, *Arizona: A History*, rev. ed. (Tucson: University of Arizona Press, 2012) provides an excellent, broad history of the state, and Donald W. Meinig provides an excellent cultural context in *Southwest: Three Peoples in Geographical Change, 1600–1970* (New York: Oxford University Press, 1971). I analyze the state's largest city in *Desert Visions and the Making of Phoenix, 1860–2009* (Albuquerque: University of New Mexico Press, 2010), and C. L. Sonnichsen examines *Tucson: The Life and Times of an American City* (Norman: University of Oklahoma Press, 1982).

The essential starting point for any Arizona political history is David R. Berman, *Arizona Politics and Government: The Quest for Autonomy, Democracy, and Development* (Lincoln: University of Nebraska Press, 1998), an outstanding blend of political history and analysis of Arizona's current political system. James. W. Byrkit explains a central dynamic in Arizona's early politics in *Forging the Copper Collar: Arizona's Labor-Management War of 1901–21* (Tucson: University of Arizona Press, 1982), and David R. Berman ably analyzes the nature of those politics in *Reformers, Corporations, and the Electorate: An Analysis of Arizona's Age of Reform* (Niwot: University Press of Colorado, 1992) and *Politics, Labor, and the War on Big Business: The Path of Reform in Arizona, 1890–1920* (Boulder: University Press of Colorado, 2012). The most comprehensive assessment of the politics surrounding the state's constitution is Mark E. Pry, "Arizona and the Politics of Statehood, 1889–1912" (Ph.D. diss., Arizona State University, 1995), while William S. Collins provides detailed information about

The New Deal in Arizona (Phoenix: Arizona State Parks Board, 1999). The political role of Arizona women is covered in Heidi J. Osselaer, *Winning Their Place: Arizona Women in Politics, 1900–1950* (Tucson: University of Arizona Press, 2009) and Rita Mae Kelly, ed., *Women and the Arizona Political Process*, Second Arizona Women's Town Hall (Lanham, MD: University Press of America, 1988).

Jason Crabtree LaBau offers an interesting assessment of factional and ideological differences among Arizona Republicans in "Phoenix Rising: Arizona and the Origins of Modern Conservative Politics" (Ph.D. diss., University of Southern California, 2010), while Elizabeth Tandy Shermer's study of *Sunbelt Capitalism: Phoenix and the Transformation of American Politics* (Philadelphia: University of Pennsylvania Press, 2013) analyzes the political dimensions of the economic development of Phoenix. Also useful are Shermer's "Drafting a Movement: Barry Goldwater and the Rebirth of the Arizona Republican Party" and Micaela Anne Larkin, "Southwestern Strategy: Mexican Americans and Republican Politics in the Arizona Borderlands," both in *Barry Goldwater and the Remaking of the American Political Landscape*, ed. Elizabeth Tandy Shermer (Tucson: University of Arizona Press, 2013). Stephen C. Shadegg, *Arizona Politics: The Struggle to End One-Party Rule* (Tempe: Arizona State University, 1986) is political history by a Republican participant that focuses on the GOP gains and election contests from roughly the 1950 to the 1970s.

James W. Johnson, *Arizona Politicians: The Noble and the Notorious* (Tucson: University of Arizona Press, 2002) provides brief, colorful sketches of 21 Arizona politicians, and, invoking Mo Udall, he attributes the national prominence of so many of them to the state's "civilized brand of politics." But once these Arizonans became nationally prominent political figures, they had little to do with state politics, and their biographers have generally followed the interests of their subjects. Still, their Arizona backgrounds and connections help to understand something of the state's political character. Among the relevant works are Robert Alan Goldberg, *Barry Goldwater* (New Haven, CT: Yale University Press, 1995); Peter Iverson, *Barry Goldwater: Native Arizonan* (Norman: University of Oklahoma Press, 1997); Dean Smith, *The Goldwaters of Arizona* (Flagstaff, AZ: Northland Press, 1986); Donald W. Carson and James W. Johnson, *Mo: The Life & Times of Morris K. Udall* (Tucson: University of Arizona Press, 2001); and J. Brian Smith, *John J. Rhodes: Man of the House* (Phoenix: Prime Publishers, 2005).

Two Arizona political leaders did have important connections with state developments, and their biographies provide valuable information. James Elton McMillan Jr., *Ernest W. McFarland: A Biography* (Prescott, AZ: Sharllot Hall Museum Press, 2004) gives a solid assessment of McFarland's gubernatorial struggles with the legislature. Jack L. August, *Vision in the Desert: Carl Hayden and Hydropolitics in the American Southwest* (Fort Worth: Texas Christian University Press, 1999) provides a useful biography of Hayden that focuses on his work on the Central Arizona Project, while Ross R. Rice, *Carl Hayden: Builder of the American West* (Lanham, MD: University Press of America, 1994) is a broader view of that notable senator.

Other biographies are mainly useful for personal information, rather than political or policy matters. Frank Asbury, *Yours Sincerely: A Biography of Jack Williams* (Phoenix: HT Press, 1994), is a popular sketch with little specific information on Williams' actions as governor; Raul Castro, with Jack L. August, *Adversity is My Angel: The Life and Career of Raul Castro* (Fort Worth: Texas Christian University Press,

2009), includes limited coverage of Castro's two years in office; and Dean Smith, *Brothers Five: The Babbitts of Arizona* (Tempe: Arizona Historical Foundation, 1989) briefly discusses Governor Bruce Babbitt. John L. Myers gives basic biographical information on *The Arizona Governors, 1912–1990* (Phoenix: Heritage Publishers, 1989). Ronald J. Watkins examines *High Crimes and Misdemeanors: The Term and Trials of Former Governor Evan Mecham* (New York: W. Morrow, 1990).

Two important legislators from the Barr era have written valuable memoirs: Stan Turley, *Kid from Sundown* (Mesa, AZ: Cox Printing Company, 2002) and Alfredo Gutierrez, *To Sin Against Hope: Life and Politics on the Borderland* (New York: Verso, 2013).

Arizona Government

David Berman's *Arizona Politics and Government* is the best guide to Arizona's political system and government, but several earlier studies of (then) contemporary Arizona politics offer useful information and insights. Roy D. Morey, *Politics and Legislation: The Office of Governor in Arizona*, Arizona Government Studies 3 (Tucson: University of Arizona Press, 1965) focuses on the making of state policy in the first two postwar decades, plus a historical context back to 1912. Bruce B. Mason and Heinz R. Hink, *Constitutional Government in Arizona*, 5th rev. ed. (Tempe: Arizona State University, 1975) describes the structure of state government in the 1970s and includes some background information. Also useful are Gerald E. Hansen and Douglas A. Brown, *Arizona, Its Constitution and Government*, 2nd ed. (Lanham, MD: University Press of America, 1987) and Donald Robinson Van Petten, *The Constitution and Government of Arizona*, 3rd ed. (Phoenix: n.p., 1960).

Efforts to reorganize Arizona government included an assessment by Robert E. Riggs, *The Movement for Administrative Reorganization in Arizona*, Special Studies 17 (Tucson: Bureau of Business and Public Research, University of Arizona, 1961). The three separate reports offering proposals for reorganization are Griffenhagen & Associates, "Report On General State Organization," unpublished report, (Chicago: n.p., 1949); Heinz Hink, "Report, October, 1967, to the Council on Organization of Arizona State Government," unpublished report, Arizona State Library, Archives and Public Records, azmemory.azlibrary.gov/cdm/ref/collection/statepubs/id/5965; and "Governmental Reorganization: Report to the Arizona Legislature," (Phoenix: Arizona House of Representatives Governmental Relations Committee, 1971), unpublished report, Arizona State Library, Archives and Public Records, azmemory.azlibrary.gov/cdm/singleitem/collection/statepubs/id/5955/rec/1.

J. Morris Richards wrote a very detailed session-by-session "History of the Arizona State Legislature, 1912–1967," 20 vols. ms. (Phoenix: Arizona Legislative Council, Arizona Department of Library, Archives and Public Records, 1990), which is invaluable for understanding the character and operation of the legislature up to the beginning years of Barr's tenure. Also useful are Dean E. Mann, "The Legislative Committee System in Arizona," *Western Political Quarterly* 14 (December 1961): 925–41; and Roderick Andrew Jacobsen, "Election of the Speaker in the Arizona House of Representatives during the Era of Coalition" (master's thesis, Arizona State University, 1967).

Reapportionment

The complex history of this process is well covered in Bruce B. Mason and Leonard E. Goodall, "Arizona," in *Impact of Reapportionment on the Thirteen Western States*, ed. Eleanore Bushnell (Salt Lake City: University of Utah Press, 1970), 49–69; J. L. Polinard, "Arizona," in *Reapportionment Politics: The History of Redistricting in the 50 States*, ed. Leroy Hardy, Alan Heslop, and Stuart Anderson (Beverly Hills, CA: Sage Publications, 1981), 36–44; and Robert C. White, "Legislative Apportionment in Arizona," Report to the League of Women Voters of Arizona, September 1978, Hayden Arizona Collection, Arizona State University Library. Evidence for how hard this hit the Arizona political world appears in the reaction of Morris K. Udall in his *Congressman's Report*: "Reapportionment—I: 'One Man, One Vote' . . . That's All She Wrote!" 88th Congress, October 14, 1964, and "Reapportionment—II: Where Do We Go From Here?" 88th Congress, December 11, 1964.

Public Policies

The various essays in Zachary A. Smith, ed., *Politics and Public Policy in Arizona*, 2nd ed. (Westport, CT: Praeger, 1996) provide an introduction to Arizona public policy. A great resource for many different policy issues over this period are the biannual reports of the Arizona Town Hall, starting in 1962. While varying somewhat in the type and quality of their coverage, they provide crucial background and contemporary information and analysis.

Water

The importance of water in Western history is evidenced by the rich literature on the subject. Useful starting points are Norris Hundley Jr., *The Great Thirst: Californians and Water—A History* (Berkeley: University of California Press, 2001); Donald Wooster, *Rivers of Empire: Water, Aridity, and the Growth of the American West* (New York: Pantheon Books, 1985); and Marc Reisner, *Cadillac Desert: The American West and Its Disappearing Water* (New York: Viking, 1986). Douglas E. Kupel considers *Fuel for Growth: Water and Arizona's Urban Environment* (Tucson: University of Arizona Press, 2003), while Rich Johnson explains the history of *The Central Arizona Project, 1918–1968* (Tucson: University of Arizona Press, 1977). Four Arizona Town Hall Reports are very valuable guides to the emerging concerns with various water issues: *Arizona's Water Supply* (1964); *Arizona Water: The Management of Scarcity* (1977); *Managing Water Quality in a Water Scarce State* (1985); and *Arizona's Water Future: Challenges and Opportunities* (2004). Dean Eldon Peterson and Larry L. Deason, "Arizona's Groundwater Problem and Proposed Legislation," Paper, New Mexico Water Conference Proceedings, Las Cruces, New Mexico, March 25, 1971, http://wrri.nmsu.edu/publish/watcon/proc16/Peterson_Deason.pdf (accessed May 17, 2012), and Robert G. Dunbar, "The Arizona Groundwater Controversy at Mid-Century," *Arizona and the West* (Spring 1977): 5–24, cover efforts to deal with the groundwater problem before the 1970s; Desmond D. Connall Jr. provides detailed coverage in "A History of the Arizona Groundwater Management Act," *Arizona State Law Journal* 2 (1982): 313–44, while Paul Bergelin assesses the lead-up to the GMA and some important consequences in "Moderating Power: Municipal Interbasin Groundwater Transfers in Arizona" (master's thesis, Arizona State University, 2013).

AHCCCS, Medicaid, and Health Care

Dennis George Preisler, "A History of the Arizona Health Care Cost Containment System Policy: AHCCCS as a Medicaid Alternative, 1981–1987" (Ph.D. diss., Arizona State University, 1998) offers a detailed narrative and assessment, while Jon B. Christianson and Diane G. Hillman offer a useful but brief historical analysis in *Health Care for the Indigent and Competitive Contracts: The Arizona Experience* (Ann Arbor, MI: Health Administration Press Perspectives, 1986). Also useful on this topic and on a range of health care issues are the published plans from the state Health Planning Authority and the Department of Health Services, while the Arizona Town Hall produced valuable reports in 1970, 1973, and 1984 that discuss the conditions of health care in the state and recommend policies.

Other Policy Areas

Town Hall reports on taxation, transportation, and education provide essential introductions to these subjects. A valuable report on taxation is Arizona House Staff, "A Historical Review of the Property Tax in Arizona" (Phoenix: House of Representatives, 1977), while *ValTrans: The People Moving Experience* (Phoenix: Regional Public Transportation Authority, 1988) helps understand transportation problems and that failed proposal.

Index

Note: Page numbers in *italics* indicate illustrative material

Adams Hotel, 126–27
AHCCCS (Arizona Health Care Cost Containment System), 162–66, 176, 177, 205. *See also* health care
Akers, Stan, 104, 115, 123, 132, 163, 174, 217
Allen, Chet, 89
Anamax Corporation, 167
Andrus, Cecil, 169
anti-Semitism, 22–23, 32
Anzio, battle of, 5, 37, 103, 205
apportionment and representation: districts/redistricting, x, 19, 86–87; one-person, one-vote rule, 63, 85–86; reapportionment, 72, 85–87, 118, 132, 139, 143, 146, 176, 217; rural interests, x–xi, 62, 71–74, 84. *See also* power
Arizona: demographics, xi-xii, 64–66, *65t*, 68, 70, 74; growth and expansion, x–xi, 16, 19, 62–71, 74, 83–84, 118, 142–43; history, 18–19, 66, 71; immigrant population, 64–66, 142; Territorial Legislature, 71
Arizona Cardinals, 210–11.
Arizona Corporation Commission, 148, 232n11
Arizona House of Representatives: Appropriations Committee, 4–5, 89; Governmental Affairs Committee report, 150; history, 71, 76–79; number of bills passed, 122–23, *122f*, *123t*; Public Health and Welfare Committee, 87–88; Republican Caucus, 4–5, 102, 109, 116, 125, 130–32, 157, 164; rule changes (1963), 77–78; Rules Committee, 76, 78, 145; Speaker elections, 75–76, *76t*, 123; State Government Committee, 88. *See also* Arizona legislature; state legislatures
Arizona Industrial Commission, 148
Arizona legislature, 71–89; assessment of, 128–29; committee system, 75–79, 77, 82, 127, 133–34, 145, 171; conflicts of interest, 116–18; consent calendar, 127; factionalism, 73, 75–79, 189; good old boy network, 127; Gung-Ho legislature, 122; House-Senate relationship, 79–85, 87, 134–35; interchamber leadership meetings, 125; interim committees, 145, 171; legislative action, 4–5, 101–11, 122–23,

Arizona legislature (continued)
122f, 191; Majority status, *130t*, 130, 133–34; organization and reforms, 69–70, 75–79, 122, 123, 127–30, 144, 219; role of women, 71, 121; special sessions, 155–56, 165, 172, 176; traditional policy priorities, 68. *See also* Arizona House of Representatives; Arizona political structure; Arizona Senate; Arizona state government; federalism; state legislatures

Arizona Licensed Beverage Association, 117

Arizona political structure, 62–89, 122–25, 220, 226n19; cultural basis, 70; history, 16–20, 53–54, 62–75, 229n76; PACs and special interests, 84, 106, 108; social basis, 64–66, 70–71. *See also* Arizona legislature; Arizona state government; power

Arizona Republic: April 1983 fiscal crisis, 5; on Barr, 31–32, 59, 89, 113, 137, 208; districting plans, 86; freshman legislator survey, 119, 120; governor's race, 181, 187, 189, 191; tax legislation, 153

Arizona Senate, 4–5, 72, 74–75, 77–78, 78, 80–82, 123. *See also* Arizona House of Representatives

Arizona state government: accountability, 138, 165; Administration Department, 117, 150; confrontational atmosphere, 208–9, 219; Constitutional provisions, 66–67, 73, 135; Council on the Organization of Arizona State Government, 145, 149–50; decentralized, 16, 66, 146, 152; governor, 66, 71–73, 130, 135–39, 146, 150; Griffenhagen Report (1949), 83, 146; gubernatorial vetoes, *137t*; history, x–xi, 66–68; inefficiency, 62–63, 122; infrastructure, 154, 157–58, 166–67, 217; reductions in government spending, 155, 156; reform and redesign, 9, 63, 85–87, 126–30, 138, 143, 144–51, 176, 216–18, 232n11; rural domination, x–xi, 62, 71–74, 84; sunset law, 150–51. *See also* budget and fiscal policy

Arizona State University (ASU), 174, 213, 233n52

Arizona Supreme Court, 152, 167

Arnold, Ben, 123

assimilation, 29–30, 31, 41, 112

Atomic Energy Commission, 151

Babbitt, Bruce, 3–4, 47, 143; and Barr, 90, 95, 100, 135–39, 177, 187, 214, 216, 218; governor's race, 181, 182, 189, 195; policies, 155–56, 157, 164–65, 168, 172

Babbitt, Ted, 47, 136

Baker v. Carr, 85

Bandouveris, Harry, 78

Barnes, Stan, 219

Barr, Burton, 38, *46*, *51*, *96*, *112*, *132*, *158*, *183*; birth, 6, 22; Bronze and Silver Stars, 37, 39; and Bruce Babbitt, 90, 95, 100, 135–39, 177, 187, 214, 216, 218; business and civilian life, 6, 43–61, 114, 212–13; childhood and education, 21–22, 29–32, 40–41, 223n5; death and burial, xi, 7, 213–14; family background, 22–25, 41; health problems, 39–40, 44, 212–13; legacy, xi, 6–7, 9, 19, 142, 156, 166, 176–78, 214–20; marriage and family, 39, 54, 56–60, *58*, 112, *183*, 227n15; military career, xi–xii, 5, 6, 32–40, *38*, 43, 49, 213–14; relationship with GOP, 113, 114, 200. *See also* governor's race of 1986; legislative career

Barr, Burton, character and personality: bipartisanship, 102–3, 140, 188, 215, 219; character traits, xi–xii, 6–7, 40–42, 48, 60, 92–97, 144, 214, 216, 226n7; flexibility, 11, 101–2, 114–15, 134, 164, 175–76, 177, 201–3, 217; ideology, 114–15, 149, 202, 203, 215–16; military career impact, 5, 35, 41–42, 91, 93, 94, 103, 107, 112–13, 198, 205; performance and appearance, 99–100, 192; pragmatism, 6, 98, 102, 113, 116, 130, 169–70, 209,

215; use of humor, 93, 100, 108, 111, 178, 194, 217, 235n46; values, 112–13; Western politics, 18–20
Barr, Burton, views on: education, 27–29, 173, 188, 191, 211–12; environment, 170, 172; federalism, 114; health care, 144, 145, 151, 160–61; Jewish identity, 31, 32, 41; leadership, 3, 80, 82, 203; need for compromise, 114–15, 124, 131, 133, 167–68, 176, 184, 189, 190, 202, 216; politics, 62, 75, 204
Barr, Charlotte, 39, *46*, 52, 54
Barr, David Samuel, 223n5
Barr, Ella Hurwitz, 24, 30
Barr, Hyman Max, 24–29
Barr, Louise, 41–42, 92–94, 117, 174, 181–82, *183*, 205, 213, 217, 227n15
Barr, Michael, 41, 57, 58–59, *183*, 206, 213
Barr, Stephanie, 21, 33, 57, 59, *183*
Barr, Suzanne, 57, *183*, 220
Barr, Wallace, 30, 40–41
Barrow, Tim, 128
Basha, Eddie, 43, 47–48, 54–55, 108, 110, 114, 173, 205, 211–14, 216
Bass, Bernard, 91, 118
Benning, P. J., 55
Berman, David, 70, 84, 131
bipartisanship: coalitions, 71, 76, 84, 87, 108, 133–34, 140, 215; consensus politics, 102–4; leadership style, 102–3, 140, 188, 215, 219; negotiation and compromise, 114–15, 131, 133, 167–68, 176, 184, 189, 190, 202–3, 216. *See also* nonpartisanship; partisanship
Bolin, Wesley, 135, 181
Boyd, Mike, 186, 192, 193, 197
Bradley, Omar, 37
Brayton, Nelson, 80
Brown, Jack, 78–79, 100, 103, 133, 149
budget and fiscal policy: April 1983 fiscal crisis, 3–5, 12, 194; Budget Division, 146, 150; centralized state purchasing, 149; debt limits, 156; Finance Department, 110; Legislative Budget Committee, 127, 146; Office of Budget Director, xi, 88; state budgets, xi, 4–5, 88, 104, 109, 133, 135, 145, 208. *See also* taxes/tax policy
Burns, James MacGregor, 11, 91, 140, 226n7
Burns, Peter, 43, 93–94, 97, 101–2, 109, 112, 129, 137, 193
Bush, Jim, 94, 95, 168, 175, 179

Campbell, Clovis, 99
Carlson, Donna, 130
Carpenter, Clarence, 62, 80, *81*
Carter, Jimmy, 14, 168
Castro, Raul (governor), 135, 164, 181
Chapman, Calder, 186
Clark, Lloyd, 43, 51
Clay, Henry, 12–13
Cold War, 16, 50
Collins, Rick, 96, 98, 101, 111, 192, 207
Congressional Medal of Honor, xi–xii, 42, 214
Conner, Pat, 119, 120, 126
Corbet, Leo, 120–21
Corbin, Bob, 186
Corpstein, Pete, 130
Corral, Nikki, 59, 95, 108, 124, 129, 133

Daley, Mike, xi, 42, 214
Daniels, Craig, 163, 220
Davis, Stephen, 115
de Berge, Earl, 200
de Uriarte, Richard, 190
DeBolske, Jack, 79, 80, 94–95, 126, 130, 158
Democratic Party, x, 13, 64, 67, 69, 72, 74–75, 133, 153, 188–89, 217; and conservatives, 64, 69, 74, 75, 84, 132, 133. *See also* Jeffersonian democracy; Pinto Democrats
DeWitt, John, 134
direct democracy, 25, 63; initiatives, 18, 67, 102, 155, 157; recall/judicial recall, 67; referenda, 18, 67
"dirty Seven," 87, 89, 128
Dolphin Group, 185, 192–93. *See also* Stitzenberger, Lee
Dugan, James I., 53
DuVal, Fred, 95

economy and commerce, 16, 64, 142–43, 148, 156–57, 175; agriculture and farming, 63, 65–66, 68, 113, 166–69, 201; Commerce Department, 151; consumer protection, 116–17; copper production, 3, 64–65, 75, 156; defense spending, 16, 68, 142; inflation, 152, 154; mining, 63–66, 68, 75, 84, 106, 113, 153, 156, 166–68, 170; railroad interests, 66, 75, 83, 153; ranching, 66, 68, 75, 113; timber and forestry, 68, 153; tourism, 188, 191
education, 173–75; Arizona Citizens for Education (ACE), 211–12, 213; Barr interest in, 27–29, 173, 188, 191; Bilingual Education Act (1982), 173; Federal Bureau of Education, 27; funding, 146, 153, 155, 156, 173, 208, 219; higher education, 173–74, 208, 212; special education, 155; vocational education, 173; voucher system, 173
Eisenhower, Dwight D., 10, 33–35, 50, 69, 95
Ellsworth, Delos, 87, 89, 128, 143
environment, 160–72; air pollution, 169–71, 189, 190; anti-smog bill, 170; auto emissions program, 95; Barr views on, 170, 172; Clean Air Act, 170; Division of Air Pollution Control, 170; hazardous waste management plan, 172; Interim Committee on Environmental Future, 171; land-use planning, 68, 138, 145–46, 166–67, 171–72, 211, 216, 218; urban lands bill, 138; vehicle emissions, 170–71. *See also* water
Environmental Protection Agency (EPA), 170–71
ethics issues and standards, 116, 148. *See also* lobbyists

Fannin, Bob, 185, 192, 193, 200, 215
Fannin, Paul, 52, 68, 80, 83, 131, 152, 174
federalism, 9, 16; Barr's ideas, 114, 151; "little federalism," 74, 123; New Federalism, 151.
FICO Corporation, 167
Fitzpatrick, Tom, 105, 117–18, 227n15
Flagstaff, 49, 50, 65, 186, 188
Flying Farmers, 84
food processing equipment, 43, 45–47, 50, 53, 55–56, 60
Forbes, Robert H., 77
Fort Lewis, Wash., 33–34
Fry, Don, 47

Gabaldon, Tom, 190
Gilbert, Jack, 87
Giss, Harold, x, xi, 62, 72, 80–82, *81*, 87–88, 120–21, 123, 126, 134, 140, 226n19
Goddard, Samuel, 73, 88, 135, 143
Goddard, Terry, 7, 93–94, 103–4, 157, 189, 204–5, 209–10, 212–15
Goldwater, Barry, xi, 9, 12, 17–18, 53, 69–71, 130–31, 180, 208
Gonzalez, Louis, 119, 121, 123
governor's race of 1986, 179–203; "Dear Neighbor" letter, 191; decision to run, 179–86, 188, 191, 217; Democratic primary, 188–89; grass roots participation, 192; issues, 188, 191, 194; negative campaigning, 196–97, 198, 205, 236n49; polls and polling, 181, 185, 186, 187, 189, 193, 198, 200; results and assessment, 7, 190–94, 198–206, 216, 229n73; strategy, 187–89, 191–94
Great Depression, 17, 31, 41, 67
Gutierrez, Alfredo, x–xii, 98; Arizona politics, 62, 80, 81, 84, 126, 127, 136, 143; Captain Chaos, 133, 212; Barr's governor race, 179, 184, 192, 194, 198, 201; leadership style, 95, 96, 97, 101, 103, 105, 106, 107–8, 111, 133–34; mentoring, 115, 141; policy leadership, 5, 142, 143–44, 162, 163, 167, 171, 173, 174, 177; post-legislative life, 7, 206, 212–13, 214, 217, 218

Hamilton, Art, 102, 106, 175, 202, 207, 217; bipartisanship, 133, 141; character and personality, 6, 164, 175–76; leadership, 95, 102, 103, 107, 110, 111, 124, 156; legislative experience, 121,

125, 133, 135, 141, 219–20; mentoring, 98–99, 141; price of power, 179, 201
Haugh, John H. "Jack," 87, 89, 125
Hawkins, Max, 195, 197, 205
Hayden, Carl, 9, 11, 19, 52, 70–71, 195
health care, 28, 158–66; AHCCCS, 162–66, 176, 177, 205; Arizona Medical Association, 162, 163; Barr views on, 144, 145, 151, 160–61; capitation financing, 165; health maintenance organization (HMO), 160, 161, 164; Health Services Department, 150, 170; hospitals, 109, 137, 159–63; indigent care, 157, 159, 162, 164, 165, 215; insurance, 160–63; Kerr-Mills Act, 87–88, 159; Medicaid/Medicare, 115–16, 159, 162–66, 177; mental health, 105, 148, 174; "socialized medicine," 160–61, 163
Herstam, Chris, 100, 107, 110, 113, 114, 125, 204, 207, 214
Heusler, Bill, 155, 156
Hill, Jeff, 107, 135
Hobart Company, 45, 55
Hoover Report (1949), 82
Hubler, Shawn, 95, 105
Hull, Jane, 103, 107, 113, 121–22, 130, 131, *132*, 192
Humphrey, Marshall "Marty," 125, 153, 192–93
Hunt, George W. P., 67
Hurwitz, Ella, 24
Hurwitz, Isaac, 22–24, 29

ideology, 9, 62, 114–15, 131, 133, 149, 202, 203, 215–16, 219. *See also* political culture
Indian tribal gaming compact, 212
Isaacson, Don, 42, 129, 165, 206, 207

Jacquin, Bill, 87, 89, 128, 143, 148, 163
Jamieson, Bill, 212–13
Jamieson and Gutierrez firm, 212–13, 214
Javelina Association, 50–51
Jeffersonian democracy, 69, 149
Jenkins, Bill, 128
Jewell, Malcolm Edwin, 72, 140, 229n76
Jewitt, Jack, 207
John Birch Society, 52–53
Jordan, Jewel, 149
Jordan, Lilian, 130

Kalil, Charles, 52–53
Kaplan, Richard, 48, 55, 56, 59, 95
Kay, Peter, 106, 176
Kelley, Frank, 123, 133, 206, 217, 218
Kennedy, Ted, 12, 160
Killian, Mark, *158*
Kimball, William F., 75
Klahr, Gary Peter, 85–86
Kluender, Al, 100, 104
Kolbe, John, 106–7, 123, 134, 138, 175, 191; character and personality, 6, 94, 115, 144, 194, 216; governor's race, 180–81, 187–88, 190, 193, 194, 205, 235n46; leadership, 90, 104, 111, 124, 155; legacy, 19, 142
Kromko, John, 126, 202, 203
Kruglick, Burt, 192, 199, 200
Ku Klux Klan, 28–29
Kunasek, Carl, 130
Kush, Frank, 174
Kyl, Jon, 19, 90, 96–97, 104, 107, 113–14, 127, 129, 134, 143, 200, 214

labor unions/union organization, 65, 66, 70
Lane, Joe,, 5, 103, 106–7, 134, *158*, 207, 209; flexibility, 102, 115; governor's race, 184, 190, 193–94, 206; legislative experience and leadership, 97–99, 105, 110, 120, 121; relations with GOP, 113
law and justice, 136, 137, 146, 175–76, 190
leadership, 90–141; approaches to, 10–12, 13, 109–10, 114, 202–3, 215–16, 219–20; assessing, 90–92, 113–16, 118–19, 122–23, 139–41, 143–46, 176–78, 190–91, 193; character traits, xi–xii, 6–7, 10–12, 14, 40–42, 48, 60, 92–119, 194, 214–16, 219, 226n7; flexibility, 11, 101–2, 114–15, 134, 164, 175–76, 177, 201–3, 217; historical

leadership (continued)
views, 10–14; impact of situation, 91, 118, 119–41; inclusiveness, 201, 215, 219; leader-follower dichotomy, 10–11; legislative partners, 129–39; legitimacy, 11, 222n15; mentoring, 98–99, 110, 120–21, 140; strategy and techniques, xi, 4–7, 9, 12, 97–112, 131–35, 171, 174–75, 176, 202–3, 228n48; types of, 140, 215–16; values and conflict, 112–18
legislative career, 90–178; early years, 6, 51–56, 60–61, 87–89, 144; Majority leader, 90, 123–35, 215–17; managing legislative business, 125–29; "Mr. Magic" label, 12, 133, 140, 202; policy priorities, 144–45, 151–52, 158–59; post-governor's race, 206–9, 212
Legislative Council, 127, 145
legislators: challenge of legislative service, 71–72, 79, 119–22; changing attitudes, 217–18; compensation, 119–20, 127, 148; experience of freshmen, 120–21; incumbents, 18, 86; women, 121–22
liquor, 67, 116
lobbyists, 84–85, 105, 125–27
Luke Air Force Base, 172

Maricopa County, x, 74, 86–87, 157–58, 163, 183, 188, 199, 200, 211
Martin Luther King, Jr., holiday, 175, 189, 191, 207, 219
Mason, Tony, 188–89
Mathews, William R., 80
Maverick Store Fixture Company, 55–56, 59, 93
Mawhinney, John, 134
McCain, John, 9, 102, 109, 165, 182, 185, 188, 193, 200, 214
McCray Refrigeration, 45–47
McFarland, Ernest, xi, 19, 50, *51*, 73
McMillen, Barbara, 50
Mecham, Evan, 52, 131, 218–19, 236n49; controversy and impeachment, 207–9, 212, 218–19; governor's race, 180, 194–203, 205–6, 229n73
Merrill, Bruce, 192
Meyerson, Bessie, 23, 24
minority population, 63, 64, 66, 69, 70, 86, 132
Mofford, Ross, 212
Morales, Mike, 105
Moss, Dave, 188, 189
Murphy, Pat, 179

Navajo County, 86, 188
New Deal policies, 67, 69
New Federalism, 151
Nilsson, Joel, 201–2
Nixon, Richard, 151, 160
nonpartisanship, 69, 149

O'Connor, Sandra Day, 100, 122, 127, 128, 143, 163, 181, 182, 214
O'Neil, Tip, 13
Osburn, Jones, 163

Parmenter, Paul, 45–46, 55
Parmenter Company, 46, 47, 52, 54–55
partisanship: increases in, 13–14, 131, 140, 189, 219; partisan balance in House, 149; and public policy, 9–10, 113. *See also* bipartisanship; nonpartisanship
patriotism, 112, 114
Peña, Manuel, 117, 121
Phelps Dodge Corporation, 65, 75, 190
Phoenix, 209–13; Chamber of Commerce, 45, 48, 194; Charter Government Committee, 69, 226n22; demographics, *65t*, 70; grocery industry, x, 46–47, 55, 56, 60; growth and development, 16, 45, 46–47, 64, 65, 74, 142–43; Stay America Committee, 52
Phoenix 40, 195–96
Phoenix Gazette, 57, 190
Phoenix Indian School, 210
Phoenix New Times, 190
Pima County, 74, 86–87, 199, 200
Pinto Democrats, 70, 74, 75, 76, 84, 87, 130, 218

policy. *See* environment; health care; taxes/tax policy; water
political campaigns: Barr legislative campaigns, 53–54; financing and disclosure, 106, 186; fundraising and distribution, 105–7, 111, 117–18, 130, 185; negative nature of, 218–19; personality-focused, 18; political action committees (PACs), 106. *See also* governor's race of 1986
political culture: anti-colonialist feelings, 15, 16, 19, 66; conservatism, 12, 17, 19, 20, 69–70, 73, 75, 113, 115, 218–19; Conservative Democrats, 64, 74, 84; Elazar, Daniel J., 70; individualism, 15, 16; liberalism, 12, 69–70; nature of Western politics, 9–10, 14–20; populism, 63, 202, 203; Progressive Era, 72; water issues, 14–15; wedge politics, 219–20
political parties, 9, 12–14, 69–70, 74, *130t*, 217, 219. *See also* Democratic Party; Republican Party
polls and polling, 181, 185–87, 189, 193, 198, 200, 211
Portland, Ore., 21–22, 25–32, 40–41, 223n5
power: balance and distribution, 62–63, 66–67, 75–79, 87, 130, 148–49, 152, 176, 216–18; institutional, 118–19, 229n76; and persuasion, 215; political costs, 201–3, 216; pragmatic response to, 67, 69; traditional powerbrokers, 63, 216; understanding its use, 66, 111, 180
pragmatism, 6, 9, 12–14, 69, 98, 102, 113, 116, 130, 169–70, 209, 215
Prescott, *65t*, 66, 71
Pritzlaff, John, 88–89, 226n31
Pulliam, Eugene, 153
Pyle, Howard, 18, 69

Reagan, Ronald, 7, 14, 182–83, *183*, 185, 200
Republican Party, x–xi, 62–63, 67, 70; Arizona House of Representatives, 74, 76, 84, 87; Arizona Senate, 67, 69, 74, 84, 87–89; Barr relationship with, 62, 113–14, 178, 187, 188, 200; conflicting ideology, 130–35, 231n100; conservatives, xi, 7, 20, 52–53, 88, 103, 113, 115, 129–35, 164, 171, 184, 187, 217–18; Goldwater prism, 20; government reform, 143, 217; growing strength of, 69–70, 74; John Birch Society, 52–53; primary voters, 185, 188; Young Republicans, 57. *See also* apportionment and representation; Democratic Party; Mecham, Evan; political culture
Reserve Officers Association, 49–51
Reserve Officer Training Corps (ROTC), 32–33
Reynolds v. Sims, xi, 85–86
Rhodes, John, 9, 69, 131
Richards, J. Morris, 62, 75, 78, 79–80, 81
Rio Salado Project, 211
Roberts, Bill, 185–86
Rosenbaum, Polly, 121
Rosenthal, Alan, 101, 104
Rosenzweig, Harry, 186
Rottas, Ray, 156
rural interests: apportionment and representation, x–xi, 62, 71–74, 84; domination of, x–xi, 62, 68, 113, 119, 218; rural-urban conflict, 64, 74, 110, 132, 153–54, 203; shifting power balance, 152, 218. *See also* urban/suburban interests
Russell, Richard, 51

Sagebrush Rebellion, 16
Salt River, 65, 68, 211
Salt River Valley, 45, 48, *65t*, 66, 166, 172
Schulz, Bill, 181–83, 205, 206, 219
Seattle, 6, 44, 49
Sharpe, James, 75
Shelp, Larry, 46, 47, 54, 55, 56, 57, 59, 60
Skelly, Jim, 91, 93–94, 100, 105–6, 109, 111, 124, 130, 131, 134, 171, 174, 184, 201
Smith, Clyde, 47, 52
Smith, Jay, 185

social policies: as Barr's legacy, 217; food stamps, 175; Friendly House, 212; group homes, 174; Housing Opportunity Center, 212; welfare reform, 212. *See also* health care
Sossaman, James, 99, 100, 103, 111, 184, 187, 190, 206
Sossaman, Sue, 194
Southern Pacific Railroad, 83, 152
Spencer, Stuart, 185
Stanton, Alan, 126
state legislatures: changing character of, 184; Citizen's Conference on State Legislatures, 128–29, 230n94, 231n95; importance of structure, 122–25; little federalism model, 74, 123; professional standards, 128, 139. *See also* Arizona legislature
Stephens, Alan, 208
Stevens, Charlie, 94–96, 104–5, 114, 126, 130, 206, 214
Stitzenberger, Lee, 193, 197, 200–201
St. John, Ron, 193
strikes, 4, 5, 6, 11, 65
Stump, Bob, 133
Symington, Fife, III, 212, 226n31

taxes/tax policy, 151–58; 1982 tax proposal, 98; cigarette and liquor tax, 153; Democratic Party, 153; education funding, 153, 155, 156; gasoline tax, 91, 109, 153–54, 157; income tax, 153, 155; irrigation pump tax, 169; property tax, 83, 126, 152–58, 163, 232n19; Proposition 13 (California), 155; Proposition 106 (Arizona), 156; rebates, 154; recapture, 156; reforms, 146–47, 176, 217; Republican party, 4–5, 70, 151–52; sales tax, 109, 152, 157, 194, 195, 205, 207, 211; sales tax on food, 102, 115, 117, 156
tax revolts, 155, 156, 157
teamwork, 5, 92, 110–11, 125, 184
TIME magazine, 122
transportation, 150, 171; highway system, 16, 142, 146, 154, 196, 211; light-rail mass transit, 211; Maricopa County, 157–58, 183, 211; State Highway Commission, 80; ValTrans, 211, 216
Truman, Harry, 14
Tucson, x, 16, 64, *65t*, 70, 74, 142–43, 167, 186–87
Turley, Keith, 201
Turley, Stan, 82, 135, 206, 217, 218; governor's race, 179, 186, 190, 195; leadership, 5, 87, 88, 96, 125, 128, 152–53, 168, 169; legislature, 119, 120, 123, 125, 226n19

Udall, Morris "Mo," 9, 71
United States Army Reserve program, 6, 49–51, 60
United States Supreme Court, 63, 85, 85–86
University of Arizona, 161, 174
University of Phoenix, 212
urban/suburban interests: growth and development, 16, 19, 64, 68, 118, 140, 142–43, 216–17; growth of GOP, 64, 67, 83–84, 130; impact on Arizona legislature, 74, 87, 130–34, 143–44, 149, 176; land-use planning, 68, 138, 145–46, 166–67, 171–72, 211, 216, 218; rural-urban conflict, 64, 74, 110, 132, 153–54, 203; shifting power balance, 152, 218; suburban conservatism, 17, 19, 20; tax policy, 153–57; water use, 166–67. *See also* rural interests
Usdane, Bob, 103, 134
utilities, 113, 153, 170, 201

voter rights/Voting Rights Act (1965), 63, 86, 132

Warner, Carolyn, 189, 191, 193, 197, 202, 205, 206
water, 166–69, 190; Active Management Areas (AMA), 169; Arizona Water Commission, 167; Central Arizona Project (CAP), 68, 166, 168, 169; Colorado River Compact (1922), 68; Critical Groundwater Areas, 167; dams, 15, 68; federal water projects, 15, 19; groundwater management,

167–69, 190, 215; Groundwater Management Act, 145, 176–77; historical patterns and usage, 9, 14–15, 64–65, 68, 166–67, 169, 201, 217; Newlands Reclamation Act, 15; pump tax, 169; Rio Salado Project, 211; Salt River Project, 166; U.S. Supreme Court water allocation ruling, 68; water quality standards, 172; Water Resources Department, 169
Watergate, 116
Watkins, Ralph, 183
Wesberry v. Sanders, 85
West, Tony, 95, 106–7, 113–15, 131, *132*, 171, 185, 197, 228n48
Whicker, Marcia Lynn, 72, 140, 229n76
Willey, Keven Ann, 5, 12, 92, 94, 97, 100, 105, 182, 192, 201, 227n15, 229n73, 236n49
Williams, Jack, 125, 135, 193
Wills, Garry, 3, 10–11, 141, 202
Wolfe, Bob, 192, 193
women, 67, 121–22
World War II, 5, 6, 32, 35–40, *36map*, *40map*, 107
Wright, Pat, 103, 130
Wynn, Bernie, 86, 91, 181

Yuma, 65, 186, 189

About the Author

Professor **Philip R. VanderMeer** has written widely on the history of legislative leadership, state politics, and Arizona. His first book, *The Hoosier Politician*, and several articles studied the legislators and leadership in the Indiana General Assembly. He has written a comparison of state legislatures and Congress, as well as articles on other legislative leaders, ranging from the Gold Democrats of Michigan to Senator Hiram Johnson of California. He has authored an essay on "The Historical Patterns of Arizona Leadership," as well as a brief sketch of Arizona's Lorna Lockwood. He has published two histories of Phoenix: *Phoenix Rising* (2002) and *Desert Visions and the Making of Phoenix* (2010). He has taught at Arizona State University since 1985.